MW01515927

The Heart of Toronto

The Heart of Toronto

Corporate Power, Civic Activism, and the Remaking of Downtown Yonge Street

DANIEL ROSS

© UBC Press 2022

All rights reserved. No part of this publication may be reproduced, stored in a retrieval system, or transmitted, in any form or by any means, without prior written permission of the publisher, or, in Canada, in the case of photocopying or other reprographic copying, a licence from Access Copyright, www.accesscopyright.ca.

30 29 28 27 26 25 24 23 22   5 4 3 2 1

Printed in Canada on FSC-certified ancient-forest-free paper
(100% post-consumer recycled) that is processed chlorine- and acid-free.

Library and Archives Canada Cataloguing in Publication

Title: The heart of Toronto : corporate power, civic activism, and the remaking of downtown Yonge Street / Daniel Ross.

Names: Ross, Daniel (Daniel G.), author.

Description: Includes bibliographical references and index.

Identifiers: Canadiana (print) 20220141797 | Canadiana (ebook) 20220141851 | ISBN 9780774867009 (hardcover) | ISBN 9780774867016 (softcover) | ISBN 9780774867023 (PDF) | ISBN 9780774867030 (EPUB)

Subjects: LCSH: Yonge Street (Toronto, Ont.) – History – 20th century. | LCSH: Urbanization – Ontario – Toronto – History – 20th century. | LCSH: Toronto (Ont.) – History – 20th century.

Classification: LCC FC3097.67 .R67 2022 | DDC 971.3/541—dc23

Canadä

UBC Press gratefully acknowledges the financial support for our publishing program of the Government of Canada (through the Canada Book Fund), the Canada Council for the Arts, and the British Columbia Arts Council.

This book has been published with the help of a grant from the Canadian Federation for the Humanities and Social Sciences, through the Awards to Scholarly Publications Program, using funds provided by the Social Sciences and Humanities Research Council of Canada.

Printed and bound in Canada by Friesens
Set in Zurich and Minion by Artegraphica Design Co. Ltd.
Copy editor: Deborah Kerr
Proofreader: Helen Godolphin
Indexer: Margaret de Boer
Cartographer: Eric Leinberger
Cover designer: Martyn Schmoll

UBC Press
The University of British Columbia
2029 West Mall
Vancouver, BC V6T 1Z2
www.ubcpress.ca

Contents

List of Figures / vii

Acknowledgments / viii

The Street and the City / 1

1 Making Downtown Yonge Street / 15

2 The City of Tomorrow / 40

3 A People Place / 72

4 Fighting Sin Strip / 99

5 Malling Main Street / 133

Remaking Downtown Yonge Street / 165

Notes / 180

Selected Bibliography / 207

Index / 217

Figures

xii / Map of downtown Yonge Street in the 1960s

18 / Yonge Street, around 1895

24 / Crowds on Yonge and Queen, summer 1929

30 / Metro Toronto in the mid-1960s

32 / The Yonge Street subway under construction, 1950

38 / Christmas lights and crowds on Yonge, 1962

47 / Postcard of Eaton's buildings, 1923

56 / Aerial view of downtown Toronto, 1967

61 / Planners and politicians at the Eaton Centre unveiling, 1966

66 / Demonstration against the demolition of Old City Hall, 1966

79 / Crowds replace cars on the Yonge pedestrian mall, 1972

83 / Promotional postcard for the mall, 1971

87 / Looking south from near College Street, 1971 or 1972

89 / Making the scene on the pedestrian mall, 1973

93 / The mall as a dysfunctional public space, 1974

104 / Men at a Cinema 2000 screening of *Vixen,* 1970

107 / Toronto's sexual entertainment district, 1974

115 / Demonstration against the sex industry, Yonge and Dundas, 1975

126 / Rally for Emanuel Jaques at City Hall, 1977

134 / The first phase of the Eaton Centre, 1977

142 / Holy Trinity Church and Trinity Square, 1972

153 / The Eaton Centre's atrium on opening day, 1977

157 / The opening of the second phase of the Eaton Centre, 1979

160 / Eaton Centre surveillance system, 1980

Acknowledgments

This book explores people's relationships to a significant place in Toronto, and how both that place and those relationships changed amid larger urban transformations. It uses historical evidence and methods to present a narrative of Yonge Street's remaking from the 1950s through the 1970s, while offering explanations of why that process turned out as it did. My own experiences are not part of that story, but they have inevitably shaped how I've told it. Like most people who grew up in Toronto, I have my own memories of downtown Yonge. I've been a consumer and a teenage loiterer there; I've shopped, had nights out, marched in demonstrations, and been stuck in traffic while parades crawled by. For a few years as an undergraduate student, I spent evenings and weekends selling boots at the Eaton Centre. Individually, none of those experiences were particularly important. But together, by showing me the street's changes and different faces over time, they helped me see the possibilities of studying a place like Yonge.

Researching and writing this book has kept me busy for almost a decade, and many people have helped and supported me along the way. I began the research for *The Heart of Toronto* at York University, where I crossed paths with a fantastic bunch of historians. I'm particularly grateful to Marcel Martel and to Colin Coates for their constant guidance and friendship. Like my other mentors in York's history department, they modeled an egalitarian style of teaching and advising that continues to shape how I approach my job today. Marlene Shore, Craig Heron, Richard White, Harold Bérubé, and Roger Keil all provided valuable feedback on earlier versions of this project. Thanks also to my fellow grad students, who exposed me to new ways of thinking about history, while showing me the value of doing that work in a like-minded community.

I'm lucky to have found a similarly supportive and enriching environment in Montreal, where this manuscript was written and rewritten in coffee shops, in my office at the Université du Québec à Montréal, and in my living room at the height of the COVID-19 pandemic. My wonderful colleagues in the history department at UQÀM, my peers at other Québec universities, and the members of the Montreal History Group continue to help me find my place at a new institution and in a new city. Thanks especially to Magda Fahrni for her advice, and to Geneviève Dorais for the friendly competition that motivated me to finally finish the manuscript. My students have continually challenged me to grow as a teacher. Their perceptive questions and comments have often inspired me to rethink the big ideas that frame this book.

Within the wider academic world, I've appreciated both the long-term connections and the chance encounters that have helped shape my work. *ActiveHistory.ca* has been a part of my life for as long as this book, offering an early publishing venue, contact with inspiring people, and a welcome escape from the most laborious moments of the research process. Over the years I've presented pieces of this project at meetings of the Canadian Historical Association, the American Society of Environmental History, and numerous other conferences, and each time I've found some new insight or idea to take away. A big thank you to the people who have kept these kinds of events going in difficult times, and to the organizers of the NiCHE summer schools for letting me tag along on the bus.

I am deeply grateful to the public institutions and funding agencies that made this project possible. My research at York was funded by the Social Sciences and Humanities Research Council, the Ontario government, and the Avie Bennett Historica Chair in Canadian History. Elements of this book took shape during a stay at the Centre for Urban History at the University of Leicester, where I was welcomed by Simon Gunn and the centre's faculty and graduate students. Costs related to additional research and rights for the book's images were generously paid for by UQÀM.

Archivists do not always get the thanks they deserve. *The Heart of Toronto* could not have been written without the careful work of past and present staff at the City of Toronto Archives, the Archives of Ontario, the Clara Thomas Archives, and the Toronto Public Library. Thanks to David Zylberberg and Sabrina Gaudreault-Drouin for helping to fill in gaps in my initial research. Thanks also to former Toronto mayor David Crombie, who gave generously of his time over a series of coffees, and to Janis Cole, who screened her documentary work for me and helped me understand life behind the scenes at Yonge Street's body rub parlours.

It has been a pleasure working with the staff at UBC Press on this manuscript. James MacNevin enthusiastically championed the project, and Ann Macklem did a great job shepherding the manuscript through the production process. Martyn Schmoll's bright cover art helped bring Yonge Street to life, and Deborah Kerr's sharp editorial eye made the text clearer and more readable. Avigail Oren and two anonymous reviewers offered thoughtful suggestions for improvement. I owe a great debt to Steve Penfold, who read and re-read the entire manuscript and gave me the constructive critical feedback I needed to make it a better book.

I would like to close by expressing my heartfelt thanks to my family. Thank you, Mom, Da, Jacob, and Anna for always encouraging me in my choices, and for supporting me with love, advice, and – more than occasionally – food and shelter. This book is dedicated with all my love and affection to Lauryn, my partner on this journey and in so much more.

The Heart of Toronto

Queen's
Park
COLLEGE ST
College
YONGE ST
CHURCH ST
Eaton's
BAY ST
Zanzibar
Tavern
Ryerson
Polytechnic
GERRARD ST
Sam the
Record Man
Bus
Terminal
EDWARD ST
St Patrick
Dundas
Dundas
Square
DUNDAS ST
Trinity
Church
Imperial
Theatre
TRINITY
SQ
New City Hall
LOUISA ST
Osgoode Hall
ALBERT ST
Eaton's
Nathan
Phillips
Square
Old
City
Hall
Loew's
Theatre
QUEEN ST
Osgoode
Queen
ADELAIDE ST
Simpson's
YONGE ST
VICTORIA ST
CHURCH ST
YORK ST
BAY ST
KING ST
St Andrew
TD
Centre
Stock
Exchange
King
WELLINGTON ST
FRONT ST
Union
Union
Station
— Subway
○ Subway station
GARDINER EXPRESSWAY
N
QUEEN'S QUAY
250 m
N
4 km
Toronto Harbour (Lake Ontario)

Downtown Yonge Street in the 1960s | Cartographer: Eric Leinberger

The Street and the City

In September 1975, Toronto threw its first birthday party for Yonge Street. Downtown businesses, civic leaders, and citizens came together to celebrate the 180th anniversary of the street's opening to traffic and to commemorate its evolution from colonial road to bustling urban thoroughfare. On the densely built stretch running north-south through the city's core, often referred to as downtown Yonge, block after block was decorated with bunting and banners advertising sales and promotions, as the owners of shops, restaurants, and bars made individual contributions to the occasion and tried to direct some of the excitement their way. Each evening for a week, this commercial corridor played host to public events and spectacles intended to draw people downtown. These included free concerts and, on the night of September 5, the lighting atop Canada's tallest skyscraper of "the birthday candle to end all birthday candles," an 11-million candlepower flare visible across the city. The next day, a thousand people watched as Toronto mayor David Crombie gave official sanction to "180 Years Yonge Week," before helping cut and share out a three-hundred-pound birthday cake in front of City Hall.[1]

The cake was decorated with a 1795 map of the British colony of Upper Canada – now southern Ontario – just one of many historical references that helped frame celebration of the street. Earlier on the same day, a line of re-enactors bearing muskets and clad in green felt marched down Yonge to commemorate the Queen's Rangers, the soldier-settlers who carved out what was then the colony's first north-south road and the basis for British settlement in the area. Past and present mingled freely as their leader, portraying Lieutenant-Governor John Graves Simcoe, bantered about the dramatic changes of the past two centuries. He expressed both pride and amazement to see the muddy little outpost of York – population six hundred in 1795 – transformed into the modern city of the 1970s, with its sprawl, skyscrapers, and subways. Yonge Street provided a rare continuity between those two scenes, and its anniversary was promoted as an important date for the entire city, not in the least by merchant association the Downtown Council, the main organizer of the event, who took out newspaper ads inviting residents to the "birthday of downtown Toronto."[2]

However, any suggestion that the intertwined stories of Yonge Street and Toronto could be reduced to two centuries of progress was complicated by the undercurrent of anxiety that ran through the festivities. Toronto chose to celebrate the street at the moment when its future seemed most in doubt. In the months leading up to the anniversary, local newspapers were full of controversy over the problems of downtown Yonge, including flagging retail sales, the proliferation of street vendors and sex shops, and speculation that the metropolitan municipality planned to widen it into a commuter thoroughfare. The Downtown Council admitted that the anniversary week was intended to draw families and middle-class shoppers back to the area and to counter the perception that it was in decline. This was not the first time that the group, formed to represent business interests on downtown Yonge and in the surrounding area, had mobilized with that goal in mind: its members had spent the first half of the 1970s lobbying tirelessly for street improvements, funding for renovations, and stronger restrictions on sexual entertainment, without lasting success. "Nobody else is going to do it for us," explained the group's managing director a month before the event, "so we've got to create some positive publicity, promote the street properly, and clean it up." Commissioned to write a song for the occasion, local crooner Tommy Ambrose captured the mood with the ballad "Long Street Winding through My Mind," whose lyrics described Yonge as a friend in need, "a loved one that has seen better times."[3] There was hope, but also concern, about what the future would bring.

The story of 180 Years Yonge Week highlights two themes that frame the arguments of this book. The first is the street's place in the civic culture and urban life of Toronto. Only a small number of the more than 2 million people living in Toronto and its metropolitan boroughs attended the 1975 anniversary, and fewer still bought Tommy Ambrose's record. But they were all familiar with the street being feted. Yonge Street ran (and runs) through most stories told about the city, from its founding myths of Loyalist perseverance to accounts of its twentieth-century growth into a North American metropolis. In 1873, one of the first histories of Toronto devoted nearly 150 pages to the "great northern highway," using a trip along its length to write the city into the larger narrative of British settlement in the region. More than a century later, a popular urban biography framed the street as a microcosm of the rapidly changing city around it. "Toronto grew up alongside Yonge Street," explained its author, "and Yonge Street is a reflection of the city itself."[4] Toronto's geography, like its past, was often understood in relation to this key artery. Centred on every map of the city, it was the main north-south reference for the street grid, the "datum line where East meets West," streets change their name, and addresses reset.[5] Like the Lake Ontario shoreline and the valley of the Don River, Yonge was an organizing force in Toronto's landscape, but it differed from those formidable natural barriers because it was a connector, pointing the way for expansion and linking the older city with its largest and most affluent suburbs to the north.

Yonge Street's hold on the public imagination went beyond its importance as a line on a map or a historic transportation corridor. People in Toronto knew it best as a place. By the 1970s, downtown Yonge's busy sidewalks and brick shopscape had played a key role in the city's commercial and public life for nearly a century. Anchored by the headquarters of department store giants Eaton's and Simpson's and crowded with music venues, theatres, and specialty shops, it was Toronto's main street, its largest – if not its most modern or attractive – retail marketplace and its showiest mass entertainment destination. Day and night, the strip running from just below Queen Street north to College was a magnet for crowds, a hub where a cross-section of the urban population converged for Friday night thrills, Saturday shopping, or spontaneous celebrations. It was the section of the city that was the busiest, that contained the most prized real estate, that evoked the most vivid memories. It was this aging but popular commercial corridor and public space that people referenced when they described 180 Years Yonge Week as "downtown's birthday bash."[6] To the merchants and civic leaders behind the event, but also for the media and many other Torontonians whose lives and livelihoods connected them to the area, this stretch of Yonge Street *was* downtown.

Second, both the festivities and the associated newspaper coverage record the ambivalence that defined attitudes toward Yonge Street during the decades following the Second World War. By the 1950s, the idea that the street had "seen better times," as Tommy Ambrose put it, became commonplace. For the first time, changes in the shape of the city and consumer tastes were not just challenging downtown's economic and social centrality, but threatening to eclipse it. Automobile ownership and mass suburbanization gave Torontonians new options for shopping, living, and working, and disrupted the metropolitan geography that underpinned Yonge Street's success. The spectre of decline, inseparable from discussions of the urban future in postwar North America, seemed to loom over its iconic commercial landscape, in many places unchanged – except for brighter neon signage and gaudier facades – since the first decades of the century. In an aspirational city, such constancy might spell stagnation, or even obsolescence. Worse still, the changes that were occurring on Yonge in the postwar decades, including the shift from mainstream retailing to nightlife and youth culture, were rarely interpreted in a positive light. Increasingly, the street was seen as both the heart of the city and the piece of the urban fabric most in need of saving.

Tension between those two identities both framed and helped drive urban transformation. In this book, I explore how a large cast of historical actors used, debated, and ultimately remade downtown Yonge, spanning a period from the 1950s through the 1970s when the street was seldom out of the news. Even as its metropolitan hegemony waned, Yonge remained a common reference point for the urban population and a symbol of Toronto whose reach extended well beyond the city limits. Variously understood as a historic landscape and an embarrassing relic, a transportation route and a people place, a laboratory for modernist urbanism and a haven for big-city sleaze, it was at the centre of efforts to reinvent downtown to keep pace with, or even lead, urban change. 180 Years Yonge Week was just one episode in that longer history, which over twenty-five years encompassed new municipal policies, grassroots cleanup campaigns, and one of North America's most ambitious downtown renewal schemes. Taking the street as its narrative through-line and spatial focus, *The Heart of Toronto* traces the history of those interventions, their successes and failures, and their connections to wider trends in the city and society. Moving from the sidewalk to City Hall, and from corporate boardrooms to suburban kitchens, this book looks at the contexts in which people became invested in the future of a key urban place and how they attempted to shape it, whether through business decisions, political action, or everyday use.

This book is about how cities change; but it is also about who has the power to shape that process. Downtown politics were defined by their publicness and by wide participation, but they were never a level playing field. Three types of power – state, corporate, and citizen – interacted unequally to set the framework for Yonge Street's remaking. For an increasingly interventionist municipal administration, Yonge was a key site for testing and expanding its influence on the urban process. Beginning in the

1950s, new strategies for promoting and controlling development, regulating streetlife and land uses, and arbitrating between diverse urban actors were all pioneered on downtown Yonge. In many cases, those innovations were responses to private decisions to invest or disinvest. Much of the dynamism in this story is supplied by a small number of corporate actors – department stores, banks, and developers – who during the postwar decades bought, sold, and rebuilt the street. A volatile market in urban land influenced Yonge's mix of economic activities and drove its creative destruction, fundamentally altering its identity and functions as a marketplace and public space. In dialogue with these changes, and as part of the surge in civil society activism that characterized the era, a range of citizens, including small businesses, populist social conservatives, and student environmentalists, mobilized politically to demand a role in working out the urban future. At no time before or since has such a diverse array of possibilities been imagined for Toronto's commercial core. The debates of the postwar decades refashioned downtown Yonge Street both physically and symbolically, and they continue to influence its development today.

Saving the Heart of the City

Toronto was just one of many cities that reimagined their downtown future in the decades following the Second World War, and in that respect *The Heart of Toronto* tells a very North American story.[7] Interventions to rebuild, clean up, and improve Yonge Street were local responses to a broader pattern of urban restructuring whose defining feature, as far as downtowns were concerned, was decentralization. From mid-century, factors including public and corporate policies, technological changes, and consumer desire interacted to accelerate the shifting of people, jobs, and investment from the centre of the city to its suburbs and hinterland. Scholarship on this process highlights the rise and rapid spread of the mass-produced automobile suburb, by 1960 firmly established as the dominant mode for new urban communities, as well as a powerful social norm.[8] Equally important was the emergent economic geography of the postwar urban region, whose sprawling landscapes included not just places to live, but manufacturing clusters, drive-in strips, office parks, and shopping malls. That last innovation was particularly significant to this story, since retailing proved to be the downtown activity that was most susceptible to dispersion. In the 1950s, central business districts began to lose customers and market share to the planned shopping centres that mushroomed up at strategic locations on the fringes of every medium- to large-sized city, fundamentally reorganizing urban commercial life.[9] In Toronto, as elsewhere, postwar decentralization broke apart the "single-focus metropolis" of centre and suburbs that had been the foundation of downtown prosperity in the late nineteenth and early twentieth centuries.[10]

Toronto's strategies for keeping Yonge Street relevant amid these changes drew inspiration from a dialogue between cities that transcended national borders. Recent research on the postwar era documents how professional networks, the movements of expert consultants, media coverage, and other circuits facilitated exchange of a shared repertoire of urbanist ideas, in the context of a larger transatlantic preoccupation with modernizing the industrial city.[11] Throughout the twenty-five years analyzed here, people in Toronto looked constantly to neighbouring communities and to others farther afield in an effort to understand what they saw as a shared set of downtown problems, including shrinking retail sales, traffic congestion, aging buildings, and the decline of civility in public space. Department store executives went on fact-finding visits to Boston and Pittsburgh to learn about their rebuilding schemes and hired top planning consultants from the United States to help them prepare their own. Merchants and activists looked to cities from Ottawa to Kalamazoo for models of a more festive, people-friendly shopping street. Media reports of crime and crisis in downtown Buffalo and Detroit fed anxieties among Torontonians that their city would be similarly afflicted and led people to connect what they saw on Yonge Street to larger narratives of urban decline.[12] The experiences of other urban centres offered both warnings and examples to follow as they worked out the downtown future.

People who were invested in that process argued that more was at stake than a specific configuration of buildings, business activities, and institutions. Seeking support for saving downtown, they turned to its decades-old identity as the vital core of the North American metropolis, insisting that – after some necessary changes – it would continue to ensure urban health and prosperity. Toronto's *Globe and Mail* echoed one of the main themes of postwar urban discourse when it wrote in 1962 that the "heart of any metropolitan city is the downtown area," before going to describe recent efforts aimed at forestalling obsolescence and "keeping the aging heart of the city beating."[13] Such organic analogies have a long history. As James Winter notes in his study of street reform in nineteenth-century London, "we have always read our built environments with our bodies," comparing cities to organisms, roads to circulatory networks, and urban problems to illness and rot.[14] In Toronto, references to downtown Yonge as the city's heart go back to the 1870s, if not earlier, but it was not until the debates explored in this book that they became a fixture of public discourse, taken up in the media, political deliberations, and promotional campaigns for the street. As in other cities, this evocative metaphor gained the most political traction in conjunction with expert diagnoses of urban "blight" and "decay," and prescriptions for their cure. Since those sicknesses were largely in the eye of the beholder – on Yonge Street they meant, at different times, aging buildings, outmoded business models, and the presence of the wrong kind of people – the image of the heart of the city helped galvanize support for a range of interventions, from the "drastic surgery" of large-scale rebuilding to more targeted "revitalization" agendas.[15]

Sprawl and uneven development, participation in transnational urban transfers, and a search for interventionist cures for downtown all place Yonge Street's remaking firmly in the larger North American context. However, in this book I argue for the centrality of place to understanding how that process was worked out on the ground. The disruptive effects of postwar decentralization were mitigated in Toronto by an activist metropolitan government, the construction of public transit, and continued demand for office space in the financial and administrative district. As a result, downtown Yonge's struggles with falling sales and a declining public image took place in a context of metropolitan connectivity, stable or rising land values, and the emergence of the command and control centre of the Canadian economy just a few blocks to the south.[16] Similarly, though policymakers and other actors in Toronto had access to the same strategies as their counterparts across the continent, ideas borrowed from other cities often failed to be "relocated" or were adapted in unforeseen ways.[17] Lacking the federal funding for private redevelopment that was the glue of growth coalitions in the United States, political and business elites seeking to imitate that model in Toronto struggled to establish anything more than ad hoc partnerships. The concept of pedestrian shopping streets failed to gain local support in the early 1960s, only to unexpectedly take on new life almost a decade later as a symbol of political reform and environmentalist critiques of the automobile. National, regional, and above all local factors play a determining role in this story.

The importance of place is even more apparent when we shift our perspective to street level. *The Heart of Toronto* is built around an empirical study of one commercial thoroughfare and the agendas, personalities, and circumstances that shaped it over a quarter of a century. Much of the action takes place on and around a ten-block strip of Yonge and is driven by a large but identifiable cast of historical actors who owned, used, managed, or otherwise asserted claims to that space. At that scale of analysis, urban change cannot be explained as the inevitable result of larger patterns of restructuring. Instead, it comes into focus as a political process, actively imagined, negotiated, and contested over time, and defined as much by contradictions and unintended consequences as by plans carefully laid and executed. Rebuilding schemes on Yonge were constrained by property arrangements and a built landscape inherited from the past, including a private land assembly that made retailer Eaton's a major player in any project, and several historic buildings whose threatened demolition forced a broad-based negotiation of the public interest. The street's centrality and regional pull facilitated its emergence as Toronto's sexual entertainment district, while at the same time giving conservative backlash against that development a constituency that extended from the city proper to its suburbs and beyond. 180 Years Yonge Week provides a vivid example of the ways in which the street's history and cultural meanings continually erupted into and influenced discussions of its economic marginalization; similar slippages and convergences defined the other debates that populate this book. Rather than furnishing a background to the action, a site where sidewalk disputes, improvement programs, or planning experiments played out, the street was a dynamic factor influencing those episodes and processes.[18]

Toronto's busiest and most unruly thoroughfare provides a privileged vantage point for thinking about some of the key themes in the history of postwar Canada and North America. Each chapter of this book pays attention to the ways in which debates over the street intersected with and were influenced by contemporary trends ranging from automobility to conservative social movement activism. This approach enriches the study in several ways. First, entangling downtown politics with larger historical processes supplies essential context for the decisions of people who were invested in the street. For example, regional and national restructuring in the real estate development and retail industries created the conditions for an ambitious redevelopment program to succeed on Yonge in the 1970s, where similar schemes had failed less than a decade earlier. Second, the approach I take in this book helps to expand the narrative of urban change beyond the vision and actions of powerful elites, suggesting ways in which other actors and ideas could – and did – influence changes in the street's form, functions, and meanings.[19] Major private and public improvement projects hogged the headlines, but I find that the political mobilization of suburban evangelicals, the get-rich-quick schemes of entertainment entrepreneurs, and the daily occupation of space by street vendors and youth also mattered to Yonge's transformation. Finally, the view from the street helps to rethink wider developments such as the sexual revolution or corporate concentration through empirical study of their interactions with place. Drawing out these connections underlines the value of doing a kind of urban history that overlaps with and learns from wider scholarship, enmeshing changes in city lives and forms in the social, cultural, and political histories of an increasingly urbanized society.[20] This book argues that there is no better place to start that project than on the street.

The Street and Its Archive

In making these arguments about urban change, downtown politics, and place, I have relied on research in a rich and varied archive. From the 1950s through the 1970s, there was seldom a moment when Toronto was not debating Yonge Street's problems and possibilities, and much of what was said and done is preserved in documentary sources from the period. Over three decades, I count at least twenty major reports on the street by City of Toronto staff, citizen groups, planners, and businesses, covering topics ranging from urban renewal to traffic to street advertising; over two thousand letters from citizens to the mayor; hundreds of photographs of buildings, people, and street scenes; and thousands of newspaper articles, all of which represented interventions, in different ways, in the story told here. Surrounding these documents is a larger collection of memoranda, meeting minutes, correspondence, and internal government reports that dwarfs them in size. Dealing with the recent past and with a topic that was of significant public interest at the time, I have rarely been faced, as many historians are, with major silences in the archival record. In telling this story, I have grappled with quite the opposite challenge: how to listen to a cacophony of voices – some much louder than others – weigh them one against another, and bring them productively into conversation.

The first and most readily accessible source employed here is the press. My research began with Toronto's three major daily newspapers – the *Toronto Star, Globe and Mail,* and *Telegram* (reborn in 1971 as the *Toronto Sun*) – as well as more selective forays into other major Canadian and, occasionally, international publications.[21] In this study, newspapers are, first of all, used as a source of information and detail. Journalists were keen observers of local affairs, including the day-to-day transaction of municipal business, with privileged access to politicians, bureaucrats, and business elites. This reporting provides the colour that brings past events to life: the attitude of a crowd; the mayor's impromptu comments to the press gallery; images of streetlife, building facades, or development plans. When followed over time, it creates a narrative of the local – with its own particular interpretations, inclusions, and omissions – that is a useful contrast to the official record.

The press also features here as an important influence on city politics. Newspapers helped mould what Torontonians thought about a range of issues, and they created a forum for public discussion, albeit one framed by distinct editorial agendas. Despite the challenges posed by changing tastes and broadcast media, the Toronto dailies remained widely read throughout the period covered here. A 1966 Canadian Facts survey of a thousand Torontonians found that most relied on the major papers for their local news: half of them read the *Toronto Star* on a daily basis, and two-thirds consulted either the *Telegram* or the *Globe and Mail*.[22] Each paper had a distinct voice: the *Globe*, "Canada's national newspaper," was business-oriented but often socially liberal; the conservative *Telegram* and *Toronto Sun* offered contrarian columnists and populist editorials; the *Star,* Canada's largest newspaper with a circulation of 300,000 to 400,000 during the period, was staunchly Liberal, with a roster of nationally syndicated columnists.[23] All three took stances on hot-button local issues such as the sex industry or downtown redevelopment and endorsed political candidates at every election. They also devoted substantial space to citizen comment through letters to the editor and the more exclusive or expert op-ed. Throughout this study, I identify instances in which coverage in the dailies influenced Yonge Street politics. Citizen activists were inspired to action by columns they read at breakfast, and business and political elites sought to use the press to take the temperature of public opinion – or to change it. By representing the city, newspapers contributed to making it.[24] Where possible, I have also sought out community papers, trade journals, and the alternative press, finding in the latter a particularly rich source of dissenting perspectives.

This study pays close attention to municipal decision making and policy, and here I draw on the vast archive produced by Toronto's two levels of local government. A substantial portion is in the public record, including planning reports, council minutes, and records of public consultations. A series of access-to-information requests and a research agreement I signed with the City of Toronto opened hundreds of previously inaccessible files for my research, including the official correspondence of the mayor of Toronto and the chair of the Municipality of Metropolitan Toronto, as well as the internal files of several units of the municipal bureaucracy. These records grew in both quality and quantity throughout the period under study. If in the 1940s and 1950s, important pieces of city business were transacted informally or the records not kept, by the late 1960s the duty to record and preserve was taken much more seriously. As this book tracks, municipal responsibilities had expanded by then, too. These files allow me to reconstruct how Toronto's bureaucracy thought, how politicians made decisions, and how both types of civic official interacted with an increasingly outspoken public. It was surprising and exciting to find thousands of citizen letters, phone messages, and petitions to the mayor concerning the state of Yonge Street. Folder after folder contained the carefully preserved voices of Torontonians from across the city, downtown, and suburbs, young and old; here was an assertive politics of place that needed to be mapped and understood. Equally significant was my discovery of Toronto councillor William Archer's documentation of the history and daily workings of the Yonge Street pedestrian mall, of which he was the principal organizer. These records highlight both the importance and the complexity of municipal governance in a period of urban transformation.

Finally, several groups of private records provide insight into the perspectives of businesses and citizen activists. This book's discussion of the politics and process of downtown redevelopment would not have been possible without the extensive archive of the T. Eaton Company, one of Toronto's most important retailers, landowners, and corporate citizens. The Eaton's archive is exceptional in that few other Canadian businesses of comparative size, and certainly none so deeply involved in urban land development, have opened up their records to the public in the same way. As a result, in Chapters 2 and 5 I am able to track nearly every aspect of the first and second Eaton Centre projects, from the negotiations to make up the land assembly to the ways in which Eaton's executives responded to public criticism and setbacks. Access to this archive allows me to present a narrative of redevelopment that moves beyond planning policy and citizen opposition to interrogate the motivations and resources of capital and the corporations that have been so influential in remodelling the central city. Other significant groups of private records include the files of environmental activist group Pollution Probe, development researchers Downtown Action, and heritage conservationists the Friends of Old City Hall. This study also incorporates several oral history interviews conducted to fill in gaps in the archival record, including a series of conversations about city politics with former Toronto mayor David Crombie and an interview with filmmaker and activist Janis Cole, who documented work in Yonge Street's body rub parlours in the early 1970s.

This archive has its absences. The files of public figures do not include the un-minuted meetings and phone calls that were crucial to the day-to-day transaction of city business; the Toronto police ignored my requests to release additional reports or internal communications for the period.

Many of the small but important players in the narrative – the Downtown Council, for example – left an incomplete documentary record. These gaps can be addressed in part through a careful reading of what is there. The extensive correspondence between police officials and the mayor and Metro chairman included reporting on the force's practices and in some cases arrest or patrol reports. Yonge Street merchants and their association worked closely with the city councillors who represented them. Other silences are the result of choices made during research. Early on, I decided to focus on the power to effect urban change and the contexts in which it was exercised, negotiated, and contested. This story is driven by investment decisions, public debates, and municipal policy, and its main actors are those who wielded the power to influence them: businesses, media, politicians, bureaucrats, and well-organized citizen activists. I have worked to include other actors and to better understand the place in the urban process occupied by everyday street politics. However, I recognize that the extensive oral history work required to do justice to the perspectives and experiences of sex workers or youth, among others, is beyond the scope of this book. The same could be said for the cultural history of Yonge Street. Other observers have highlighted its role as a hub for the arts – particularly music – or traced echoes of its resonance for Torontonians in film and fiction.[25] In this book, I take the street's role in collective memory and cultural production seriously, but I analyze them in depth only where they intersected with downtown politics.

Outline of the Book

The Heart of Toronto explores the remaking of Toronto's Yonge Street over five thematic chapters, presented in roughly chronological order. Chapter 1, "Making Downtown Yonge Street," provides an extended introduction to the street, the city, and some of the key concepts and historical actors that feature throughout the book. Beginning in the 1790s, it traces how Toronto and Yonge Street developed in tandem over a century and a half, linking the making of the street to the larger process of urbanization that took place along and around it. Throughout, I argue for understanding Yonge, like other central thoroughfares, as a complex and changing human creation. This sets the stage for the following chapters, which foreground the street's remaking as a product of both structural transformations and the individual decisions of the people who used and debated it.

Chapter 2, "The City of Tomorrow," places Yonge Street and its largest retailer at the centre of Toronto's postwar debates over urban modernization. It shows how, beginning in the 1950s, municipal authorities and corporate elites converged around the idea that comprehensive physical transformation would save the aging central city, and how department store Eaton's extensive properties became the focus for that vision. The result was the Eaton Centre (1956–67), a modernist complex of towers and plazas promoted as "a new heart for old Toronto," before being cancelled amid debates over its financial viability and its planners' cavalier attitude toward the area's historic structures. Tracing the history of this unbuilt megaproject reveals the economic imperatives, political alliances, and ideas behind Toronto's postwar drive to rebuild. It also gives us a fresh perspective on the department store as a historical actor, highlighting how changing markets and political pressure cast Eaton's – however reluctantly – in the role of urban powerbroker.

Rebuilding was a strategy out of reach of all but the most powerful commercial institutions. With Chapter 3, "A People Place," I shift my focus to the loose coalition of downtown actors, including independent businesses, who did not see their interests and aspirations reflected in projects like the Eaton Centre. Instead, they articulated an alternative future for Yonge, premised on protecting and developing its assets as a historic shopping street and public space. The result was the Yonge pedestrian mall, which closed the street to vehicles and opened it to shoppers and strollers for four summers from 1971 to 1974. Invested with great hopes, the pedestrian mall was both popular and controversial. As the experiment expanded in scope, the street was appropriated in unexpected ways, demonstrating the public's appetite for new and better shared spaces while at the same time foregrounding anxieties around youth, bad behaviour, and declining urban civility.

Chapter 4, "Fighting Sin Strip," explores the rise of a sexual entertainment district on Yonge Street in the 1970s, and the barrage of interventions made to regulate or eliminate it. Toronto's "Sin Strip" gained national celebrity with the murder of 12-year-old shoeshine boy Emanuel Jaques in summer 1977, but the story I tell here is larger than that single episode. This chapter traces how a half-decade of political change, citizen mobilization, and sensationalist media coverage contributed to labelling Sin Strip as an urban problem, and made downtown Yonge a key testing ground for new policies of sexual regulation. While the rise of Toronto's postwar sex district connects Yonge Street with wider changes in sexual morality, the law, and entertainment across North America, its suppression in the wake of the Jaques murder provides a striking example of the influence of populist conservative activism in a period often remembered for its progressive politics.

In Chapter 5, "Malling Main Street," I return to the Eaton Centre and to rebuilding as a path to downtown transformation. The flagship project of a new wave of downtown redevelopment, the second Eaton Centre (1970–79) was a pioneering urban adaptation of one of the era's most profitable architectural forms, the suburban shopping centre. Over the course of its planning and construction, debates over the impacts of "malling" Yonge played a key role in the emergence of a new politics of development in Toronto, rooted in participatory democracy and critiques of the corporate city. More than any other intervention of the era, the construction of the Eaton Centre fundamentally transformed the street. Bringing downtown life indoors created prosperity for the Centre's investors and for many Yonge Street businesses, while at the same time introducing powerful new dynamics of centralization, privatization, and control.

Finally, in the conclusion to *The Heart of Toronto* I return to the book's main arguments, highlighting how over nearly three decades downtown Yonge Street's remaking was central to debates over the urban future in Toronto. I also continue the story up to the present day, exploring how historical dynamics established in the postwar period have continued to shape downtown Yonge and the surrounding area. Massive capital investment in redevelopment has dramatically altered block after block of the street. Yet amidst this transformation, attachment to Yonge's iconic shopscape has inspired grassroots efforts to improve and celebrate the street, whether through festivals, documentary film, or architectural preservation campaigns. Debates over civility, use, and behaviour continue to erupt periodically in this busy public space, prompting new policing and planning interventions aimed at securing its value as a metropolitan shopping and entertainment destination. Much changed in form and character since the 1950s, downtown Yonge Street remains vibrant and contested, a microcosm of the North American city that has grown around it over the last seven decades.

1

Making Downtown Yonge Street

Streets change. Familiar names and routes might provide the illusion of continuity, but like the cities they run through and organize, urban thoroughfares are dynamic human creations. Brick by brick, their built landscapes are demolished and reconstructed, incorporating new techniques and materials and providing scope for new activities; populations come and go, inhabiting those environments differently and changing them along the way; images of the street evolve and clash as people try to understand it and influence its future, often with unintended consequences. This process occurs in a historical context shaped by setting, economic trends, and other material circumstances, but those impersonal forces alone do not explain why and how it unfolds. This book argues that streets are made and remade by the people who use them, by individual decisions and collective projects, long-term plans, and the routines of everyday life. Since this is a process that happens over time, each new intervention is shaped by the accumulated weight of those that came before – that is, by the street itself, actor in its own production.

From Colonial Road to Commercial Street

Before it became an urban artery, Yonge Street was a colonial road, part of a British imperial project to secure and develop the colony of Upper Canada. It was named for Sir George Yonge, a British parliamentarian who never set foot in the colony but was a friend of the lieutenant-governor and known for his particular interest in roads and roadbuilding.[1] Cleared by soldiers and settlers in the mid-1790s, it ran northward from the tiny colonial capital of York, parallel to long-established Indigenous trading routes linking the Lower and Upper Great Lakes. Maps from this period depict Yonge Street as an arrow-straight line traversing an otherwise trackless wilderness, a confident projection of British ambitions to organize and populate a region on the edge of empire.[2] In reality, it remained a rough cart-track until well into the nineteenth century. Ill-suited for anything but local transportation, Yonge functioned principally as a vector for expansion of the settlement frontier during the late eighteenth and early nineteenth centuries. It was along this colonial road that Europeans moved north from Lake Ontario into lands newly claimed from the Mississaugas and other Anishinaabe peoples, taking part in the transformation of Upper Canada from a string of garrison outposts into an enduring settler society.[3]

By the 1820s, British and American settlers had established a string of villages and agrarian townships along the fifty-kilometre length of Yonge Street, the north-south baseline for land subdivision in the region. The colonial road became a highway, carrying people and produce south to market, and commercial goods and an intermittent stream of migrants north. Following a long-established pattern in North American urbanization, York grew through acting as a hub for this traffic with its rural hinterland, transforming from a "government village" – administrative buildings, a fort, and a handful of private homes – to a port and market centre.[4] With a population of nine thousand in 1834, the year it incorporated as the City of Toronto, it was beginning to look like an urban settlement, albeit a muddy and disorganized one according to contemporary observers.[5] A growing number of brick and stone buildings dotted the shoreline and filled in the small commercial and administrative district developing just to the north on King Street. Yonge Street bisected the city into east and west, as it still does today, but it was far from being an urban thoroughfare. Toronto, like York before it, continued to face the harbour that was its main link with the outside world, and development spread east and west along the shoreline.

This changed in the second half of the nineteenth century, amid the larger urban transformations that accompanied Toronto's entry into industrial modernity. In the 1850s, railway lines began to radiate outward from the city, consolidating its dominance of the regional economy and facilitating the arrival of tens of thousands of migrants from the British Isles, reinforcing the city's already strong Anglo-Celtic character. Toronto's population expanded to forty-five thousand in 1861 and to eighty-six thousand in 1881, making it the second-largest urban centre in the new Dominion of Canada, after Montreal. Virtually the entire city was rebuilt to accommodate this rapid growth. With encouragement from the new entrepreneurial elite, manufacturing followed the railways into the heart of the city, creating an industrial corridor along the shoreline that effectively cut Toronto off from the lake. Estates granted decades earlier to the colonial aristocracy were swiftly – and profitably – subdivided to create neighbour-hoods of workers' cottages and middle-class houses, filling in most of the undeveloped sections of the city and increasing separation between resi-dential and business districts. Those who could afford it fled the noise and smoke to elite enclaves, including the garden suburb of Rosedale, furthering the ongoing sorting of the urban population by class and ethno-religious identity.

Yonge Street became a vital thoroughfare in the Victorian industrial city. Having turned its back on the lake and reaching its natural limits to the east and west – the Don River and Garrison Creek – Toronto's urban expansion began to track northward along Yonge, giving the city a rough inverted T-shape that is still visible in the density of development today. For the first time, the street was not just a corridor, but a destination. Commercial development crept north, following the urban centre of gravity and responding to the availability of land outside of the cramped King Street district. On Yonge, a nearly unbroken row of three- and four-storey Victorian brick buildings replaced wooden houses and garden plots; construction followed the line of the road allowance as originally surveyed, creating a street that measured sixty-six feet (or one colonial survey chain) across, from storefront to storefront. Its lower stretches were paved and gas-lit, and tracks were laid for the city's first horse-drawn street railway. In 1873, local clergyman and historian Henry Scadding marvelled in his vivid *Toronto of Old* at the speed at which the street had been "so solidly and even splendidly built up":

> It seems in the retrospect but a very short time since Yonge Street [was] an obscure allowance for road, visited seldom by any one, and for a long while particularly difficult to traverse during and just after the rainy seasons. Few persons in the olden time [ever] dreamed that the inter-section of Yonge Street and King Street was to be the heart of the town.[6]

With his nostalgic account of rapid urban change, Scadding was one of the first Toronto observers to see Yonge Street as the vital heart of a city in transformation.

The newly urbanized strip of Yonge running north from King Street was dominated by one sector of activity: buying and selling. By 1881, approximately half of the city's 150 retail stores were located on this short stretch, where intense competition created a charged, exciting atmosphere

A key thoroughfare in the Victorian city. Yonge looking north from Queen Street with street railway tracks in the foreground, around 1895. | McCord Museum MP-0000.25.179

for passersby, as merchants posted eye-catching signs, distributed handbills, and regularly rotated door and window displays to attract customers.[7] A developing subset of services for shoppers – tea rooms to rest and take refreshment, seamstresses to alter purchases – were interspersed between these stores. Much of this was entirely novel in provincial Toronto, the first glimpse of the way in which industrial innovations and new consumer spending were revolutionizing shopping elsewhere in the world. Throughout the Victorian era and beyond, Yonge Street was a laboratory for changes in the retail trade and patterns of consumption. In their quest to capture the spending of the growing population of white-collar and industrial workers, merchants specialized, increased their staff, and deployed new offerings, advertising tactics, and credit schemes – not to mention new technologies, including Toronto's first electric arc lights, installed on the street in 1881.

Making Downtown

Whether contemporary observers appreciated or criticized it, from Henry Scadding onward they acknowledged lower Yonge as the city's main shopping street and its centrality to the urban experience in Toronto. Attempting to convey the dynamism of the new culture of consumption to its readers, the *Globe* described the scene on a Saturday evening on Yonge Street in 1881:

> people began to pour from all parts of the city ... to see, and mayhap to be seen, upon Yonge Street. In half an hour both sides of the street were thronged with a perpetual human strain [and] the buzz of merry chat ... Every store or shop seemed like a hive, every clerk was at his best to serve the waiting customers; the door never ceased to open and shut and people to come out and go in. The whole street may be said to have the same relation to the city as the main artery has to the human body.[8]

Other accounts were less positive. In 1879, another *Globe* column complained of the young single workers of both sexes who mixed and loitered on gaslit Yonge Street after dark, arguing that their flirtatious behaviour created a sexualized space in which even "respectable" women were subject to catcalls and propositions. The shopping strip, the paper noted, was one of the best-policed areas in the city, but that made little difference; its crowds and commercial atmosphere invited transgression.[9] This reaction to shifting social categories and norms – in this case, the terms for class and gender mixing in public space – is just one example of the fundamental ambivalence toward urbanization that characterized elite discourse in late-nineteenth-century Canada, particularly in a largely Anglo-Protestant city then aspiring to temperance and a renewed moral order.[10] Ambivalence regarding the changing city would endure, resurfacing in the anxiety and excitement that accompanied later periods of intense growth.

Changes on Yonge Street announced the emergence of a new urban place in Toronto: downtown. The concept, historian Robert Fogelson reminds us, originated in Manhattan's north-south – up and down – geography in the early nineteenth century. From there, the term was adopted by cities across the continent to describe a new spatial and social reality produced by the era's urban transformations: the modern business district, which centralized economic activity and public life in space to an unprecedented degree.[11] The word "downtown" was first imported to Toronto in the 1860s, but it did not enter regular usage until the early 1900s.[12] By that point, it was widely understood to refer to the roughly one-kilometre-square urban core centred on Yonge and King Streets, an area with virtually no residential population that was distinctive for its high land values, dense built form, and concentration of retailers and wholesalers, financial institutions, offices, and the apparatus of local government.[13] As a growing network of electric streetcar lines enabled further residential dispersion east, west, and north, this functional segregation became more apparent, although it was never total: industry spread along the railway corridors, and grocers and other low-order retailers thrived on neighbourhood strips. Still, if home and neighbourhood were local and private, downtown was decidedly metropolitan and public. It was where mass transit lines crossed, where city council deliberated, where Toronto's heterogeneous population – which reached 200,000 in 1900 through in-migration and annexations – came to work, transact business, and shop.

A New Retail Paradigm

They did so in a built environment and business context that were constantly evolving: downtown Yonge Street did not stay still. The most important change of the late Victorian era was the rise of the department store. Until the 1880s, the retail landscape in Toronto was defined by a high number of small shops competing fiercely for customers on a roughly equal footing. On Yonge Street, they occupied premises on narrow lots with twenty-odd feet of sidewalk frontage, a dozen or more per block, employed a handful of male clerks – often family members – and had similar access to wholesale goods, which they sold mostly on credit. By the end of the century, this model had been disrupted, in Toronto as in other large industrial cities, by a small number of merchants who used large-scale capital investment in real estate and new retail practices – including cash-only policies, direct buying, and in-house manufacturing – to dominate the market.[14] Timothy Eaton was one, and Robert Simpson another, both British immigrants. In the early 1880s, these businessmen began an aggressive expansion of their operations at the strategically key intersection of Yonge and Queen. By the end of the decade, Eaton's four-storey, fifty-thousand-square-foot store, employing three hundred men and women and equipped with new technologies including electric lights and elevators, was the most modern and successful in Canada. Simpson's was not far behind.

Competition between Yonge's department store giants and their continued physical expansion remade consumption in Toronto, while branch stores and catalogue sales extended their economic dominance and cultural influence throughout the emerging "retail nation" of Canada.[15] Even as

Toronto's population grew at unprecedented speed, reaching 375,000 in 1911 and half a million in 1921, the number of its retailers shrank, reflecting centralization of consumer spending in large- and medium-sized stores, and most of all on Yonge Street.[16] Some smaller shops on the strip specialized in certain market niches – furs, shoes, and discount merchandise, among others – to benefit from the additional foot traffic attracted by major retailers; others were replaced as land values increased and competition for key retailing sites, especially corner lots, stiffened.[17] At the start of the First World War, both Eaton's and Simpson's were block-sized retail palaces built through the demolition of dozens of the small shops that characterized the street in Henry Scadding's day. Interviewed by the *Globe* in 1908, former Yonge Street merchant John Wanless expressed regret to see the business he had established in 1861 close its doors. The progress-oriented newspaper was more sanguine, calling the closing of the Wanless store "time's advance ... mak[ing] room for new enterprise," in this case the relentless expansion of Simpson's retail empire.[18]

The rise of the department store helped shift the gender dynamics of downtown. Simpson's and Eaton's built big, not just to profit from economies of scale, but to put into action a new selling strategy centred on customer experience that had been pioneered in the department stores of Paris, London, and New York. The targeted client for that strategy was unquestionably female. Both stores worked to attract women consumers of all classes and their growing spending power, employing girl clerks and attendants and offering an array of services including coat and luggage storage, restaurants and refreshment rooms, and toilets. By designing their retail palaces as "downtown destinations for women," the department stores provided refuges from the inconvenience, dirt, and noise – not to mention the omnipresent male gaze – that defined women's experiences of the urban core in the Victorian era. These accommodations fit into a larger process, ongoing across North America by the early 1900s, by which downtown spaces opened up to, and were claimed by, women.[19] If, in the *Globe*'s 1879 reporting, mentioned above, it was difficult for a "respectable" woman to find her place on Yonge Street, this was no longer the case by the First World War. Other key factors in this shift included wider female participation in the downtown workforce and the expansion of gender-mixed commercial amusements on Yonge.[20]

The Electric Street
The growth of entertainment on Yonge was a second important trend shaping the street in the first half of the twentieth century. In 1894, the

monumental Massey Music Hall opened just off Yonge, where it would play host to symphony, opera, and other high-brow cultural performances. Meanwhile, just steps away, an inter-class mass entertainment district sprung up around Yonge and Queen. Like the department store, commercial amusements were the result of technological and cultural innovation, on the one hand, and the drive to increase the profitability of downtown land, on the other. Retail and entertainment – day and night – were interdependent, relying on similar marketing strategies to attract the attention of the same public of consumers. The nascent technology of cinema played an important role in this process, as it morphed from a curiosity to a highly profitable cultural product that found willing consumers in Toronto. According to Paul Moore, eight cinemas had opened their doors on Yonge Street by 1920, including a seven-storey stacked double theatre with a capacity of 3,500 spectators built by New York theatre magnate Marcus Loew in 1913–14; a further eleven were located in the immediate vicinity.[21] Interspersed with these places of amusement were lunch-counters, drugstores, and other inexpensive eating places catering to both daytime shoppers and cinema-going crowds.

By night, the theatre's flashing marquees were the brightest spots on an electric street fed by Ontario's plentiful, cheap hydroelectric power. Contemporary photographs show a streetscape aglow with the light of triple-globed streetlamps, shop signs, and flashing cigarette billboards; electric streetcars slowly move people up and down the strip.[22] The brightness of the strip contrasted sharply with the darker, quieter east-west cross streets that intersected it. Yonge's centrality was emphasized by the lack of substantial commercial development on most neighbouring streets. One city desk reporter described in 1912 how Yonge Street, alone of Toronto thoroughfares, had banished the night. "Always there are people on Yonge Street," he explained. "All through the night [it is a] link between the feverish life of one day and another." Observing the street's nightlife, he emphasized the ways in which electricity created a unique ambience of public sociability. Flashing billboards and illuminated window displays captured attention and tempted strollers to linger; the sidewalks were transformed into exhilarating "lanes of light," while the darkness beyond hid the rough edges of the city and of the crowd.[23] At all times, but especially at night, Yonge Street in the twentieth century was a spectacle of downtown life.

A Public Space

Site of mass retail and entertainment, Yonge was widely understood as an important urban public space. In a modern metropolis fragmented along class, ethnic, and other lines, it was made to symbolize the North American ideal of downtown, an essentially democratic place where citizens met on terms of equality.[24] In 1906, a *Globe* columnist explained how Yonge brought together Toronto's far-flung population in space and purpose. Downtown, he argued, was "a frequent word in the northern resident's vocabulary, for the shopping district has been turned into a gigantic lodestone, whose mystic power is felt in the very remotest corners of the city ... All the diverse units that make up our civic whole seem poured together in one jostling but good-humoured mass in the city's retail quarter."[25] In this idealized view, shopping was an act of civic communion that united as few other activities could. Yonge Street's crowds – "loitering crowds, hurrying crowds, window-shopping crowds, buying crowds," explained a journalist at Christmas in 1925 – were thus a sign not just of economic success, but of social cohesion. Yonge was Toronto's "testimony of metropolitanism," proof of its capacity to thrive as an aggregation of diverse neighbourhoods and populations.[26]

Some commentators struck a note of caution, acknowledging that not everyone shared equally in the prosperity. Among the crowds spilling off Yonge's sidewalks, downtown observers in the early decades of the twentieth century counted individuals – the hard-working washerwoman, the shabbily-clothed immigrant – whose lot was to look, never to buy. These were simplified urban types that nonetheless reflected the changing social landscape of the city. The Yonge Street shopping area bordered on and was economically intertwined with some of Toronto's most impoverished residential areas. Just to the northwest of Yonge and Queen was St. John's Ward, home to a multi-ethnic population that included recent Jewish immigrants from eastern Europe, African Canadians, and a small Chinatown. Many men and women in "the Ward" worked in the factory lofts that supplied Yonge Street shops with inexpensive, mass-market clothing, including the Eaton's factories adjacent to the company's flagship store.[27] Accounts of Yonge Street did not, however, dwell on the difficult day-to-day reality facing newcomers or racialized communities, or on the ways in which their labour contributed to the street's prosperity. Instead, they emphasized that the very presence of these groups attested to the essentially democratic character of the strip. In one writer's words, the differing crowds attracted by fine-goods stores and cheap luncheonettes made the sidewalks a place of frequent "mingling of the splendid and the shabby."[28] If the conditions of the private lives of Torontonians varied sharply, according to this hopeful interpretation they could nonetheless all partake in downtown's public life.

Crowds and congestion on Yonge at Queen Street, summer 1929. Simpson's department store is on the far left (west) side of the image, and Eaton's is farther north, opposite Loew's Theatre. | City of Toronto Archives, fonds 16, series 71, item 7172

Civic ceremonies and celebrations reinforced Yonge Street's role as a central public space. From 1899, Toronto's elected officials and commercial magnates transacted business side-by-side, as the municipal government and courts followed the north-westward movement of downtown's centre to Yonge and Queen Streets. The presence of the impressive Romanesque City Hall building just west of the Eaton's and Simpson's stores further entwined Yonge in the city's official life. Soldiers went off to two world wars marching down Yonge Street; crowds at the dedication of the city's First World War cenotaph in 1925 spilled over into the retail area, as did victory celebrations in 1945. Toronto's Labour Day and Orange processions both routed down Yonge Street until the mid-twentieth century, but by far the most important event for the shopping area had little do with reinforcing class or ethno-religious identities. The cavalcade of fantastic floats that was Toronto's Santa Claus Parade, organized and financed by Eaton's, wound its way through downtown Toronto each year from 1905 with a stop in front of the company's flagship store. Somewhere between a Christmas pageant and a circus, the parade had become Canada's foremost commercial spectacle by the 1920s, watched by thousands of sidewalk spectators and diffused to many more across the country through newspaper, radio, and television coverage.[29]

Aspirations and Ambivalence

Downtown mattered in an aspirational city whose boosters sought to surpass Montreal as Canada's economic capital.[30] From the early twentieth century, Toronto celebrated Yonge Street first and foremost for its obvious prosperity. Counting crowds and the retail receipts were common ways of measuring success. Another was in observing the continued physical evolution of the urban landscape. In the late nineteenth and early twentieth centuries, Toronto joined other major North American towns in a wave of vertical expansion that transformed it into a skyscraper city, prefiguring the post-1945 tower construction explored later in this book. In 1891, it had four office buildings that were over six storeys in height. By 1931, there were forty-nine, with eighteen located on or immediately adjacent to the south end of the Yonge commercial strip. Much like the city's new department stores and cinemas, these skyscrapers expressed not just technical innovation, but changes in the organization of capitalism: in this case the expansion of Toronto's economic hinterland, the rise of the modern corporation, and the resulting growth of white-collar jobs downtown.[31] The impact on Yonge was significant. Shops and entertainment were displaced to the north as Yonge at King Street was hemmed in by stone-clad corporate towers, including the fifteen-storey Canadian Pacific Railway Building (1913) and thirty-four-storey Commerce Court (1931). Meanwhile, the growing service economy brought thousands and soon tens of thousands of office workers – and potential customers – to the centre of the city each weekday. By the 1920s, the vertical expansion of Canada's fastest-growing business district – "Toronto's wonderful boom," according to the elated *Globe* – and the intensifying of financial and other tertiary activities were also elements of Yonge's identity as a downtown street.[32]

Yonge's busy sidewalks, bright lights, and modern constructions occupied a key place in the aspirational city, which located urban success in their continued thriving and improvement. Visions for the future, however, are rooted in critiques of the present. By the interwar decades, celebration of Yonge Street in Toronto was tempered by dissatisfaction and the first noteworthy public debates over its future. The first critique to emerge in this period was aesthetic and civic, anchored in the rise of architectural and planning expertise as a voice in urban affairs in Toronto. Following the example set by their peers in cities such as Chicago, Buffalo, and New York, leaders in these professions proposed a series of plans – much discussed but never implemented – for rationalizing and beautifying the heterogeneous urban landscape created by decades of growth.[33] The hegemonic City Beautiful ideal, with its emphasis on monumental buildings, wide boulevards, and aesthetic harmony, was particularly influential. From this perspective, downtown Yonge Street was consistently singled out as an example of the faults of the unplanned city. According to its expert critics, Yonge was narrow and cramped, creating congestion and providing no space to step back and appreciate city form. Not that there was much to appreciate, despite the street's exuberant modernity – in 1927, renowned architect John Lyle spoke for his frustrated profession when he asked whether "any city in the world of a similar size can show a shabbier street than Yonge street; a meaner lot of shops, or a worse conglomeration of false fronts ... Toronto has outgrown the mining camp idea of what a metropolitan retail street should look like."[34]

In other words, Yonge must be improved to reflect and contribute to Toronto's growing economic prosperity and civic importance. To fix this situation, Lyle proposed that merchants and the municipal government invest in removing billboards, projecting signs, and wiring, and that future constructions be held to higher standards. Doubtless, he was motivated by the fact that his award-winning Beaux-Arts style Thornton-Smith building, recently completed on the west side of Yonge, was hemmed in by two much more utilitarian shop structures in unremarkable Victorian red brick. Around the same time, other experts and concerned citizens began to focus on the idea of widening the street. This plan promised not only to improve the flow of foot and vehicle traffic, but also to encourage building owners to replace shabby shops with grander constructions set back along the new property line. Some proponents of widening called for replacement of the current sidewalks with arcades set into existing buildings, offering a "sheltered shopping promenade" that would protect pedestrians from the weather while encouraging them to linger at merchants' window displays.[35] These renovation schemes consistently foundered on the City's inability to compel property owners to rebuild. But the idea that Yonge's unplanned built landscape demanded improvement stayed in circulation into the postwar period and influenced the first serious efforts to comprehensively plan downtown.

The second critique that drew public attention during the interwar decades came not from elite urban experts, but from Yonge Street business owners. If architects like John Lyle understood Yonge's rapid unplanned growth primarily as an aesthetic problem, some merchants saw it as posing an existential economic threat. A coalition of retailers mobilized to highlight the ways in which the last few decades of downtown prosperity had been unequally distributed. Faced with major increases in property tax assessments in 1911 and 1921, they argued that they were bearing more than their share of the burden of a speculative land market. "The simple fact is business men on Yonge street cannot pay that assessment," explained furrier and milliner William Dineen in a 1921 deputation to the city's Board of Control. "It will drive them away." Another delegate stated that, despite rising land values, the vast majority of Yonge merchants were losing money due to traffic congestion and the economic slump that followed the First World War.[36] Political lobbying around this issue made obvious the fact that different types of businesses had experienced Yonge's economic ascension very differently, creating not one but several interest groups on the street. Small- and medium-sized merchants protested in an angry, even desperate tone individually or through the Retail Merchants Association, a lobby group that had opposed department stores' aggressive business practices in the past. Meanwhile, the big department stores and banks, whose property transactions and redevelopment projects were among the main causes of increasing land values, were largely silent.

People who wanted to change Yonge converged in their assumption that local government was the natural place for criticisms of the street to be heard and acted upon. Both elites and merchants called for Toronto's municipal administration to solve the street's perceived problems, whether by compelling improvements or reducing taxes on business. This marked the arrival of a new paradigm in urban governance in Toronto. As in other major Canadian cities adapting to industrialization and growth, the power of Toronto's municipal government was expanding during the first decades of the twentieth century. This occurred despite the presence of a local culture of fiscal restraint, encouraged by yearly elections that often hinged on responsible spending. During the interwar period, the "service city," providing utilities, security, transportation, and other essential public goods to its citizens, definitively replaced the "private city" of the nineteenth century.[37] Reliance on various agencies and departments of the municipal state for solutions to downtown problems – or at the very least as arbiter of divergent interests – would become the norm in the second half of the century, as explored later in this book.

Decentralization and Motorization

Critics of Yonge Street felt that it was out of step with the needs of the growing city. Proposals to widen it were rooted not just in the drive to beautify, but also in a desire to use the street to bind together an increasingly decentralized urban region. By the onset of the Great Depression in 1929, Toronto had 600,000 inhabitants, with another 200,000 people living in connected suburbs. The low-density sprawl of the second half of the twentieth century had not yet arrived, but population dispersion to streetcar suburbs and fringe neighbourhoods was already well under way, destabilizing the centralized city of the nineteenth century.[38] Whereas higher-order retail and corporate power were almost entirely concentrated downtown, ribbons of dense commercial development became well established during this period, following major streetcar routes such as the Danforth and Bloor, Queen, and College Streets. Neighbourhood cinemas, restaurants, discount stores, and new chain retailers offered a growing range of services and goods; employing the downtown model, they organized to beautify their shopping areas and to encourage nearby residents to "shop at home." In this context, downtown merchants located the cause of reduced sales receipts in the inability of shoppers from the urban fringe to easily reach their stores and actively sought to encourage greater metropolitan mobility. Some thought the solution was to increase the number of streetcar routes connecting directly to the shopping strip, and they successfully lobbied the City, which took over public transportation in 1921, to do so.[39] But most interwar critics who wished to maintain Yonge's relevance focused on accommodating the private automobile.

Downtown Yonge was profoundly affected by the popularization of this new transportation technology. Though we often associate car culture with the second half of the twentieth century, the years up to 1930 saw the automobile already transforming the city. In 1904, a few hundred cars were registered in Ontario; by 1930, there were half a million, 80,000 of them in Toronto alone.[40] Rapid motorization prompted the City to create traffic police, deploy signage and automatic signals, launch safety campaigns, and divide the street into separated vehicular and pedestrian spaces.[41] Yonge Street was particularly affected, as a key route into town for the affluent northern suburbs, whose population was among the first to adopt the car for commuting or shopping.[42] It was also one of the most congested sections of town, where regular friction between road users was highest. As a result, in the 1920s and 1930s Yonge Street merchants played a central role in pioneering debates over traffic regulation and the place of the car in the city, just as they would in the 1960s and 1970s with the question of pedestrianization. Downtown Yonge was the first locale where private parking garages were constructed, or where one-way routing, parking restrictions, and even streetcar removal were debated, as merchants lobbied the City to help them cater to the growing number of customers arriving by car. Here, again, differences between larger and smaller businesses were evident. From the mid-1920s, both Simpson's and Eaton's offered valet parking to their customers, while other shops largely depended on curbside spaces or nearby garages, limiting their ability to adapt to motorization.[43]

Downtown in the Polycentric City

These two trends, decentralization and motorization, became more pronounced after the Second World War. By that point, Toronto, like the rest of the country, had struggled through a decade of severe economic depression and six years of the wartime economy, years in which people spent less, the municipal government launched no major projects, and the building industry – a key indicator of urban prosperity – significantly reduced its activities. From the late 1940s, pent-up demand for housing drove a new wave of urban expansion that burst the bounds of the streetcar city, already stretched to the limit by wartime crowding. Over the next two decades, more than 1 million people settled in a ring of large suburban municipalities – York, North York, East York, Scarborough, and Etobicoke – that occupied twice the area of the old city. Many of those who opted for the suburbs were middle-class families moving outward from the core, the only part of the city where population steadily declined – by roughly twenty thousand, or 14 percent – in the two decades following the Second World War.[44] Others were newcomers from elsewhere in Canada, or among the more than half a million immigrants who remade Toronto's postwar social fabric. As elsewhere in North America, the shift to low-density sprawl was facilitated by government policy, the rise of land development corporations, and mass automobile ownership. In 1941, there was 1 private car registered in Ontario for every 6 inhabitants; by 1961, the ratio was 1 to 3.5, and it continued to shrink.[45] Automobile suburbanization brought with it not just new built landscapes and demographic realities, but also a new tier of urban governance. From 1953, the Municipality of Metropolitan Toronto,

A Growth of Toronto to the mid-1960s

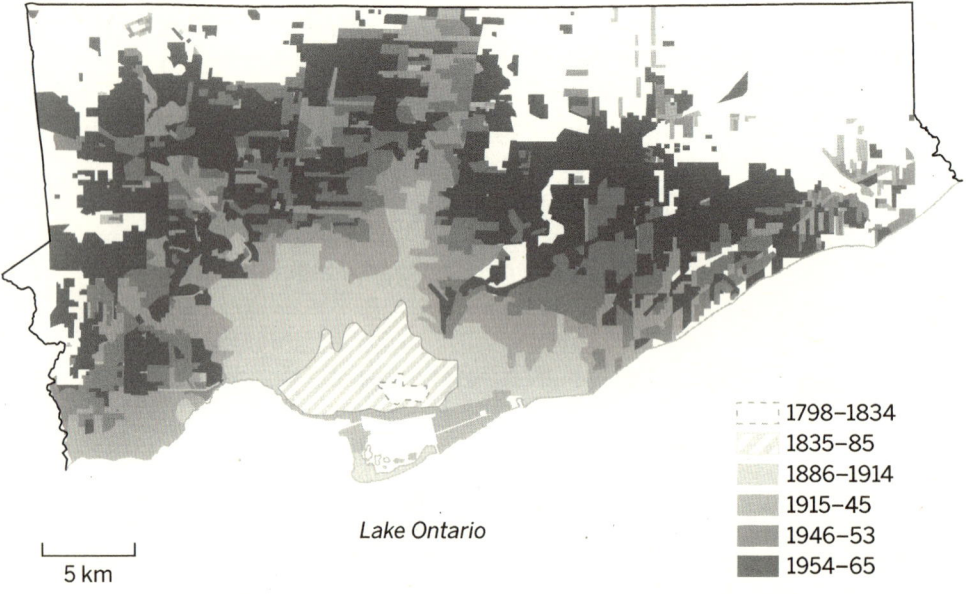

1798–1834
1835–85
1886–1914
1915–45
1946–53
1954–65

Lake Ontario

5 km

B Municipalities forming Metro Toronto, 1967

NORTH YORK

SCARBOROUGH

YORK

ETOBICOKE

EAST YORK

TORONTO

Lake Ontario

5 km

Metro Toronto in the mid-1960s | Cartographer: Eric Leinberger

or Metro, was responsible for regional-level planning and infrastructure, binding Toronto together with surrounding communities in a program of decentralized urban growth.[46]

Sprawl represented both opportunity and an unprecedented threat to downtown Yonge's business model. In terms of the former, Toronto's new urban fringe offered an expanding, underexploited customer base. There was a lag between residential and commercial development in Metro's new suburban neighbourhoods, and until the mid-1950s what was being built – mostly automobile-oriented commercial strips – could not compete with the selection, prices, and atmosphere of downtown. Leading business experts in the 1950s, including the Toronto chapter of the American Marketing Association and celebrated United States retail consultant Larry Smith, argued that downtown could dominate the affluent suburban market, but only if the City prioritized mobility between the centre and the fringe.[47] Yonge Street businesses had in fact been saying this for decades. Postwar, both the larger stores and the smaller concerns, the latter represented by a new group, the Downtown Businessmen's Association, renewed their lobbying for a more automobile-friendly downtown, with expanded parking, one-way streets, and expressway connections.[48] In this view, increased metropolitan mobility was the key to maintaining Yonge's centrality: given the right conditions, the suburbs would come to downtown.

One major new connector for suburb-centre flows was Toronto's first subway line, constructed for seven kilometres underneath Yonge Street, including the downtown shopping area, between 1949 and 1954. Tunnelled transit had been discussed in the city since the early 1900s, but the project did not become financially and technologically viable until the postwar decades.[49] People who were invested in Yonge Street viewed the short-term impacts of this major public works project almost exclusively in a negative light. The cut-and-cover method adopted by the Toronto Transit Commission on Yonge – less expensive than tunnelling – meant that the busiest sections of the strip were subject to years of traffic diversions, cancelled streetcar service, noise, and dust. In 1951, a reporter for the *Globe and Mail* claimed that a "once busy commercial thoroughfare today looks more like a combination of dirt track and sand pile." Despite special sales and promotions of the subway dig as a tourist attraction, retailers reported drops in receipts as high as 20 percent and in several cases threatened legal action against the City to recover their losses.[50] These disruptions ended, however, with the opening of the Yonge subway line in 1954, and merchants organized a parade to mark the street's "resurrection [after] six years of being a no-man's-land, chopped, chewed, excavated and pushed around."

**Construction of the Yonge Street subway, looking north from just south
of Richmond Street, 1950.** | City of Toronto Archives, series 574, item
49503

Their hope was that this new public technology would remind citizens that
Yonge Street was "Toronto's premier shopping district."[51]

Despite major investments in metropolitan public transit, the car remained the conveyance of choice for suburbanites accessing downtown.
The reshaping of the pre-automobile landscape, begun in the interwar
decades, intensified, and by the 1960s it was impossible to ignore the
widespread material impacts of the private car on downtown and surrounding neighbourhoods. Each day, tens of thousands of private vehicles
poured into Toronto's core area, filling its streets beyond their capacity and
adding to long-standing problems of congestion and air pollution. This
flow also prompted new uses of urban space. In the 1960s, parking was the
second-fastest-growing land use in downtown Toronto – after offices – with
spaces for ten thousand new cars constructed during that decade. At the
end of the decade, as motorization reached its peak in the downtown, a

staggering fifth of the land in the central business district was given over to automobile storage, often as a temporary use in preparation for re-development.[52] The traffic jam, the multi-level parking garage, and the demolition site repurposed as a parking lot became typical features of the landscape.

Amid these efforts to bring people and spending from the urban fringe into the centre, a major restructuring in urban commerce was doing just the opposite: shifting downtown functions to the suburbs. At the centre of this trend was the planned shopping centre, which from 1953 to 1969 accounted for 90 percent of retail growth in the Toronto region.[53] The shopping mall revolutionized consumption by transplanting an idealized – and motorized – version of the downtown experience to the urban periphery. With its dense concentrations of shops and entertainment, attractive pedestrian concourses, and ample parking, it was an effort to construct "a more perfect downtown," without the inconveniences of traffic, changeable weather, or unsavoury streetlife.[54] By the end of the 1960s, there were 280 shopping centres in the Toronto region, including a dozen major enclosed malls with more than fifty stores each. North York's Yorkdale, the largest in the city – and, briefly, in the world – was explicitly promoted as a mod-ernized, automobile-friendly alternative to Yonge Street. Marketing ma-terials for its opening in 1964 proclaimed that "downtown has moved uptown," explaining that its more than one hundred tenants included "Eaton's, Simpson's, restaurants, theatres [and] 70% of the best-known stores in the core area of downtown Toronto."[55] As this list suggests, by the 1960s the "best known" Yonge Street businesses – essentially the depart-ment stores and chain retailers – had embraced suburban expansion. Those who could not, the vast majority of Yonge's independent businesses, felt the impact of downtown's falling market share all the more viscerally. Urban experts exhorted them to modernize and focus on "quality and novelty"; in the larger scheme of things, they were doing just that, but as much through failure and succession as through adaptation.[56]

The postwar reality in Toronto was that growth and dynamism had shifted to the urban periphery, something that anyone who was invested in downtown understood. What was less understood was the extent to which the shape of the city was changing in ways not captured by the suburb-downtown opposition of the streetcar era. The new metropolis emerging in the postwar period was more than an enlarged version of the old: it was a different entity, an urban region in which people, cap-ital, and other flows moved not just in and out of the centre, but along and between other corridors and nodes. During the second half of the twentieth century, Toronto became not only suburban but polycentric, a process that was already well under way in the 1950s and 1960s.[57] It was politically polycentric, with the rise of the new suburbs as (junior) partners in the metropolitan government and increasingly important municipal actors in their own right. It was economically polycentric too, with the dispersal of jobs and commerce into office parks, shopping centres, and arterial strips, and from the deindustrializing core to the industrializing fringe. Finally, Toronto was more and more culturally polycentric, developing as a patchwork of differing urban landscapes and communities with their own reference points and interconnections, not necessarily dependent on the central core. The key challenge for downtown Yonge Street in this period was to adapt to its new status as just one hub – albeit the most important – among many in the suburban metropolis.

Walking the Postwar Street

What kind of a place was produced by the century and a half of change described in this chapter? Perhaps the best way to understand downtown Yonge Street in the postwar decades is by viewing it from street level. In tracing this busy thoroughfare, we follow in the footsteps of more than a century of Toronto *flâneurs* – from clergyman historian Henry Scadding in the 1860s to psychogeographer Shawn Micallef in the 2000s – who have relied on walking this street to better understand the changing city.[58] Our urban explorer might begin where Yonge meets Lake Ontario, the starting point for countless similar journeys from the colonial era onward. Here, at the foot of the street, ferries full of passengers depart for the Toronto Islands, offering people in central Toronto neighbourhoods a cheap escape to fresh air, beaches, and mass amusements. Apart from the ferry terminal, there is little at a human scale on the industrialized, motorized waterfront. Here, rubble extracted during the subway dig on Yonge has been dumped in the lake to create additional space for development. As automobile traffic speeds by, our flâneur passes parking lots and manufacturing complexes such as the Redpath Sugar Refinery, all built on construction infill. After a few hundred metres, the stroller (carefully) crosses an on-ramp and walks underneath the arches of the elevated Gardiner Expressway, a key link in the freeway network built by Metro Toronto in the 1950s and 1960s. Like the vast railway sidings behind Union Station just to the north, the concrete ribbon of the Gardiner is a testament to the size of the region that has developed around Yonge Street since the city's Victorian beginnings.

Walking north and uphill, the flâneur emerges into the city proper at Front Street and immediately sees a change in scale. Once it enters the confines of the nineteenth-century core, Yonge Street is no longer a barren industrial arterial road, but a densely developed urban thoroughfare. Most buildings are constructed right to the edge of their lots, fronting on narrow sidewalks to create an urban canyon. This is the heart of the office district, home to Canada's principal stock market and the headquarters to a range of companies – mining corporations, advertising agencies, insurance conglomerates – with national and international reach.[59] Corporate cathedrals dominate this first stretch of the street, ranging from ornate eight- to ten-storey blocks built during the Victorian and Edwardian office boom to taller, more recent stone-clad or glass-and-steel bank skyscrapers clustered around Yonge and King Streets. Chances are that as our pedestrian moves north, evidence of a new wave of creative destruction of the urban fabric will become more visible. After a virtual halt during the Depression and the Second World War, once again from the early 1950s buildings are being demolished, lots consolidated, and the skyline filled in. While industrial jobs relocate to the margins and traditional retail stagnates, the office district is experiencing a boom that brings tens of thousands of additional workers downtown each day.[60] More than any other development of the period, the growth of white-collar employment brings home the fact that the different sectors of the downtown economy experienced postwar decentralization very differently.

Banks and insurance companies lead the most dynamic sector of the downtown economy. But the centre of human activity – of buying and selling, work and leisure – remains farther north, on the ten-block, 1.5-kilometre-long commercial strip running from just south of Queen Street to College Street. Despite the challenges of the postwar period, this strip retains its Victorian-era identity, that of a bustling urban artery offering consumer goods and mass entertainment to a wide cross-section of Torontonians. Commercial development does not stop at College Street; small businesses flank both sides of Yonge more or less continuously to Bloor Street and the elite residential suburb of Rosedale. But the iconic Yonge Street strip – and debates over its future – effectively ends at College. Here the sidewalks are the busiest in the city, but the pedestrian feels less hemmed in than among the bank towers at Yonge and King. In comparison to the office district, or to nearby University Avenue, widened and rebuilt in the first half of the twentieth century, this stretch of Yonge is remarkable for its lack of stately buildings, aesthetic coherence, or open space. Instead, its greatest strength is its human scale, allowing our urban observer to see what is happening on the other side of the street – and to jaywalk in relative safety.

By far the largest structures on this part of Yonge, and the first to draw the stroller's attention, are the flagship stores of the Eaton's and Simpson's chains, facing one another at the south end of the shopping area. Since the end of the nineteenth century, both have expanded to occupy entire blocks rebuilt to six, seven, or eight storeys, maximizing retailing space and frontage on Yonge's busy sidewalks. Farther up the street, Eaton's impressive Art Deco College Street store provides a northern bookend for the commercial strip. Its construction in 1930 marked the tail end of the golden age of department store dominance; nonetheless, Eaton's and Simpson's continue to exert a tremendous influence on downtown. They are two of the largest employers in the urban core, pulling thousands of men and women to Yonge Street each day to work in their stores, offices, and warehousing operations. Elaborate seasonal and themed window displays, sales, and celebrations stimulate Yonge's street life and attract consumers. In the early 1950s, a survey of a key category of Metro consumer – women homemakers – found that approximately one-third of every dollar they spent on retail goods (and three-quarters of their downtown spending) went into the coffers of one of the two giants.[61] Thanks to the competing presences of Eaton's and Simpson's, the corner of Yonge and Queen remains the most trafficked retail crossroads in the country, with the highest land value per square foot in Toronto's downtown, or almost anywhere else in Canada.[62]

Despite the continued dominance of the retail giants, there is room for smaller businesses to thrive on Yonge Street. Bracketed by the two Eaton's stores, the stroller moves through a dense and varied commercial area defined by large numbers of independent local businesses, mostly housed in three- or four-storey brick structures erected on narrow lots before the First World War. Just as in earlier decades, postwar urban critics expressed disappointment with this chaotic built landscape, seemingly always in the process of becoming.[63] But they also recognized that it possessed something unique. In the 1950s and 1960s, downtown Yonge Street was home to some three hundred shops and small businesses accounting for more than 1 million square feet of retail floor space: twice that of any other part of Toronto and equivalent to all but the largest of North America's suburban shopping centres.[64] A closer analysis of one stretch of the street – the east side of the block from Shuter north to Dundas – emphasizes its heterogeneity and diversity of uses. In the early 1960s, it boasted two taverns, five restaurants ranging from a burger joint to an expensive supper club, the Imperial Theatre, thirteen shoe and fashion outlets, three jewellers, and a drugstore with a late-night snack counter. Of course, life did not stop at street level. Above these ground-floor uses were additional layers of activity that included hair salons, a Trinidadian social club, a private detective agency, and dozens of offices ranging from dentists to architects, wholesalers to lawyers. Few landscapes better exemplified Jane Jacobs's 1961 description of dense urban environments as "natural generators of diversity and prolific incubators of new enterprises and ideas of all kinds."[65]

Lingering on the strip, our flâneur watches it undergo its nightly transformation into an electric street. Since the 1920s, white light has been replaced by colourful neon. The density of entertainment outlets also increased, particularly on the east side of the street, as they proved more able than traditional retailers to weather changes in consumer markets. On the cutting edge of liberalization of the city's nighttime economy, Yonge played host to Toronto's first cocktail lounges from 1947 and to the burgeoning blues, jazz, and rock and roll scenes. Throughout the 1950s and 1960s, venues such as the Edison Hotel, the Colonial Tavern, and the Coq d'Or hosted major American musicians on circuit and acted as laboratories for home-grown talent. Meanwhile, the city's largest record stores were among a growing list of hubs for a youthful consumer culture that included denim emporiums, poster shops, and pinball arcades. In 1969, local rags-to-riches retail and entertainment mogul "Honest" Ed Mirvish would describe the social mixing and vitality of the strip in terms reminiscent of those employed nearly a century earlier:

> People! People! People! Here is Bassel's restaurant, where you might find the mayor sitting next to a truck driver. The bars, go-go parlours, jazz combos, arcades, noise. A & A Records and Sam the Record Man. This noisy, busy strip, beautiful in its ugliness, contrasting with the stark, cold white skyscrapers of University Avenue just a few short blocks to the west.[66]

As Mirvish's comment suggests, the vitality of Yonge has always been measured in human traffic. Its sidewalks buzzed with people headed to and from appointments, shopping trips, and lunch breaks. At night, a corridor of neon signage shone on symphony-goers, tourists, and cruising carloads of teenagers. Crowds meant not just bargains and thrills, but also livelihoods. This busy street was a workplace for thousands of people, whether shop clerks, servers, accountants, or cab drivers. Among those working on the street, our downtown flâneur would note activities that had disappeared from the rest of the city. In an era when the Metropolitan

The electric street. Christmas lights and crowds on Yonge looking south from Gerrard Street, 1962. | Frank Grant/*Toronto Star* 499294709 via Getty Images

Toronto police are heavily motorized, downtown Yonge is one of the last areas still patrolled by "beat" cops on foot. In warmer weather, street vendors selling hot chestnuts, flowers, or candles are ubiquitous on the strip. They are joined by adolescent shoeshine boys, often drawn from the working-class neighbourhoods of the inner core, who set up their shops – a portable stool and polish kit – in doorways and on corners. Postwar observers tended to romanticize "Donnie the bootblack" and his companions as street-savvy entrepreneurs or as elements of Yonge's diverse human landscape, much as earlier commentators spoke approvingly of the presence of the washerwoman or the poor immigrant.[67] As explored later in this book, by the end of the 1970s Torontonians would come to see the shoeshine boy as a powerful symbol of innocence lost.

OUR EXPLORER'S TRIP up Yonge might end in several ways. Block after block of window displays and promises of sales and entertainment might weaken even the most dedicated flâneur's resistance, prompting a foray into Eaton's, Athens Restaurant, or the Rio Cinema, to participate in sustaining the city's largest consumer marketplace. Toronto's continental Great Lakes climate might also influence this decision, tempting the pedestrian with an escape from summer humidity or grinding winter cold. Or, perhaps it is time to return home. Chances are that in the 1950s or 1960s that journey would be much longer than in 1860 or 1920, although made more comfortable by changes in transportation technology. Collecting a car in one of a ring of downtown parking garages, catching a streetcar west or east, or descending to subway level to travel north, the flâneur becomes a commuter, joining the daily flow of thousands of metropolitan Torontonians in and out of downtown Yonge. Although it is no longer the centralizing hub it was in previous eras, downtown remains, in this respect, a shared experience for a significant cross-section of the urban region's dispersed population. Postwar, even people who seldom share in that experience recognize that this quality makes it unique as a place and as a symbol of urban life and its possibilities. Such common reference points become rarer as we leave downtown and move into the sprawling urban region that has developed around Yonge Street since the industrial era.

2

The City of Tomorrow

On March 1, 1966, Toronto turned to department store Eaton's for a glimpse of the urban future. In a gallery overlooking downtown Yonge Street, company executives, politicians, and the press crowded around a scale model of the Eaton Centre, a colossal modernist complex of towers and plazas proposed by the retailer for the area surrounding its flagship store. Encompassing twenty-two acres – six city blocks, including four fronting on the west side of the Yonge strip – it was the product of a decade of efforts by political and business elites in Toronto to promote the comprehensive rebuilding of the downtown core. The Eaton Centre would be a "new heart for old Toronto," ensuring the commercial strip's continued economic and civic vitality – and the Eaton company's centrality to it.[1] The road to this imagined urban renaissance would prove to be rocky. Still, under the lights of Eaton's showroom in March 1966, the future looked bright.

The department store occupies an important place in the histories of business, consumption, and labour in Canada.[2] This chapter considers it in another light: as an actor wielding considerable power in urban development. Just as Eaton's early expansion helped make downtown Yonge Toronto's main commercial area, in the decades following the Second World War Canada's largest retailer was at the centre of plans to rebuild the street. As it adapted to changes in markets and urban geography, its corporate ambitions and extensive downtown landholdings brought it into an uncertain partnership with pro-development municipal officials. The result was the first Eaton Centre (1956–67), one of the largest of a series of postwar projects that sought to align private profit and the public interest to modernize North American downtowns.[3] Its planners envisioned Yonge

Street radically remade, the low-rise heterogeneity of a century of unplanned growth replaced by a unified megastructure under corporate
control. In the short term, that dream remained unrealized, and the centre
joined the long list of unbuilt utopias that are one of the legacies of mid-
century urban modernism.[4] But the project and its promises for the future
persisted, transforming the Yonge Street property market, redefining the
politics of redevelopment, and laying the groundwork for the physical
transformation of the street over the following decade.

The Ethic of City Rebuilding

The Eaton Centre was emblematic of the drive to drastically refashion
the urban environment that spread from city to city and across national
borders in the mid-twentieth century. Urban centres from Winnipeg to
Boston to Berlin emerged from the Depression and the Second World War
seeking to address long-standing problems of the industrial city and to
plan their adaptation to new challenges, including mass automobility,
decentralization, and wartime destruction. The solutions proposed varied
according to local and national contexts, but everywhere they were articulated in the same language of progress, modernization, and rationality.
National governments created new institutions to finance or incentivize
the construction of housing, expressways, and other capital-intensive
projects; municipal bureaucracies expanded in size and scope, hiring from
a growing pool of credentialed experts – traffic engineers, planners, architects, and others – who moved easily between the private and public sectors;
and politicians and businesses formed local alliances to rebuild deteriorating districts, protect existing capital, and attract new investment to their
cities. This urban renewal order, animated by an expansive vision of the
city remade, would have a significant impact on postwar cityscapes in
North America, western Europe, and beyond.[5]

During the 1940s and 1950s, an ethic of city rebuilding took root in
Toronto politics and civil society.[6] Its advocates were not a formal coalition or party, but a constellation of institutions, groups, and individuals
that included housing reformers, elected officials, newspaper editors, labour
unions, and the Toronto Board of Trade.[7] Their proposals for rebuilding
downtown and surrounding neighbourhoods varied widely, from demol-
ishing declining blocks to erect public housing and parks to widening
congested streets and their connection to the planned metropolitan expressway network. This was not the first time that these kinds of schemes
had been presented in Toronto. However, the postwar context, with its

combination of optimism for the future, interventionist government, and faith in expertise and centralized planning, proved particularly receptive to their implementation. Whereas early-twentieth-century plans for urban improvement were "lost in management," and housing activists of the 1930s were frustrated by government parsimony, postwar Toronto accepted renewal as a precondition for future prosperity.[8] The key question was not whether the older city should be modernized, but how such change would be accomplished – and what roles public powers and private capital would play in that process.

National and local factors configured and constrained Toronto's responses to this challenge. Canadian advocates of rebuilding drew on the same vocabulary and the same repertoire of modernist urbanist ideas as their American counterparts, and they professed interest in solving the same perceived urban problems.[9] This led to interventions – expressways connecting downtown and suburbs, large-scale public housing projects such as Toronto's Regent Park (begun in 1947) – that were virtually indistinguishable from similar projects in Boston or New York. But state-sponsored urban renewal in Canada was less far-ranging than in the United States, where it financed not just public housing and transportation infrastructure, but stadiums, office buildings, and even for-market residences. Whereas in cities south of the border, federal funding provided the glue for local growth coalitions between government and business, in Canada public-private redevelopment partnerships were generally informal and ad hoc.[10] To this was added Toronto's local political culture, in which interventionism was tempered by populist fiscal conservatism.[11] In contrast with Metropolitan Toronto, which centralized decision making in the person of its founding chairman, Frederick "Big Daddy" Gardiner (1953–61), the City of Toronto's frequent elections and weak mayoral system tended to produce city councils that were fractious and slow to act.

These limitations prompted progress-minded urbanists in Toronto to look enviously at the ongoing transformations in the United States. In 1956, the Liberal, pro-renewal *Toronto Star* observed that

while Toronto frets and wonders where the money is to come from, American cities have for seven years been doing something about "downtown blight" – that seemingly inevitable disease of modern city life which produces slums, gives motorists ulcers, and sends shopkeepers out into the suburbs. From the "high-riser" apartment projects of New York to the multi-lane expressways of Los Angeles, some 297 projects are currently underway in 195 centres to redevelop blighted areas.[12]

The *Star*'s expansive definition of "downtown blight" – encompassing not just degrading built environments but traffic jams and decentralization – and the metaphor of disease are both typical of an era in which city problems were viewed as systemic and interrelated. Over the next two decades, downtown freeways and apartment densification would lose much of their popular appeal, and critics would question the effectiveness of large-scale redevelopment in solving metropolitan problems. But in the mid-1950s, rebuilding – bigger, higher, and more efficiently – was viewed as a cutting-edge intervention that would save the North American city.

The Politics of Redevelopment

Discussion of rebuilding was often framed in terms of large-scale social and economic goals – housing the poor, improving competitiveness – or the prestige of modernization. But the politics of redevelopment in Toronto revolved most of all around its important contribution to municipal revenues in a period of growth. Building roads, sewers, and other infrastructure to accommodate sprawl and augmenting administrative capacity to govern a burgeoning population meant an unprecedented expansion of municipal government, a process ongoing throughout Canada at the time. After decades of near inertia, the City of Toronto's expenditures grew five-fold between 1945 and 1966, and after 1953 Metro Toronto's budget expanded at a similar rate. Property taxes underwrote this growth, accounting for 80–90 percent of Toronto's revenues and 50–60 percent of Metro's throughout the period and making both municipalities dependent on a constantly growing tax base to finance expansion.[13] In the older city, that meant encouraging redevelopment at higher densities. Replacing the low-rise Victorian streetscape with new high-rise development had the potential to create new tax revenues while reversing nearly two decades of decline in property values. This was particularly true in commercial and industrial districts such as downtown Yonge Street, which because they were densely built and taxed at a higher rate than residential neighbourhoods accounted for two-thirds of the City's tax revenues.[14] Redeveloping downtown became policy not just because it created employment or promised to revitalize business, but because it provided the financing that was the engine of metropolitan expansion and governance.

To this end, Toronto's municipal administration systematically mapped the urban landscape, considering the condition of buildings (good, fair, poor), how they were used, and the current and potential tax value of each property. Toronto's first *Official Plan* (1949) included a map of "uneconomic areas" that were suited to rebuilding, and in the mid-1950s its new Planning Department amplified this assessment work with a comprehensive survey of downtown and surrounding neighbourhoods. The key idea operating here was that of the best and most economic use of land, a judgment based on calculations that included comparing municipal services provided against taxes paid, and the assessed value of buildings against the value of the land on which they sat. Viewed through this lens, properties in poor condition, districts that absorbed more services than they funded in taxes, and other "uneconomic uses" of space were a fiscal problem for the City.[15] These assessments were used to plan the location of public housing and were the basis for the creation of a policy of designating downtown "redevelopment areas" in which the City would use its powers to assemble and clear land for private development.[16]

In parallel, a new interventionist politics of development emerged in Toronto. Led by Mayor Nathan Phillips from 1954, a series of Toronto politicians won elections on pro-rebuilding platforms, promising to use public powers and expenditures to encourage private investment downtown. Until the late 1960s they held the balance of political power in the city, despite opposition from more fiscally conservative members of council.[17] Phillips and his successors presided over the planning and construction of Toronto's New City Hall and the civic square (1965) named in his honour, a project that numerous urban observers have cast as Toronto's coming of age, or a marker of its entry into the ranks of the world's great cities.[18] Today, Finnish architect Viljo Revell's distinctive curved towers are still one of the most recognizable structures in Toronto and a key element in the city's visual branding, appearing in its logo and on its official flag. It is less well known that this civic symbol was intended, as Mayor Phillips put it, to "spark redevelopment in a manner and to an extent which is today difficult to conceive."[19] It was framed as a catalyst for a larger downtown transformation, a $60 million stimulus package that would raise the value of nearby properties and offer private developers an example of the successful clearance and replacement of uneconomic elements – in this case, thirteen acres of aging commercial and residential buildings in the largely low-income St. John's Ward, located just west of the Yonge Street strip.

Public investment was meant as the spark for rebuilding; the fuel would come from private capital. Nathan Phillips and his allies sought to enlist business in their political project and to identify investment in rebuilding with good corporate citizenship. In 1959, this approach was formalized with the creation of the Toronto Redevelopment Advisory Council (RAC), a corporate "brain trust" with a broad mandate to advise the City on downtown planning and to promote new construction.[20] The RAC was a who's who of the Anglo-Canadian business elite, composed of fifteen executives from the largest downtown corporations, including three banks and Eaton's and Simpson's department stores. It was criticized as a special interest group, "big business gathered together to divide the spoils," according to one critic in the labour movement, but its members saw themselves in different terms. The RAC shared with pro-development officials the idea that "keeping the aging heart of the city beating" was a civic goal that transcended individual interests or party politics.[21] The group's founding chairman, Simpson's vice-president G. Allan Burton, developed this idea in a 1963 speech in which he emphasized that his fellow members' experience, networks, and significant stake in the downtown future – according to him, their businesses paid 60 percent of the district's property taxes – made them uniquely qualified for the job.[22] The RAC's influence played a significant role in the creation of the Development Department (1962), a City agency whose mandate was to work with private developers to promote and expedite new building projects and in formulating the City's pro-redevelopment *Plan for Downtown Toronto* the following year.[23] The group also helped insert Toronto into larger North American discussions around downtown renewal, flying in prominent American redevelopment consultants and meeting with business leaders and politicians in Pittsburgh, Boston, Newark, and other cities in the throes of major rebuilding projects.[24]

The Eaton's Lands and Project Viking

Each member of the RAC was expected to provide corporate leadership, but none was more important to this redevelopment vision than Eaton's. In part, this expectation was associated with the company's long history in the city. Historian Donica Belisle traces how, beginning in the late nineteenth century, Eaton's wove itself into both local communities and larger national narratives of progress in Canada.[25] This process was most visible in Toronto, the company headquarters and home of the Eaton family. By the mid-twentieth century, generations of Torontonians had experienced Eaton's as a dominant corporate presence in the city: a commercial institution, an employer, and a cornerstone of downtown. At the same time, they could not avoid familiarity with the lives and philanthropy of Timothy Eaton's dynastic succession, in its third generation by the mid-twentieth century. Both Eaton's and the Eatons themselves were strongly identified with good corporate citizenship and progress well before the founding of the RAC. The construction of the retailer's monumental Art Deco College

Street store (1930) – seen, amid economic depression, as an important contribution to downtown – was accompanied by an agreement with the City to widen and beautify a stretch of Yonge Street into a boulevard. In subsequent decades, Eaton's helped popularize the municipal administration's plans for modernization and renewal. In spring 1945, it hosted a public exhibit entitled "City for Tomorrow," which presented models, maps, and diagrams prepared by City agencies based on their plans for the postwar period. Over four weeks, sixty-seven thousand people visited the store to tour "the Toronto of the future ... planned as a whole instead of a random-growing mass ... with proper housing adequately spaced ... rapid transit system, super-highways, and widened streets ... a Toronto transformed from deterioration into modern comfort and convenience!"[26] During the 1950s, Eaton's continued to display the city of tomorrow to the public, with exhibits celebrating the construction and completion of the Yonge Street subway line and presenting architectural models submitted to the design competition for New City Hall in 1958.

For proponents of rebuilding, this record of corporate citizenship and interest in civic improvement mattered less than Eaton's considerable property portfolio. By the 1950s, the company and its subsidiaries had been accumulating property on and around downtown Yonge for eighty years, making Toronto the central element in a corporate land bank that included properties in downtowns across the country. The retailer's holdings on the commercial strip between College and Queen encompassed not just its two block-sized stores, but the bulk of six other blocks, including warehouses, factories, and mail-order buildings, a discount annex, and a parking garage.[27] This land bank, the largest concentration of property in private hands in downtown Toronto, had for decades been at the core of Eaton's business model, providing premises for its expanding operations and allowing it to raise capital through resale or the issue of millions of dollars in mortgage-backed bonds, as it did in 1929 to finance construction of the College Street store.[28] In addition to these commercial properties, Eaton's real estate subsidiaries owned more than one hundred properties unrelated to the retail business in Toronto – including several blocks of aging two- and three-storey houses – bought opportunistically in the first decades of the twentieth century.[29]

Postwar, Eaton's rethought how best to use its property empire. Robert Lewis and Paul Hess document how it lobbied the City of Toronto to create its first "redevelopment area" near Yonge and College in 1952, in the hopes that the designation would facilitate the sale of company-controlled residential lots near its store and ensure that they were quickly

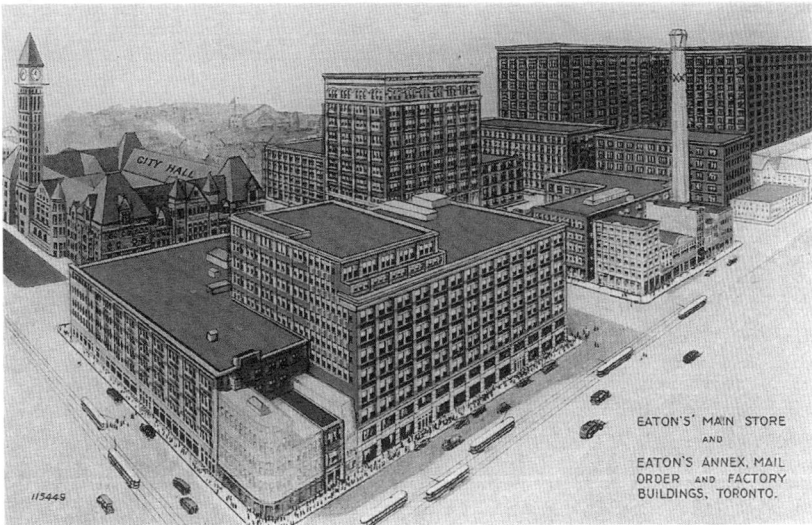

Eaton's illustrated postcard showing the extent of its Toronto land bank, 1923. Yonge Street runs diagonally along the right side of the image. | Eaton's/Wikipedia, http://upload.wikimedia.org/wikipedia/commons/d/d4/ Eatonstoronto1920MainStore.jpg

developed into modern apartment buildings.[30] This set an early precedent for alignment between the interests of the company and the municipal administration in redevelopment. However, the future of Eaton's commercial properties was a more difficult question, with much higher financial stakes. Apart from its newer College Street store, the retailer's physical plant was aging and underutilized. Executives frequently discussed the deteriorating condition of the Queen Street store, whether prompted by letters of complaint from customers, criticism in local tabloids, or an insurance assessment that pointed out serious structural weaknesses in the building.[31] Just to the north, the twelve-storey factory complex, which had employed thousands at its peak in the 1920s, shut its doors as the production of Eaton's house brands was outsourced to more modern operations. At the same time, neighbouring St. John's Ward, home to many of the immigrant women and men who laboured in the factories, was in the process of being bulldozed to make way for New City Hall. Finally, in 1956 the company moved its mail-order division to the northern suburbs, where land was cheaper and transportation links better.[32] Some of the buildings left empty were levelled and converted into surface parking lots, which facilitated access to the store but did not come close to realizing the potential value of the land. This was particularly the case after 1954, as the completion of the Yonge Street subway raised the development prospects around the station intersections of Dundas and Queen Streets that bookended the Eaton's lands.[33]

This value gap preoccupied Eaton's corporate leadership as much as the condition of the main store. By the second half of the 1950s, the company was shifting to a new retail strategy in the Toronto region, based on a combination of aggressive suburban expansion and consolidation of its downtown operations. A report commissioned in 1954 from influential United States retail and redevelopment consultant Larry Smith highlighted the urgency of both goals. Smith's research showed that since the end of the war, Eaton's and other downtown retailers had been losing ground to suburban alternatives. Though the company's sales remained larger than those for any other single retailer, its market share in the metropolitan area had dropped from 30 to 20 percent, as new customers overwhelmingly chose to shop in automobile-oriented plazas and commercial strips.[34] To stop this trend, Smith argued that Eaton's would have to build suburban branches in Toronto – which it did, beginning with two stores in 1962 and the Yorkdale mall development in 1964 – and modernize its Yonge Street properties, possibly by closing one store and expanding the other. By 1957, the retailer was committed at the highest levels to tearing down and re-building its Queen Street store, at an estimated cost equivalent to the re-cently approved New City Hall project next door.[35]

Project Viking, named dramatically after the Eaton house brand, was an effort by the municipal administration to transform these plans for a new store into a larger rebuilding project. It was spearheaded by Matthew Lawson, the City of Toronto's first head of planning since 1954, one of dozens of British and European planners and architects whose migrations to Toronto brought new modernist ideas and ambitions to the city's urbanist discussions.[36] In May 1956, Lawson and planner Gordon Stephenson – a former acolyte of modernist icon Le Corbusier and Canada's foremost expert on urban renewal – met with Eaton's representatives to discuss the future of the company lands. In a follow-up memorandum, Lawson ex-plained his vision for the site: the construction of a modern commercial complex that would replace Yonge Street's outmoded low-rise shopscape:

> We in this office believe that the erection of a downtown shopping core would be of enormous advantage to Toronto. The present centre was built on a layout which does not lend itself to present-day needs, whereas

a new one could be both efficient and attractive ... Where Toronto is almost unique is that without undergoing extensive wartime destruction or major upheaval, it is in a position to achieve this objective ... through co-operation between the T. Eaton Company, the City and others concerned.[37]

The potential that Lawson detected was not obvious from street level. The six blocks where his staff had conducted a comprehensive building survey, the quadrangle bounded by Yonge, Queen, Bay, and Dundas Streets, were typical of the unplanned, lot-by-lot construction that had characterized downtown development over the last century. They contained more than one hundred individual properties, many in poor shape, or containing uses – tea rooms, auto shops, the disused Eaton's outbuildings – that planners saw as "inappropriate for the very heart of the city."[38] What excited Lawson was visible only from above, in the synoptic view that underpinned the practice of modern urban planning. First, there was the area's concentration of ownership. Of the twenty-three acres included in the study, ten were controlled by Eaton's and a further eight by the City of Toronto, including the soon-to-be obsolete 1899 Old City Hall and a series of cross-streets that could be closed to create new space for development. Of the remaining five acres, the only structure considered of architectural significance was Holy Trinity (1847), a small Anglican church that sat at the centre of the study area, surrounded by Eaton's factory buildings.

Equally important was the close relationship between the company's lands and the future civic centre, just steps away. One of Lawson's major contributions to postwar planning in Toronto was to integrate the redevelopment dreams of politicians like Nathan Phillips into a large-scale modernist vision for the downtown core. At the heart of this vision, first made public with the *Plan for Downtown Toronto* in 1963 but already emerging in the development of Viking, was the idea of a downtown divided into quadrants, with New City Hall and the civic square at the centre as the "new fulcrum of downtown activities."[39] In that geography, the Eaton's lands formed the core of the northeast quadrant, dedicated to retail shopping; to the south were two distinct office areas and to the west an administrative district. This level of segregation and organization of functions – core tenets of mid-century modernism – was the ideal toward which downtown planning would strive throughout the 1950s and 1960s. It was accompanied by a concern for connectedness and coherence of form across functional groupings. Lawson and his successors believed that construction around the civic complex – including any redevelopment of the Eaton's lands – should be "complementary in design" and envisioned tying the four quadrants together with public spaces and pedestrian paths.[40]

Project Viking sought to accomplish all of these ambitious goals by bringing together Eaton's properties with the City of Toronto's municipal powers and urban expertise. Thinking big was another crucial component of modernist planning and architecture, and Viking certainly had what planning scholar John Gold calls the "allure of scale."[41] As laid out in the detailed plans and models submitted to Eaton's in 1958, it was a radical reimagining of urban space.[42] Smaller streets within the assembly would be closed, and the six blocks of the study area fused into a comprehensively planned superblock, with a single, limited-access surface road and extensive underground parking and service tunnels. On the east side of this unified complex, the Eaton's store would be rebuilt at nearly double its current size; the 1,500,000 square feet that the company forecasted would allow it to dominate downtown retail. Running north from the store, a pedestrianized retail plaza connected it to Dundas Street. The west side of the site was given over to four twenty-storey office blocks. The entire complex was sketched out in the concrete, glass, and steel vernacular of urban modernism, then the cutting edge of architectural practice in Europe and the United States. It was Toronto's version of the British postwar shopping precinct or Victor Gruen's 1956 plan for Fort Worth, both of which presented a comprehensive modernist remaking of the city centre, emphasizing pedestrian plazas, retail arcades, and the mixing of commercial and civic spaces.[43] As daring as this vision was, Viking was conservative when it came to the area's older structures, calling for the preservation of Holy Trinity Church and Old City Hall.

From Viking to the Eaton Centre

Nothing like Viking had been attempted in Canada up to the late 1950s, and it is unsurprising that Eaton's was initially hesitant to commit to its construction. The company knew what it wanted from its new store and considered the profitable disposal of its aging downtown physical plant a high priority. But it had little experience with the logistical, financial, and political challenges involved in a development on the scale of Viking. Nor did the City of Toronto's planners, despite their enthusiasm. There was the land assembly to complete, including private purchases and negotiating terms for the transfer of municipal property. Demolition and construction on the site would have to be staged and kept to schedule, and a team of architects, engineers, and other experts would need to be brought in and made to work together to achieve the goals of the plan. Most importantly, Viking entailed substantial financial risk. Construction would have to be financed at the level of tens of millions of dollars yearly, and it would not produce revenue in the form of rents or boosted sales for a long time. The municipal administration was certain that Viking would help achieve its planning goals while significantly raising tax revenues, but there was no consensus in the private sector whether this scale of development, involving offices, retail, and other uses, could be profitable without hefty government subsidies. Eaton's responses to Matthew Lawson's office were guarded; however, it was sufficiently intrigued by the idea to put planning of a stand-alone replacement for its Queen Street store on hold in 1959 while it examined the possibility of a larger development.[44]

Eaton's understanding of what was possible for its Yonge Street properties was profoundly shaped by one much-publicized project: downtown Montreal's Place Ville Marie. As presented to the public in 1956, it proposed to transform a neglected Canadian National Railway site into an integrated office and shopping complex that would be Canada's most valuable commercial property.[45] On its opening in 1962, Place Ville Marie was applauded locally and nationally as a symbol of progress and renewal; well before that date, its signature skyscraper – a forty-two-storey cruciform tower set in a wide square – was already iconic, deployed in print advertising as an emblem of modernity.[46] Don Nerbas argues that Place Ville Marie represented a new paradigm for the capitalist production of space in urban Canada. Its promoter, American developer William Zeckendorf, viewed real estate as a financial services industry and its built products as investments that could be sold, leveraged, and leased to create value from thin air.[47] Like many major developers of his generation, Zeckendorf benefited from federally funded urban renewal projects in the early 1950s, before moving on to the construction of office towers and shopping malls over the subsequent decade. Place Ville Marie was typical of his private-sector work in that it was speculative, heavily debt-leveraged, and dependent on his ability to manufacture and sell corporate prestige to prospective tenants. Zeckendorf's publicly traded company, Webb and Knapp, although the largest development corporation in North America, constantly teetered on the brink of bankruptcy.

William Zeckendorf first expressed interest in the Eaton's lands in 1956, and by the time the Viking plans were produced in 1958 he had confidently promised Toronto's business community that he would be "doing comparable operations [to Place Ville Marie] in Toronto very shortly."[48] During the intervening two years, Webb and Knapp Canada had expanded rapidly, becoming Canada's leader in shopping mall and office construction, and one of only a few companies in the country with the expertise and capital to manage large-scale downtown redevelopment. It was also Eaton's partner in postwar expansion. In 1958, the retailer agreed to be the principal tenant in Webb and Knapp's Wellington Square (1960) in London, Ontario – one of Canada's first wave of enclosed, climate-controlled shopping centres, and the only one located in a downtown setting. The two companies also began the negotiations that would lead to the Yorkdale mall project in the Toronto suburbs. Eaton's seems to have been confident, despite Zeckendorf's record of financial instability, that his staff could turn Viking into a viable plan. By 1960, it had signed an agreement giving Webb and Knapp exclusive rights to prepare a redevelopment plan for its downtown Toronto properties.[49]

Until contracting with Webb and Knapp, Eaton's had managed to avoid public scrutiny of its rebuilding plans, but this became impossible with the involvement of William Zeckendorf. He deliberately cultivated publicity wherever he went, with his flamboyant personality and grandiose schemes – to build Toronto's New City Hall or to buy and sell the Brooklyn Dodgers.[50] His participation concentrated media attention on Eaton's and led to the public getting its first glimpse of Viking in 1962. That summer, writer and television personality Pierre Berton published a front-page series in the *Toronto Star* – where he was an associate editor – focusing on downtown rebuilding, which he called Toronto's most glaring example of "unfinished business."[51] Berton lavished praise on Place Ville Marie, then just opened, stating that it presented a model of private-public partnership that Toronto must follow:

> Here is an oasis, seven and one-half acres in size, in a concrete desert – a place where pedestrians may stroll about without the confinement of narrow streets or the harassment of traffic. Here the elegant shops, smart theatres, sidewalk cafes, plazas, promenades, offices, hotel and railway stations are all interconnected as part of a single plan ... [Place Ville Marie] has demonstrated that you can have comfort, dignity, beauty, and profit all at the same time. It is a money-making proposition created by free enterprise with an assist from the city.[52]

Such sentiments were nothing new for Toronto's redevelopment lobby, who had been making similar arguments for years, although Berton's status as a national media figure made his voice one of the loudest. His intervention was novel, however, in that he described Viking in detail and published sketches drawn from both City planners' 1958 scheme and the latest plans prepared by Webb and Knapp's house architect, the prolific I.M. Pei.[53] These confidential documents were probably leaked by someone on Zeckendorf's staff in an effort to create public interest in the project. For the first time, the public saw bird's-eye and street-level views of the plazas, office high-rises, and commercial arcade planned to replace Eaton's dusty brick empire. Despite Viking's scale, the sketches emphasized its people-friendly orientation, depicting contented shoppers and office workers sauntering through tree-lined plazas and ice skating in a sunken rink resembling New York's Rockefeller Center. The only obstacle to the realization of these plans, Berton insisted, was lack of vision. The "decision is Eaton's," he argued, explaining that with the plan in place, a word from company head John David Eaton would suffice to install a "Montreal wonderland" in downtown Toronto. "Seldom," he wrote, "has the fate of one metropolis rested to such a degree on the decisions of a single mercantile enterprise."[54] The image of the Eaton family holding the keys to the city's future was a powerful one that would resurface in later debates over the project.

Other factors converged in 1962 and 1963 to place additional pressure on Eaton's to determine the future of its downtown properties. In early 1963, the City of Toronto's *Plan for Downtown Toronto* was published to sustained media attention.[55] In addition to its general emphasis on a future shaped by privately led redevelopment, the plan made specific reference to the important place of Eaton's in that vision. The section on the Yonge Street shopping district directed attention to the Eaton's lands, calling on the company to take advantage of what it called "an excellent opportunity for redevelopment [of] great public importance," including shopping and "prestige offices."[56] With this publication, Viking effectively became part of official City planning policy. Planning head Matthew Lawson emphasized in media interviews that Eaton's and competitor Simpson's would be the anchors and prime movers in the modernization of the shopping district.[57] In a meeting during the lead-up to the release of the plan, Eaton's Executive Committee agreed that its publication would place the company "under considerable pressure" and that consequently redevelopment of its downtown holdings should be given the highest priority.[58]

The business case for a Viking-scale project was improving. Between the mid-1950s and the early 1960s, private redevelopment in Toronto sped up, driven by demand for housing and commercial rentals, as well as the relatively low cost of centrally located land. A 1967 study by geographer Larry Bourne shows a city undergoing significant renovation, as more than a thousand buildings – mostly nineteenth-century homes – were demolished each year and replaced by denser, larger constructions. New building in the City of Toronto climbed from a wartime low of $6 million annually to $80 million in 1953 and to $167 million in 1964.[59] An apartment boom began in the residential neighbourhoods adjoining downtown, and several smaller office tower projects crept northward from the financial district up Yonge Street.[60] In addition to Eaton's, two other members of the Redevelopment Advisory Council were planning major investments in downtown real estate. The new headquarters of the Toronto Dominion Bank, a superblock development announced in spring 1964 for a site a few blocks southwest of Eaton's, was hailed as a model redevelopment and proof of the RAC's success in promoting corporate "faith in Toronto's future."[61] Following the pattern set by Place Ville Marie, the TD Centre included an underground mall and pedestrian plaza in a complex centred on two glass-and-steel towers, which were designed by renowned modernist architect Mies van der Rohe. A few months later, Simpson's announced store renovations and construction of a thirty-three-storey tower on the south side of Queen Street, facing the Eaton's site.[62] The suburbs remained the preferred locale for investment, but by the mid-1960s the dreams of Toronto's rebuilding lobby seemed poised to come true.

In this context, Eaton's made a decision that would have seemed incredible just a decade earlier: to take on Viking in its entirety as a company project, with all of the risks and potential rewards that entailed. In 1962, Webb and Knapp had abruptly withdrawn from its development agreement with the company. Even as Place Ville Marie neared completion and work began on Yorkdale mall, the developer was in serious financial difficulty, as nearly a decade of overextension and speculative borrowing caught up with it.[63] Negotiations between Eaton's and an alternative partner, Canadian Equity and Development, the real estate arm of Canadian industrialist E.P. Taylor's investment empire, also soon soured.[64] Heavily committed to profitable and logistically simpler residential projects in suburban Toronto, Canadian Equity was daunted by the cost of land assembly, demolition, and construction for Viking, estimated by this point at between $150 million and $200 million. As one *Toronto Star* reporter would later point out, that was roughly equivalent to two TD Centres, or one-sixth of all planned construction in Metro Toronto that year.[65] Despite these warning signs, Eaton's was committed to leading the project. There was even speculation that the first stage of the complex could be opened in time for the company's centenary in 1969.[66]

This new state of affairs was formalized in August 1964 when working titles for the scheme, including Viking, were abandoned in favour of the

Eaton Centre. The name change was significant, and not a step that company executives took lightly.[67] Attaching the storied Eaton's brand and the Eaton family to the redevelopment clearly identified them as the prime movers behind it, a decision that gave it solidity and would probably boost confidence in its completion, but that also meant staking their reputation on its success. The new name invited comparison with another powerful mercantile family that had made its mark in downtown redevelopment. The construction of Rockefeller Center (1930–39), largely financed by the Rockefeller family after other major investors pulled out, was widely viewed as a significant act of corporate citizenship in Depression-era New York. In choosing to rename Viking the Eaton Centre, Eaton's made just one of the many implicit and explicit references to that landmark development – to its size and design, its civic purpose, or to the role of private capital in making it happen – that would contribute to branding its project as "Canada's Rockefeller Center."[68]

Progress and Its Discontents

The Eaton Centre was a complex and costly enterprise that extended Eaton's operations in both familiar and new directions. The project hinged on centralizing control of the patchwork of public and private properties that made up its six-block site. Eaton's began by buying out the small shop buildings that lined Yonge Street north of its store. In mid-1964, it acquired a batch of ten properties for $2 million, while beginning negotiations to purchase a further thirteen from individual owners, leaving just a few holdouts outside of company control.[69] To mask the coordination behind these purchases and thus prevent price inflation, it created a real estate subsidiary, Sunjam Ltd.[70] Despite this gesture toward anonymity, public discussion of the Eaton Centre precipitated a steep rise in the speculative value of real estate on downtown Yonge Street. If in 1964 the company was able to buy a hundred feet of low-rise retail on the strip for half a million dollars, by the next year a comparable stretch of frontage was selling for $1.7 million. Eaton's correspondence suggests that by mid-1965, Sunjam was competing with several speculative investors – including major Canadian banks – to snap up the remaining lots in the assembly. Despite the poor condition of existing buildings, as the assembly proceeded this competition drove prices as high as one hundred dollars per square foot, or twice the average price paid during the TD Centre assembly just a few years before.[71] In addition to these purchases, Eaton's began negotiations with Metro Toronto in early 1965 to buy the largest piece of the superblock not under company control – Old City Hall. Metro viewed the building as

Aerial view looking south over downtown Toronto, giving a sense of the scale of the Viking/Eaton Centre project, 1967. New City Hall is at the centre of the image, Old City Hall just above. The financial district, including the distinctive black TD tower, is at the upper right. | Boris Spremo/*Toronto Star* 502832641 via Getty Images

a burden, and saw in its sale and demolition a chance to meet several organizational and planning objectives, including financing a modern courthouse and police headquarters, and widening and straightening the crooked Bay and Queen intersection.[72]

Parallel to its land assembly, Eaton's began to hire planners, architects, and other consultants to create a plan for the site, bringing some of the most important figures in North American urban modernism to Toronto. Its rotating cast of experts included shopping mall builder Victor Gruen, office tower firm Skidmore, Owings, and Merrill, and traffic engineer George Barton. In spring 1965, it hired David Owen as managing director of Eaton Centre Limited. A former vice-president of Webb and Knapp Canada, Owen was one of a small pool of Canadians who had acquired experience of large-scale redevelopment while working on Place Ville Marie. Eaton's was aware, given its reputation as a Canadian retailer and the 1960s climate of growing economic nationalism, that there was considerable symbolic value in appointing a Canadian to a visible position of power on the Eaton Centre.[73] One journalist likened Owen to "executive producer" of the development.[74] The comparison to a Hollywood film was apt: in the planning stages, there was something unreal or fantastic about the Eaton Centre. The huge sums of money involved, the complexity of the plans, the transformative agenda attached to them – all of it seemed precarious, and at times too grandiose to be true. Confident in his ability to usher in "the Toronto of the twenty-first century," Owen brought a cool arrogance to the work of convincing Torontonians to share in that vision.[75]

There was little convincing to be done among the pro-rebuilding majority in Toronto's civic administration. Throughout 1965 and 1966, Eaton's was in regular contact with its municipal allies, including Metro Toronto chairman William Allen, Development Department head Walter Manthorpe, and Toronto mayor Phillip Givens, nicknamed "go-go" Givens for his impatient pro-development stance.[76] Informal, private meetings between these important public figures and Eaton Centre principals were the norm at this stage, as was their advising the company on how best to satisfy the civic administration's demands, often before they had been formally presented. The sale of Old City Hall is one example. David Owen and Eaton's executives met with William Allen or his representative four times over the spring and summer of 1965, each time coming closer to a price for the building; all of this occurred months before Allen had been given a mandate to negotiate its sale. In September 1965, it was Allen who led the first significant press briefing on the Eaton Centre, from his position of authority as Metro chairman, while using materials supplied by Eaton's PR consultants.[77] If the sober Allen was the project's municipal spokesman, Phillip Givens was its cheerleader, confidently attaching every superlative possible to the plan and assuring the public that its construction would "tremendously enhance the downtown area."[78]

The Eaton Centre captured the imagination of most Toronto politicians, not the least with its promise of new municipal revenues. It was widely reported in the press that the complex would boost the City's annual tax income by a staggering $11–12 million – approximately 8 percent – the kind of evidence of good governance that won elections in Toronto.[79] No one disagreed with the desirability of the project or that income. However, the Eaton Centre also became a pretext for criticism of the pro-development consensus, most prominently by central Toronto councillor William Dennison. A fiscally conservative former CCFer, Dennison had never been, in Nathan Phillips's words, "one of the boys"; rather, he had built his reputation on opposition to pro-growth policies.[80] In 1940s and 1950s debates over downtown apartment construction and the Regent Park complex, he argued against expropriation and derided the redevelopment process as catering to speculators while hurting individual ratepayers. His position on the Eaton Centre was that "Old City Hall is not for sale," although he was less concerned with the building's historical value, he asserted, than with accountability. Selling Toronto's largest and most architecturally impressive public building to a major corporation based on private negotiations was an embarrassment for a city that had lately wasted millions in cost overruns on the New City Hall project. Dennison's views put him in a tiny minority in Toronto City Council, but he found allies among suburban populists in Metropolitan Toronto, including the outspoken social conservative East York reeve True Davidson.[81]

Following publication of Eaton's letter of intent to buy Old City Hall in December 1965, this small group of elected officials was joined by other voices – the Friends of City Hall. In a development that surprised both the retailer and its allies in the civic administration, a campaign to save Old City Hall from the wrecking ball coalesced around James Acland, a University of Toronto professor and a major figure in Canadian architectural circles, who also chaired the Friends. Alongside him were a slate of public figures that included internationally known Metro Toronto planner Hans Blumenfeld, former governor-general Vincent Massey, and Eric Arthur, elder statesman of Canadian architecture, one of the first members of the City's Planning Board and an advisor on the New City Hall project.[82] Over the next year, the Friends campaign would transform approval of the Eaton Centre and the sale of Old City Hall into major public issues, carving out a space in the conversation for increased public participation and a politics of urban conservation that would have a significant long-term impact on the city's form.

The Friends of Old City Hall received the support of several Canadian and international architectural or planning organizations.[83] Their fight was important enough within the profession to merit mention in United States journal *Architectural Forum* in early 1966.[84] Not all Canadian urbanists supported preservation. In February 1966, *Canadian Architect* published a special forum section on Old City Hall, and nearly half of a dozen contributions urged demolition if the plan for the site were strong enough.[85] But the Friends stance was influential, drawing as it did on a larger sense that Toronto's historic architecture was being indiscriminately bulldozed in the short-sighted push to rebuild the city. Even before the announcement of Eaton Centre, Eric Arthur spoke to a growing constituency in Toronto when he wrote that

> in the march of progress, we have ruthlessly destroyed almost all of our older architecture; street names cherished for a hundred years or more have been altered to suit the whims of the people on the street, and even our most treasured buildings, Fort York, going back to the beginnings of British settlement, have recently been threatened because the historic soil on which they stood interfered with the curvature of a modern expressway.[86]

This interpretation of postwar rebuilding as casually destructive was not confined to urban professionals. During the previous decade, debates over other structures and sites had fostered a politics of heritage preservation in Toronto, as in many other North American and European cities coming to grips with the disruptive impacts of modernism.[87] For heritage-minded Torontonians, the Old City Hall debate was a continuation of battles to save Fort York – mentioned by Arthur – or the neighbouring University Avenue Armouries (1891), torn down in 1963 to make way for a new courthouse adjoining New City Hall. In the latter case, architects and other experts were just one element in an anti-demolition coalition that included retired soldiers, local historical societies, and the United Empire Loyalists.[88] A similar demographic rallied to the Friends of Old City Hall, allowing its spokespeople to claim six hundred pledges of support by the start of 1966.[89] Concerned by the dangers of being labelled as anti-modernist cranks or a "rent-a-crowd" (in the words of one *Globe and Mail* columnist), James Acland and other experts made efforts to establish the group's authority as "informed professionals and community leaders."[90] In an era in which expertise played a key role in constituting political authority, they, like Eaton's, would rely heavily on the perceived ability of experts to determine the best course for the future.[91]

In their public statements, letters to the editor, and deputations to council in early 1966, the Friends of Old City Hall and its allies presented their case for the building's preservation. The tone ranged from the professorial to the sentimental, reflecting the diverse coalition assembled around the issue. Much was made of the building's unique place in architectural history. Under the years of grime that obscured its stone facade, it was "a national monument," one of the most impressive Victorian buildings in

Canada.[92] Support for this view was anchored in an appeal to professional authority: Old City Hall was one of only three Canadian buildings singled out in the definitive international history of architecture; it was considered one of the best existing examples of Romanesque Revival style in North America; the jury in the New City Hall competition, all renowned architects, had applauded its "rich design" and judged all submissions in relation to it.[93] In place of demolition, the Friends insisted, Toronto should find a new public purpose for the structure. Proposals for doing so included transforming the hulking and expensive-to-maintain building into everything from an art gallery to an adult education centre.[94]

Other Friends took a different tack, stressing personal and communal attachments to Old City Hall as a key physical element of downtown. "This building has meant more to the life of our City than possibly any other," wrote a Scarborough man; others called it a "tangible link to the past," mentioning homecomings from war, celebrations of sporting victories, and the way in which the edifice dominated views north along lower Bay Street. Positioning themselves as taxpayers, voters, and concerned Torontonians, these Friends thought that not just a structure, but a principle, was at stake. Their concern was that in embracing development and change, the city was losing its formerly strong sense of itself: "How can you measure progress if you have nothing of the past to compare with the present?"[95] This conservative critique of progress had a social dimension as well, with James Acland and others suggesting at Friends meetings that 1960s disorder and delinquency were consequences of a lack of reverence for the past. Several vocal members of the Friends campaign would resurface in the 1970s, calling for a cleanup of the sex industry on Yonge Street.[96] Some of these citizen activists attacked the Eaton Centre concept, at times in emotional terms; charges of "philistinism" and "vandalism" were common. Their critiques had an impact. Faced with delegation after delegation opposing demolition, Metro agreed to defer a final decision on selling Old City Hall until its planners had reviewed a detailed development plan for the Eaton Centre.[97]

Selling the City of Tomorrow

The unveiling of a master plan for the project on March 1, 1966, was Eaton's chance to reassert control over the image of the Eaton Centre. Every aspect was planned and stage-managed, from the choice of location – a showroom "on the company's own ground" in a recently purchased Yonge Street property – to the invited audience, composed of journalists, provincial and City politicians, and senior bureaucrats.[98] The centrepiece of the room

The City of Tomorrow. The Eaton Centre planners and municipal politicians including William Dennison (with moustache), at the project unveiling, March 1, 1966. | Barry Philp/*Toronto Star* 502839151 via Getty Images

was a detailed scale model of downtown Toronto, completed and re-assembled on-site just days before. Against a backdrop of older, mostly low-rise structures – the city of the past, intentionally made nondescript with darker colouring – the gleaming white towers of the Eaton Centre, New City Hall, and the new Simpson's development presented a dramatic vision of the city of tomorrow promised two decades before. The presentation was broadcast on the CBC, and the press were encouraged to photograph Metro and City politicians interacting with the model and discussing its attributes with the centre's planners. The resulting photos, published in every major Toronto paper, projected a powerful image of collaboration between civic leaders from the public and private sectors.[99] The postwar dream of elite partnership in creating the city of tomorrow had never seemed so close.

The Eaton Centre master plan expressed the firm faith in urban progress through physical transformation that underpinned the rebuilding ethic.[100] The project's authority was established by expertise. "We have subjected our thinking and our objectives for this area," explained Eaton Centre vice-president Greg Kinnear in his opening remarks, "to appraisal by the finest specialists we could find in Canada and outside of Canada."[101] The Eaton Centre would transfigure the Bay-Dundas-Yonge-Queen superblock into a "megastructure" integrating every conceivable downtown function: a hotel, convention centre, transportation hub, shopping arcade, and four soaring office/residential towers. It was a city within a city, projected to draw 200,000 persons per day. Many of the original ingredients from Viking were present but magnified. A sixty-nine-storey tower would give Toronto the world's tallest building outside of Manhattan, alongside a five-level enclosed retail centre containing two hundred specialty shops; David Owen boasted that this made the development three times the size of Place Ville Marie. All of this was promised in two construction phases over fifteen years, at an estimated cost of $260 million.

How would a project of this scale reconcile private profit and the public interest? A few months before the unveiling, Eaton's directors met to outline the company's internal objectives for the project. The tone of that meeting was set by its first point: "Creation of a department store of unrivalled supremacy in Toronto."[102] The message was different at the March unveiling, which emphasized the plan's strong engagement with the public interest in revitalization. The project's principals emphasized that the centre was in continuity with the company's past civic engagement in Toronto. "When you have done business in a community for nearly 100 years," Kinnear went on, "you acquire a deep sense of obligation to the people of that community in addition to becoming deeply rooted in it. [That] is why we have not confined our plans to a retailer's basic objectives ... but extended them to encompass the entire 22.5 acres bordering the new City Hall and Nathan Phillips Square."[103] Referencing Viking, he positioned the Eaton Centre as "the culmination of eight years of planning" for the economic revitalization of downtown Toronto. Its construction would rid the core of substantial blight, clearing and replacing blocks of "underdeveloped, predominantly substandard buildings." That most of those buildings had been allowed to deteriorate by their owner – Eaton's – was not mentioned. The new department store and shopping arcade would also confirm downtown Yonge Street's place as the city's primary retail district, pushing back against the decentralization of commerce by making it competitive in ambience and offerings with suburban alternatives. Aesthetically, it would complement and accentuate New City Hall, and like that structure it would become "the image of the new city, the new city of Toronto ... a recognizable visual symbol of the city as a whole."[104]

The project would also reinvigorate downtown's social and civic life. "Perhaps the greatest gift of the Centre to the city," stated consulting planner James Murray, "is the gift of space. Space not empty but lively. Space for the daily tasks of the thousands who work or shop. Space for the enjoyment of those who stroll or rest or play ... space as a setting for great architecture."[105] With space came life. Civic revitalization meant addressing the concern that the downtown was becoming a desert outside of working hours – in Pierre Berton's words, a "vast, forbidding prison from which we gratefully make our escape at 5 p.m."[106] At street level, landscaped plazas and courts would set off the larger towers and add to the walkable space provided by Nathan P hillips Square. The Eaton's store would be linked to retail tenants by a multi-floor glass-domed gallery recalling a European arcade. Most dramatically, the entire complex would be built on a pedestrian podium designed by Vincent Ponte, another former Place Ville Marie collaborator whose modernist vision of the "multi-level city centre" was garnering attention across North America.[107] He envisioned the Eaton Centre as the hub of an underground tunnel network that would bind the core's financial, government, and retail districts into one cohesive whole, ending forever the "fragmented city" of small-scale developments so criticized by city planners.[108]

Building the city of tomorrow would be an act of creative destruction, forcing a significant break with the past. This was perhaps most evident in Eaton's stance on Old City Hall, which – whatever its architectural or historical merits – was "the very key to the complex" and must be cleared.[109] In an effort to offset this, the Eaton Centre master plan also attempted to establish continuities. Project planners claimed that their proposal had a real "sense of history."[110] In the weeks before the March 1 presentation, Eaton's staff were busy making lists of historically significant names that could be given to the complex's buildings and public spaces: Simcoe, Champlain, and Iroquois, among others. In the same vein, the press kit distributed at the announcement included a handout on Eaton's history in downtown Toronto and Canada, emphasizing that despite expansion and modernization, it remained the same family-owned, square-dealing business established by Timothy Eaton in 1869.[111] This was a familiar narrative, a story that the company had been telling to Canadians since the start of the twentieth century.[112] Other continuities would be established in the spaces of the new development. The master plan stated that it would preserve and "release the Church of the Holy Trinity from its present environment and return it to a setting in which its battlemented turrets may be seen against the sky." In place of a tight cluster of factory and warehouse buildings, the church would be set in a "cloistered garden space" – albeit, as the scale model demonstrated, one hemmed in on three sides by skyscrapers.[113] In a similar vein, Old City Hall's clock tower and First World War cenotaph would be retained, surrounded by a new "Tower Square" appropriate for Remembrance Day ceremonies.[114]

The initial reception of the master plan was enthusiastic. All three Toronto dailies gave it front-page treatment, beginning with photographs, planning sketches, and fawning prose in the evening edition of the *Telegram,* a publication in which the Eaton family had long held a financial interest.[115] The next day, editorials in both the *Globe and Mail* and the *Toronto Star* endorsed the project, the latter arguing that its combination of private enterprise and public initiative would create "a new heart for old Toronto."[116] In a period of high newspaper readership, the editorial stances taken by these papers mattered. A later poll would find that, among Torontonians who were interested in the project, the dailies were their main source of information. Half of the thousand people surveyed read the *Star* daily, and two-thirds opted for the *Telegram* or the *Globe and Mail.*[117] Ripples of the project announcement were felt beyond the local level. Eaton's used its substantial corporate communications network to distribute press kits and information to media throughout Canada. Beginning with a special edition of *Eaton News,* the company's redevelopment plan was featured in trade and business journals across the continent. Nearly every account of the master plan saw its approval by the civic administration, and subsequent transformation of downtown, as virtual certainties. "Farewell to Hogtown" – an unflattering nickname for provincial, Victoria-era Toronto – wrote the Canadian edition of *Time* just a few days after the centre went public.[118]

City politicians who attended the unveiling spoke glowingly of the plans, and an on-the-spot survey by the *Globe and Mail* found that two-thirds favoured their implementation.[119] Influential private-sector groups also publicly pledged their support. The Toronto Board of Trade asserted that the plan's "realization will have a decisive influence upon patterns of future growth and will contribute in substantial measure [to] ranking Toronto among the foremost of the world's cities." The RAC was laudatory, underlining the centre's social and civic benefits and urging that "no obstacle" – clearly a reference to Old City Hall and the Friends – "should be permitted to forestall it."[120] Both levels of municipal government fast-tracked reports related to the development. The only note of caution came, surprisingly, from the planner behind Viking, Matthew Lawson, who set out a fourteen-point plan for public participation in the development. His points, endorsed by the City Planning Board, ranged from the practical and specific ("direct connections to the subway system") to the general ("the centre must be a place of appeal to the public at large ... active night and day"). Their overall goal was to make the civic objectives outlined by Eaton's concrete and actionable.[121] In contrast, development commissioner Walter Manthorpe's report was uncritically approving of the project and focused mostly on the logistics of its rapid implementation.[122] This reflected the significant divergence in objectives and mandates emerging between the two City of Toronto agencies tasked with rebuilding downtown. Whereas the Development Department worked to promote and facilitate redevelopment, planners sought to control and direct it.[123]

However, rather than silencing critics, as Eaton's had hoped, the release of the Eaton Centre master plan gave them fresh ammunition. There was, first of all, professional skepticism about the project drawings and models. Noted local architect George Banz dismissed the complex as "a monstrous thing – a huge collection of boxes"; his criticism of the centre's monumental, square-edged modernist style was soon taken up by others.[124] More weighty was increasing popular approval for the Friends of Old City Hall campaign, which, with the additional publicity, was winning new support. On March 10, David Owen was greeted at a public presentation on the project with boos and derisory comments from an audience packed with hundreds of Friends and sympathizers.[125] Similarly, an open meeting of Metro Council on March 22 drew a crowd of 250, the vast majority there to express criticism of the sale. Opposition to the Eaton Centre development was acquiring countercultural cachet: while ratepayers' groups and professional planners made deputations in the council chamber, students from neighbouring high schools picketed across the street, waving signs reading, among other things, "Eaton's is culturally bankrupt."[126] Calls to "Save Old City Hall" were now beginning to be joined by censure of Eaton's corporate goals. Was the retailer serious with its public-spirited urban objectives, or was it simply justifying a profit-oriented plan with ideas borrowed from renewal scripts written a decade earlier for use in American cities?

Star columnist Ron Haggart, a long-established critic of the status quo in Toronto municipal affairs, suggested the latter, calling the master plan a collection of "magical words and mystical imagery of dreamland cities."[127] There were, he pointed out, no guarantees that Eaton's would ever build more than the first phase of the project; in effect, Toronto would be sacrificing a major public building in exchange for a new Eaton's department store and an office tower. Haggart was an influential local journalist. The questions he raised were discussed in council meetings and on newspaper opinion pages, and citizens who wrote to the City on the subject quoted him or, as Mayor Givens commented derisively, "scrawled" their messages

While Metro Council deliberates, high school students demonstrate against the demolition of Old City Hall, March 22, 1966. | York University Libraries, Clara Thomas Archives, Toronto Telegram Fonds, ASC60811

on clippings of his column.[128] In subsequent articles, Haggart continued to attack the civic administration's secretive negotiations with Eaton's and unquestioned acceptance of the company's good intentions. To illustrate his argument, he drew the public's attention to the neighbouring city of Hamilton, where Eaton's had in 1955 bought a former city hall building similar in style and age to Toronto's, promising to include the property in an expansion of its nearby store. After demolition, Eaton's abandoned its development plans, citing complications due to a federally funded urban renewal scheme then in the works for the area.[129] Without guarantees, argued Haggart, Toronto might face a similar future.

Running through all these critiques were increasingly strident demands that a broader range of Toronto citizens be given a voice in downtown rebuilding. The Eaton Centre project drew new constituencies into a discussion that had been dominated by urban experts, major corporations, and elected officials for more than a decade. This was most visible in the evolving strategy of the Friends of Old City Hall. In place of its earlier focus on detached, expert opinion and elite leadership, the group placed an appeal to participatory democracy at the heart of its campaign. In a letter to Friends members, James Acland emphasized the importance of ongoing popular involvement in the project's negotiations: "a continuing dialogue must be maintained between the citizens of Toronto and the developers of the Eaton Centre ... Only you can save our square from being crushed by a badly conceived development scheme."[130] By mid-1966, Acland's group boasted of having filled the message trays of Metro and Toronto officials with 1,368 letters, telegrams, and messages, a point that it underscored to establish its new legitimacy as a citizen movement. Nearly half of these citizen interventions originated in Toronto's suburban boroughs, demonstrating the metropolitan reach of what had previously been viewed as a downtown issue. Geographically dispersed, Friends supporters were nonetheless predominantly drawn from a largely Anglo-Canadian, middle-class demographic that was comfortable writing to elected officials and otherwise intervening in the political process.[131]

Aware that public engagement with the centre was expanding, Eaton's sought to counter the perception that its plan pleased politicians while ignoring the input of ordinary Torontonians. It hired Canadian Facts, the country's top polling firm, to interview more than one thousand Metro residents in their homes. The results demonstrated just how effective both the project's publicists and its critics had been in reaching citizens. Ninety-one percent of interviewees had heard of the Eaton Centre. However, of all the facts and ideas they associated with the project, the one mentioned most often was "controversy over Old City Hall," ahead even of basic identifiers such as "tall buildings" or "shopping mall."[132] When asked if they supported the demolition of Old City Hall to fulfill the Eaton Centre plan as presented in the press, a substantial majority – two-thirds – answered positively. The question did not exactly reflect the decision faced by Toronto politicians, since it assumed a direct link between demolition and completion of the plan. Still, for the first time Eaton's believed it could demonstrate public approval of its scheme, and it made the most of it. Publication of the poll was delayed until early June, just before a council meeting at which Old City Hall's lease and demolition were easily approved by Metro Council. On what the *Toronto Star* gravely called a "day that will decide the future of Toronto," there proved to be little common ground between the project's critics and its supporters. Both claimed a monopoly on the public interest, whether in the name of citizen participation and historical conservation or civic progress and prosperity.[133]

The Downtown Future Deferred

By the fall of 1966, after a decade of planning and a year of public debate, the Eaton Centre seemed poised to become reality. But its confident image of the city of tomorrow was built on a fragile foundation. This was brought home when on May 18, 1967 – just under fifteen months after the announcement of the master plan – the centre made front-page news again, this time with its abrupt cancellation.[134] Suddenly, Old City Hall was saved and the project's opponents vindicated, but at the cost of leaving the City's carefully laid redevelopment plans in shambles. That morning, Eaton's executives crossed the street to New City Hall to deliver the message in person, along with a letter from John David Eaton explaining his decision. Reaffirming his company's good faith and commitment to "underwrit[ing] Toronto's future as one of the world's great cities," Eaton explained that he was bowing to the will of the people:

> As we stated when the conceptual plan was presented, we do not presume to judge for the citizens of Toronto what they want this city to be. The plan which we presented represented our conception – and that of the best advisors we could get – of a revitalized downtown core that would inspire and stimulate the growth and redevelopment of our city. This was a proposal we submitted to the judgement of the people of Toronto ... In view of the fact that our enthusiasm for the plan is not matched by some groups in the municipality and some members of the municipal government, we do not believe that workable financial conditions can be negotiated.[135]

The tactfully expressed message was that the Eaton Centre had been doomed by its small-minded critics, and in the following days and months that became the main public narrative about the cancellation.

Negotiations between Eaton's and the municipal administration had indeed slowed. In the December 1966 municipal election, William Dennison surprised nearly everyone by winning the mayoralty, putting an end to more than a decade of growth boosters in this key office. He had campaigned without a single endorsement from any Toronto newspaper – the *Globe*, for example, thought he was out of step with the "dynamic thrust of modern Toronto" – using his stance on Old City Hall to his advantage, defining himself as more concerned with neighbourhoods, fiscal responsibility, and history than with expressways or office towers.[136] This set him apart from incumbent Phillip Givens, who continued to champion the Eaton Centre "dollar planning": the evaluation of development proposals based on the tax revenues they would bring in.[137] Flushed with victory, William Dennison pledged to take a harder line in bargaining with Eaton's over Old City Hall; addressing a meeting of the Friends in early

1967, he even hinted that he might revisit the decision to demolish the building if public opinion were with him.[138] Following the Eaton Centre cancellation, these statements made Dennison an easy target for blame. The *Telegram* lamented that "no other city would have piled obstacles in the way of this development ... [Dennison and supporters] have set Toronto back years." In fall 1967, a feature article in *Toronto Life,* a style and urban affairs magazine, opened with a full-page caricature of a drab, bucktoothed Dennison, whom it accused of "bungling" the Eaton Centre with unnecessary red tape.[139]

This was the public narrative, but Eaton's communications reveal that external factors were much less important than the project's internal collapse. When John David Eaton wrote his May 1967 cancellation letter, the Eaton Centre's financing was in disarray. By that point, Eaton's had made significant financial commitments to the project, including more than $2 million spent on planning and consultants' fees, and around $8 million on land assembly. The company raised additional funds in late 1965 through the sale of $25 million in mortgage-backed bonds.[140] It was understood among Eaton's leadership that the remaining cost of construction would be funded with outside capital, and from 1965 to 1967 David Owen and Eaton Centre Ltd. spent considerable time pitching investors on the project. But of the sixteen international corporations and investment groups that showed interest, ranging from Metropolitan Life to the Rothschilds, not one produced a tangible offer. During a meeting with Rockefeller Center Inc. in Manhattan – at the heart of the development that had inspired the Eaton Centre – Owen was told that the project was too ambitious for a city of Toronto's size. Other investors expressed concerns about the size and placement of the Eaton's store and the project's dependence on continued bullish office markets.[141] Failure to attract a major investor was compounded by dwindling projections of the income that would be made available by phased construction and in particular by leveraging the prestige office tower slated to replace Old City Hall.[142] By early 1967, the Eaton Centre's profitability and viability were in doubt. In February, David Owen quietly resigned as director, and he was not replaced.

The significant financial problems might have been overcome, but the corporate will was not there. Throughout the centre's public life, Eaton's sought to present a face of confidence to the public, but behind that veneer was growing ambivalence about its role as an urban developer. Much time and money went to measuring what today would be called the "brand risk" posed by the project's construction – its potential to negatively affect Eaton's reputation and sales. Throughout 1965 and 1966, the Eatons and their executive team followed closely any public criticism of the centre, the store, or the family itself. They read *Canadian Architect,* instructed staff to attend and report on meetings of the Friends of Old City Hall, and researched each of the individuals and groups that had made deputations to Metro Council opposing the centre. Most of all, company staff catalogued letters from Toronto customers who threatened to take their business elsewhere if Old City Hall were torn down, writing back with fulsome, thoughtful replies.[143] Eaton's public relations consultants were increasingly critical of the idea of the company spearheading the project. "The most important point to bear in mind," argued a 1966 report,

> is the fact that this company is in the retail trade business – not the real estate business. It therefore depends on the goodwill of the general public – all of it. Eaton's cannot consider action on any project with which its name is associated in isolation from this fact. A land developer may be said to have won his point if he has the support of a simple majority of the general public or of a municipal council. This is not the case with Eaton's.[144]

A year later, when the cancellation decision was made, an internal position statement contended that this conflict between the roles of retailer and land developer had placed Eaton's in an "impossible position" that could be resolved only by abandoning one of the two roles. There was no question as to which that would be. The memorandum went on to militate against an idea that had animated more than a decade of policy and planning: that "any single corporate citizen" could take on the fraught task of rebuilding the heart of the city.[145] In this light, the idea of downtown redevelopment as an elite partnership seemed at best unrealistic, and at worst naive.

THE CANCELLATION OF the Eaton Centre in 1967 marked the end of the fraying consensus around downtown rebuilding in Toronto. For more than a decade, planners, politicians, business elites, and prominent public personalities had sought to mobilize government and private resources to transform Toronto's business district. Although they varied in approach and objectives, advocates of redevelopment subscribed to the idea that both the public interest and private profit could be served by replacing older urban forms with modern structures and more efficient uses. This vision was embodied in new municipal agencies, plans, and policies for downtown, including the formation of the Redevelopment Advisory Council and the Development Department, the crafting of the *Plan for Downtown Toronto,* and the construction of Toronto's New City Hall and civic square. It also influenced a series of corporate decisions to invest in large-scale modernist reconstruction, including the Toronto Dominion Centre, the Simpson Tower, and, most dramatically, the Eaton Centre.

Proponents of private-public partnership in 1950s and 1960s Toronto were perhaps idealistic, but they were not naive. In the absence of America-style funding for urban renewal, municipal officials leveraged their limited resources to enlist private capital in their redevelopment dreams. In the case of the Eaton's lands, the civic administration offered municipal property, planning expertise, and the prestige associated with corporate citizenship. In exchange, it hoped to raise tax revenues, beautify the landscape, and ensure urban prosperity in a period of decentralization and suburban competition. Eaton's and the Eaton family became invested in this idea, enlisting some of North America's most renowned downtown planners and revitalization experts to devise a complex that reconciled these public goals with their own strategies for adapting their business to the postwar era. The civic administration and Canada's largest retailer became partners in making a new heart for old Toronto because for a time they believed that their interests could be made to align, bringing significant benefits to both.

However, as this chapter has revealed, there was nothing simple or straightforward about putting this vision into practice. In the decade between the Project Viking proposal and the Eaton Centre's announcement, downtown rebuilding was tested by economic realities, public scrutiny, and the sheer complexity of the existing landscape. It was almost inevitable that the 1966 master plan could not live up to the rhetoric that accompanied its generation and public presentation. The project's failure underlined how ill-equipped Eaton's was – good corporate citizen or not – to plan and finance redevelopment on such a scale. It also demonstrated the potential influence of well-organized citizen groups such as the Friends of Old City Hall on the redevelopment process, which until that point had been a closed negotiation between experts, elected officials, and the private sector. With the collapse of the rebuilding consensus, a new politics of urban development was in formation in Toronto during the late 1960s and early 1970s, and downtown Yonge Street would be one of its main battlegrounds.

3

A People Place

On the last day in May 1971, the front pages of all three Toronto dailies reported on a dramatic downtown transformation. "People take over Yonge St.," read the *Toronto Star;* the *Telegram* showed two views of the shopping street, first as "its usual dreary self, dominated by cars, with people confined to the cramped, crowded sidewalks," and second as a "people's freeway," with four lanes of vehicle traffic replaced by linden trees, outdoor cafés, and, above all, crowds.[1] Tens of thousands of people shopped, strolled, and loitered on downtown Yonge Street that weekend, inaugurating a four-year experiment in pedestrianizing Toronto's busiest retail strip. Between 1971 and 1974, the Yonge pedestrian mall grew from a brief festival to a mile-long public space that was closed to cars – and open to other uses – throughout the summer months. As reports of its opening suggest, the mall was popular, bringing crowds downtown and generating excitement with its disruption of everyday urban routines. But it was also controversial, most of all because the change focused public attention on Yonge's perceived problems – old and new – while frustrating hopes that they could be addressed by physically reconfiguring the street.

Toronto's "people's freeway" was the product of a decade of efforts to articulate an alternative future for downtown Yonge, in the face of the program of creative destruction pursued by municipal and corporate elites. Between its arrival in Toronto during the late 1950s and its implementation on Yonge in 1971, the idea of pedestrian malls mobilized a series of actors who did not see their interests or ideas reflected in the drive to redevelop downtown. To small businesses and their allies – including urbanists, downtown politicians, and environmental activists – Yonge's unplanned streetscape, narrow right-of-way, and mix of commercial uses were not obstacles to progress, but unique assets. Whereas the Eaton Centre promised to save the heart of the city by rebuilding it, reimagining it as a people place was a strategy to develop what was already there. Intended not just to protect livelihoods, but to encourage sociability, boost citizen participation, and contest the dominance of the automobile, the Yonge Street pedestrian mall was entangled with many of the major urban issues of the day. This was highlighted as the experiment expanded in scope and its shared spaces were appropriated in unexpected ways, shifting the focus of Toronto's debates over the downtown future from economic decline to the everyday politics of public space.[2]

Downtown Planning for the Motor Age

The North American pedestrian mall was a product of the motor age, an urban intervention that became widespread from the 1960s in the context of transformations facilitated by mass car ownership. Its popularity, like that of the suburban cul-de-sac and the climate-controlled shopping centre, expressed a central irony of automobility: the more people participated in building a city around the car, the more they wanted places where they could escape it.[3] Such spaces had been the norm in most Canadian and American cities prior to the 1920s, but by mid-century they were few and far between, as cars filled the streets of the industrial city and enabled new urban expansion well beyond its boundaries. Municipal governments and planners in the postwar era focused on accommodating the automobile, but they were also preoccupied by its domestication, deploying new expertise and traffic management technologies to make its use efficient and safe. Providing respite from the noise, pollution, and physical danger of traffic was a form of therapy for a population that increasingly lived, worked, and shopped in car-dependent landscapes.[4] Car-free, human-scaled spaces could also be profitable. The curvilinear, maze-like layouts of tonier residential subdivisions – designed to frustrate through-traffic and to foster green, safe streets – and the era's increasingly elaborate enclosed shopping malls were successful, reproducible business models that addressed people's ambivalence about automobility. So, for a while, were the pedestrian streets that began popping up in downtowns across the continent at the end of the 1950s.

Pedestrian malls offered an alternative to the downtown rebuilding projects of the 1950s and 1960s, but the two approaches also had common roots. Both the first car-free streets and many of the era's major commercial redevelopments were based on the premise that struggling downtown commercial areas would benefit economically from transposing the most successful features of the suburban shopping centre – attractive, pedestrian-only areas with ample parking nearby – into the centre of the city.[5] No one better embodied the conceptual links between these different forms of retail planning than Victor Gruen, who designed North America's first indoor suburban shopping centre (Minneapolis, 1956) and first downtown pedestrian mall (Kalamazoo, 1959) before moving on to produce a set of plans for the Eaton Centre in 1964.[6] There were, of course, major differences in the execution of such projects: redevelopment was premised on using massive outlays of capital to replace the existing landscape, whereas pedestrian malls left it intact, closing public streets to change how it was accessed and used. Gruen's mall in Kalamazoo, Michigan, was the model for this approach, a two-block car-free section on a street already lined with shops, with added aesthetic features such as benches and trees giving it an idealized pre-automobile, Main Street feel. Requiring little in the way of property or power to implement, such malls became the intervention of choice for urban actors who possessed neither, but who still hoped for downtown transformation.

The few scholars who have studied pedestrian malls have focused on their failure to live up to hopes for economic revitalization.[7] Tremendous enthusiasm accompanied the early examples – including Ottawa's Sparks Street, first opened in 1960 – and for a time it seemed that removing traffic would allow traditional downtown retail streets to challenge the ascendant suburban shopping centre and "beat suburbia at its own game."[8] Just two months after the opening of Kalamazoo's mall, a *Life* feature gushed that sales and property values were "booming," and the local press went so far as to claim that the city's "bold auto-ban plan could become the salvation of Downtown America."[9] However, by the 1970s these initial successes had given way to renewed reports of decline. In the long term, it became clear that localized, largely aesthetic solutions such as pedestrianization could not address the larger structural challenges facing downtown. And yet, cities continued to close streets to traffic, in growing numbers and, in many cases, for new reasons. Research in the late 1970s found that roughly twice as many pedestrian malls had opened during that decade than in the previous two, and that this new wave of experiments focused as much on fostering civic pride and improving the downtown environment as on boosting retail trade.[10] The history of Yonge Street's pedestrianization bears this out, highlighting the flexibility of the mall idea and its capacity to integrate – at least temporarily – the agendas of a range of downtown actors.

Pedestrian Malls in Toronto

The concept of pedestrianization arrived in Toronto in the mid-1950s, with the small cohort of experts hired to staff the City's first permanent Planning Department. Influenced by urban modernism as practised in Britain, Europe, and the United States, they proposed a series of interventions to order and improve the central city, including a network of separated pedestrian pathways and spaces that would move people more efficiently, make walking more pleasant, and beautify the drab "surveyor's grid" that defined downtown Toronto.[11] In response to the much publicized openings of the Kalamazoo and Sparks Street malls in 1959–60, Toronto planners began to direct their attention to closing existing streets to make pedestrian malls. In their opinion, downtown Yonge could particularly benefit from more people space, at least in the interim before its redevelopment. In discussing the idea, they stressed that Yonge was already "primarily a pedestrian way," with more foot traffic than vehicular traffic on any given day. Malling would recognize this, while at the same time providing some aesthetic coherence to the street's "heterogeneous jumble" of storefronts.[12] These exploratory ideas were first published in the *Plan for Downtown Toronto* (1963) and were widely reported in local newspapers, through which the idea of creating pedestrian malls entered public discourse in Toronto.

Shortly after that plan was published, independent merchants on Yonge seized on the mall idea and made it their own. A spring 1963 letter to the Planning Board, signed by the owners of seventeen shoe, clothing, and specialty shops, described in vivid detail their ongoing struggles to maintain their business model in the context of decentralization and uneven access to metropolitan mobility. "Shopping centres on the outskirts of the city have taken many people away from downtown Yonge," they explained, but suburban competition was not the only problem.[13] The removal of the streetcar in favour of tunnelled transit a decade earlier had reorganized street traffic to favour the large department stores, while punishing smaller outlets. The subway, the merchants noted, funnelled people straight into Eaton's and Simpson's – both located immediately above subway stations, with their own direct entrances. This arrangement was convenient for shoppers, but it effectively cleared the sidewalks of the foot traffic upon which the merchants depended. To illustrate their predicament, they appended a photo of an empty sidewalk, taken in the middle of a business day. For businesses that had long associated success with the bustle of crowds, there could be few more easily recognizable images of failure.

Calls to install a pedestrian mall on Yonge were just the latest in a series of postwar appeals by these merchants and their neighbours for municipal intervention on the street. Previous requests for property tax relief, the removal of parking restrictions, and other measures designed to combat shrinking sales had produced little in the way of concrete action.[14] Unsurprisingly, given these precedents, their request exuded a tone of desperation. They portrayed the problem of downtown decline as both personal and existential: "For small independent retailers, the downtown area has become a 'decaying heart city.' It is not a matter of earning a living, or making a profit, but rather a question of who can afford to lose money and hang on the longest!"[15] Their bleak prognosis flew in the face of the optimism of corporate groups such as the Board of Trade and the Redevelopment Advisory Council, for whom the key indicators of downtown prosperity were a surging commercial real estate market and growing white-collar employment – not everyday levels of foot traffic on Yonge Street. It was these larger lobby groups, much more than independent merchants, whose voices carried weight with the municipal administration. After receiving their letter, City of Toronto officials gave a sympathetic hearing to a delegation of small Yonge Street businesses as they pleaded for a pedestrian mall. But just a few months later, the idea was shelved after resistance from the Redevelopment Advisory Council, for whom limiting traffic circulation on major streets could only impede the more important business of rebuilding downtown.[16] In the wake of this rejection, several of the letter's signatories would sell their properties to Eaton's, then in the process of completing its land assembly for the 1966 Eaton Centre.

In parallel with the merchants' campaign, interest in street closures developed in a very different context: that of the youth counterculture. By 1965, the Yorkville "Village," an area of inexpensive Victorian housing and shops just north of downtown along Yonge Street, had supplanted Gerrard Street as Toronto's bohemian hub. There, as in San Francisco's Haight-Ashbury and other hip enclaves across the continent, rebellion from the mainstream became a spectator sport. On summer evenings and weekends, Yorkville Avenue was packed with cars, motorcycles, and people, making it impossible to say who was "making the scene" – and who was simply observing it.[17] In an effort to push back against cruising vehicles, gawkers, and journalists, a few Yorkville villagers proposed converting the street into a pedestrian mall. Not only would this allow them to assert their ownership of the space, but the idea of banning the car – that potent symbol of consumer capitalism and suburban conformity – also fit into a larger counterculture social critique. By the summer of 1967, the mall proposal had become a flashpoint of tension between hip youth and the civic administration, reaching a peak early in the morning of August 21, 1967, when a mass sit-in calling for pedestrianization was violently broken up by police, who made fifty arrests. Yorkville villagers followed up with a "sleep-in" in front of City Hall that, though it failed in its objective of securing a meeting with the mayor, generated media attention and popular support for pedestrianization.[18]

As Yorkville's countercultural scene ebbed, new champions of downtown malls emerged along with Toronto's nascent environmental movement. The young, policy-oriented anti-pollution activists of Group Action to Stop Pollution (GASP, founded 1967) and Pollution Probe (1969) were not particularly bohemian, but they shared the Yorkville villagers' conviction that the private automobile was a destructive force and that banning or restricting its use in the city – even on a limited basis – could be a powerful symbolic victory.[19] For these two groups, pedestrianization was less an end in and of itself than a means to engage the public and build awareness of the negative impacts of the car on the urban environment and human health. To that end, in summer 1970 the centrepiece of their program of urban activities was "Leave the Car at Home Week," which proposed to convert several downtown thoroughfares into pedestrian malls, while encouraging commuters to walk, cycle, or ride public transit to work. Following on the heels of the first Earth Day events in April of that year – including New York City's environmentally inspired closure of Fifth Avenue to cars – the idea was surprisingly popular with downtown politicians, the press, and the public.[20]

This was in part due to the growing environmental awareness of which Earth Day was just one manifestation; it was also a result of local questioning of the place of the car in the city.[21] By 1970, Toronto was in the grips of an extended public debate over the construction of the Spadina Expressway, a north-south freeway planned to run through the west side of downtown. Often framed as a battle between "people power" and technocratic planning, the project generated significant citizen opposition in the middle-class and gentrifying neighbourhoods along its route, while moving critiques of automobility into the political mainstream and connecting them to other causes such as neighbourhood preservation.[22] The organizers of 1970's Leave the Car at Home Week were unsuccessful in closing downtown thoroughfares, but municipal support for the idea led directly to the Yonge Street pedestrian mall of the following summer.[23]

From second-tier planning concept to revitalization project, countercultural protest to green planning, a series of very different actors incorporated pedestrian malls into their agendas over the course of a decade.

This distinguishes Toronto from cities such as Kalamazoo or Ottawa, where pedestrianization experiments were driven almost entirely by the lobbying of downtown businesses. That a broad range of local actors had visions for downtown and, increasingly, the political space to express them speaks to the upsurge in civil society engagement that characterized the late 1960s and early 1970s in Toronto and cities throughout North America.[24] The activism of the Friends of Old City Hall and its contribution to the election of Mayor William Dennison were early examples of a larger phenomenon. By the early 1970s, municipal politics in Toronto were being remade through the mobilization of dozens of citizen groups ranging in size and political orientation, including a powerful network of middle-class rate-payers' associations, but also ethnic organizations and working-class housing advocates.[25] The most politically astute were the "new middle class" described by David Ley; young, educated, professionally successful urbanites who had recently rediscovered central-city neighbourhoods and were eager to participate in shaping them.[26] This population produced a series of municipal politicians, often referred to as reformers or reformists, who won elections on platforms of increased citizen participation, neigh-bourhood preservation, and environmental awareness. They also offered sustained opposition to what they saw as the destructive technocratic planning of the past two decades, as embodied by the Spadina Expressway and Toronto's experiments in residential urban renewal.[27] By the start of the 1970s, the phrase "planning for people" seemed to be on everyone's lips, even officials at the business-friendly Development Department.[28] No project was better poised to benefit from this shift than downtown pedes-trian malls.

The People's Freeway

> *Yonge Street will be a pedestrian mall from 00.01am Sunday, May 30th ... There [is] no list of charges. There will be no ticket collectors because the street is being opened up for people and will be free for all ... There will be no special briefings for the Press ... The judge and jury for the success of the mall will be the people of Toronto.*

As captured in this 1971 press release, the Yonge Street pedestrian mall was imagined and promoted as a "people place," an identity that encom-passed both its planning and daily functioning as a public space. It was widely understood as a grassroots initiative. Not only was the mall idea already associated with civil society activism, but from the start its

A "people place": crowds replace cars on the Yonge Street pedestrian mall, summer 1972. View north from Adelaide Street. | Graham Bezant/*Toronto Star* 502842709 via Getty Images

planning was infused with the enthusiasm for participatory democracy and community-based initiatives that would characterize so much of downtown politics in 1970s Toronto. That meant public meetings, citizen committees, and other efforts to involve a wide range of municipal actors who had supported street closures in the past or might do so in the future.[29] Closing Yonge to cars remained a municipal project, with the bulk of the work done by a small group of downtown politicians and City employees, led by area councillor William Archer. They worked closely, if not always harmoniously, with the Downtown Council, formerly the Downtown Businessmen's Association. But the involvement of other activist groups such as Pollution Probe in the mall's implementation, as well as the general atmosphere of volunteerism that surrounded it both contributed to its image as a citizen project unlike other planning interventions of the period. Nothing expressed this perception better than the decision of the Toronto branch of the Ontario Association of Architects to break with tradition and present its 1972 Design Award – normally bestowed on a member of the profession – to "the citizens of Toronto" for their role in creating the mall.[30]

The Yonge mall was a street without cars, unique in Toronto's thoroughly motorized downtown core. The project's planners used barriers and traffic police to divert cars, buses, and trucks – and the noise and fumes they generated – onto other streets, tripling the space available to pedestrians. This was transformative, given that in the early 1970s downtown Yonge's four-lane roadway was used by approximately twenty-five thousand vehicles daily – one every three seconds on average, with much higher rates during morning and evening rush hours. In their place came crowds. Pedestrian counts in 1971 suggest that tens of thousands of people visited the mall each day, and at peak times – evenings, weekend afternoons – more than ten thousand moved hourly through each block, two to three times more foot traffic than during an ordinary rush hour.[31] The sheer numbers and mingling of these crowds defined the mall as a people place. Journalists tended to divide its users into a series of types according to gender, age, and their perceived use of the space: lunching office workers; "little old ladies"; appreciative out-of-towners; fashionable young women; and unconventional but essentially harmless "hippies."[32] The overall image conveyed by these reports was that of a vibrant human ecology that varied according to the hour, the weather, and the location. Each year, the mall took place between May and September; within that season, rain tended to empty it, whereas sun and warm summer evenings filled it with people.

Torontonians celebrated the mall for its fulfillment of the ideal of encounter and social mixing among a heterogeneous urban population.[33]

Both the major newspapers and citizens who wrote to mall organizers referred to the "miracle" of the mall, portraying it as the birthplace of a new urban sociability. With the stress and noise of traffic removed, people were friendlier: commuters slowed down on their usual rushed walks to work; strangers mingled and shared tables in the streetside cafés; and Yonge became a "sea of smiles."[34] There was a widespread sense that the mall's vibrant – even somewhat disorderly – streetlife signalled a larger trans-formation in the city. *Toronto Star* columnist Jack McArthur captured the hopeful, self-congratulatory mood when he observed that the city was preparing a future as a "people-oriented, loveable, small town," rather than an impersonal, business-oriented metropolis.[35] Urban experts rejoiced at the creation of new public space in a downtown where virtually every empty lot was either allocated to parking or slated for office tower redevelopment. After walking the mall with a reporter in tow, noted Canadian architect and urbanist John C. Parkin announced that it marked the end of "Toronto the dreary ... the city of corridors without a living room," which he had criti-cized in the past.[36] The closure of Yonge Street to cars was imagined as the creation of a public good – open space – for the democratic enjoyment of all. Within a week of its opening, the press and the project's supporters were calling for downtown Yonge to be permanently off-limits to traffic.[37]

The public targeted by the mall was one that was increasingly ethnic-ally diverse and supportive of celebrations of cultural pluralism. The Yonge Street closures occurred at a moment when Toronto was redefining itself as a multi-ethnic city, reflecting both local realities and larger national trends. Although migration had long fuelled its urbanization and growth, its Anglo-Protestant identity would not significantly alter until the post–Second World War decades. Between 1951 and 1971, Metro Toronto was the settlement choice of half a million immigrants, a quarter of those who arrived in Canada during the period. The non-British share of the city's population rose quickly to 54 percent, as large-scale migrations from southern and eastern Europe – and smaller movements from Asia and the Caribbean – contributed to creating a multi-ethnic, if still overwhelm-ingly white, urban population.[38] Franca Iacovetta shows how in the postwar decades Toronto civil society groups responded to these changes by pro-moting a liberal, cultural pluralist nation-building program that prefigured the official multiculturalism policies of the 1970s. Festivals, cultural ex-changes, and other public activities generated in partnership with ethnic organizations staged a (mostly European) multi-ethnic mosaic as spec-tacle, offering citizens a chance to experience the foods, customs, and folk culture of their new neighbours.[39]

Like other festivals and municipal pageantry of the period, Toronto's downtown pedestrian experiments put its identity as an emerging multi-ethnic metropolis centre stage. In 1971, two of the biggest draws during the Yonge closure were Wednesday's Caribbean steel band and limbo competition, and a Friday-night gala featuring the costumed Zemplin Slovak dancers and other folk dancing groups.[40] Following this success, in 1972, the mall's ethnic content was significantly increased. The Community Folk Arts Council, one of Toronto's major multicultural bodies and the coordinator of the annual Metro International Caravan Festival, collaborated with mall organizers to dedicate each of the event's seven weeks to showcasing a national culture. British Week, Italian Week, and Caribbean Week, among others, provide excellent examples of the growing importance of expressions of cultural pluralism to Toronto's public culture in the 1970s.[41] They also demonstrated the ease with which ethnic folk culture could be appropriated and packaged to boost sales of T-shirts, pizza, or handicrafts, and more generally as a means to revive interest in flagging commercial areas. This would become a strategy of choice for ethnic entrepreneurs in 1970s Toronto, beginning with the car-free Dragon Mall organized on nearby Elizabeth Street, the historical heart of the city's Chinatown.[42]

Selling on the Mall

People mattered to the Yonge mall not just as citizens, but as consumers. The street was Toronto's largest retail marketplace and entertainment destination, lined with independent merchants and entertainment entrepreneurs who depended in all seasons on its sidewalks and foot traffic for their livelihoods. Whereas other observers saw the mall's success in its provision of public space, excitement, and sociability, for businesses on the strip its value was most of all commercial. They hoped to measure its impact at the cash register and at the lunch counter, in sales receipts and resurgent profits. For a car-free Yonge to be successful, it needed not just to attract people in the abstract, but the right kind of people: shoppers, diners, customers with money to spend. At a time when economic dynamism and demographic growth were concentrated on the urban fringe, Yonge Street merchants saw these qualities as synonymous with middle-class suburban consumers, who might otherwise be spending their money at Yorkdale Shopping Centre, Sherway Plaza, or another of the metropolitan area's dozen self-contained suburban marketplaces.[43]

To this end, businesses on Yonge Street leveraged the pedestrian mall as a marketing strategy. The Downtown Council and the larger stores

A better version of the North American downtown. Promotional postcard for the mall, featuring its popular street cafés, 1971. | Author's collection

bought radio spots, subway car posters, and full-page ads in local newspapers, promising thrills, special sales, and places to relax and linger: "Live it up downtown! ... the most pleasant shopping experience you will find anywhere."[44] Eaton's organized street fashion shows with store merchandise, and the Downtown Council paid for clowns and other street performers to encourage a diverting "family-oriented" atmosphere. Businesses with smaller budgets placed stereos in front of their stores, set up sidewalk displays, or hired teenagers to hand out coupons and advertisements. Eager to dispel any suggestion that downtown Yonge was in decline, merchants branded it "Main Street Canada," referencing the North American myth of Main Street (and, perhaps, Disneyland's Main Street U.S.A.), with its associations of small-town friendliness, safety, and plain dealing.[45] This image went over particularly well in Detroit, Buffalo, Rochester, and other neighbouring US cities, where Toronto marketed itself as a better functioning, more harmonious version of the North American metropolis, devoid of the racial tensions and rising crime rates that characterized the 1970s urban crisis.[46] "People along the border," explained the city's tourist bureau, "would rather come to Toronto than to any American city because it is cleaner and safer." A 1974 survey found that just over 10 percent of mallgoers were from the United States, suggesting that targeted promotion of the mall was succeeding.[47]

More importantly, merchants' dreams of competing with shopping centres for suburban customers also seemed to be coming true. According to that same 1974 study, one mallgoer in three came from the city's five suburban boroughs; a door-to-door survey conducted in the inner suburb of North Toronto in 1973 revealed that three in four respondents had visited Yonge Street during that summer's closure.[48] Early on, small-business interviewees glowingly claimed that the mall was "attracting people who haven't been downtown for [years]," and nearly all the businesses participating in the experiment reported increased foot traffic and sales.[49] Some were better able than others to leverage the mall's spaces to create value, however. By the second and third summers, it was becoming increasingly clear that the greatest beneficiaries of the experiment were not established merchants such as Clark Shoes or Business Girl fashions, but discount retailers offering impulse purchases, as well as Le Coq d'Or, Circus-Circus Pub, and the other taverns and restaurants that had capitalized on the closure to offer food and (especially) alcoholic drinks on the street. Between 1971 and 1973, while retailers reported modest increases in receipts, the number of licensed patios on the mall grew from two to ten, boosting the street as a nightlife destination unique in the city. People loved this aspect of the experiment, the first time in the post-Prohibition era that Toronto had legally sanctioned outdoor drinking. "It's just like Paris," exclaimed one woman, summing up the warm response to the introduction of "European-style" café culture in the heart of downtown.[50]

Alongside this "official" marketplace, a fantastic range of informal commercial ventures competed for space on the mall. Some were viewed positively, such as the preteen shoeshine boys, already an established feature of downtown life in Toronto, who set up their stools in doorways and rest areas. In 1971, a *Toronto Star* journalist used an interview with "Little Jimmy Crouse" to press home the point that Torontonians of all types approved of the experiment. This reflected a common understanding of this marginal trade. In the 1960s and early 1970s, Jimmy and his peers were often uncritically celebrated in the press as examples of entrepreneurism or big-city colour, glossing over the circumstances that prompted dozens of working-class youngsters, often from immigrant families, to spend their evenings and summers working informally on the street.[51] There was also a certain sympathy for the unlicensed performers who congregated on Yonge during its closure: jugglers, magicians, and most of all buskers, who seem to have found the mall lucrative enough to stay. Prior to the 1970s, busking entertainers were a rarity in Toronto, but after several summers of pedestrian closures they had become a near-constant feature of the Yonge Street scene in warm weather.[52]

Entertainment was encouraged, but the Downtown Council vigorously protested other types of informal commercial activity and especially street vending. Like their more established counterparts, dozens of street merchants attempted to cash in on the mall's crowds of strollers by selling candles, flowers, sunglasses, personalized portraits, and jewellery from blankets and tables. Some sold mass-produced products at a discount, others specialized in leather and beadwork and handmade pendants in bone, silver, or wood that reflected the natural aesthetic of the 1970s counterculture. Yonge's independent merchants saw this as direct competition and protested the fact that these "capitalists of the counterculture" had free access to mall-going customers, when they themselves had been obliged to pay municipal taxes and subscriptions for mall entertainment for that privilege.[53] Mall organizers responded to this lobbying by reconfiguring the space, attempting to corral vendors into "street fair" areas away from the storefronts and the flow of foot traffic. Still, like buskers and shoeshine boys, vendors preferred to stay where the action was. This led to frequent confrontations with neighbouring shop owners, and with City officials who tried to move them along or issue tickets for the bylaw infraction of vending without a permit. The latter approach generally proved unsuccessful, since tickets were commonly ignored or if the relatively low fines were paid, they were simply seen as a cost of doing business on Toronto's busiest street.[54]

Some of Yonge's most dedicated entrepreneurs were selling ideas. From opening day, the pedestrian closure attracted a wide range of people who were eager to exploit its crowded spaces as a political stage or recruiting ground. Alternative educational experiment Rochdale College held its 1971 graduation ceremony on the mall, mocking the formality of convocation at the nearby University of Toronto with a kazoo orchestra; federal Conservative leader Robert Stanfield and virtually every municipal politician in Toronto used the mall to "meet the people" and pose for photo opportunities with supporters.[55] A stroller making her way up Yonge Street might receive en route a copy of the *Radical Humanist* (a "monthly newspaper on alienation"), an ad for an anti-war music festival ("End Canada's complicity in Vietnam!"), and an invitation to a folk-music night at the nearby Scientology coffee house (a "night especially for people to be themselves"). She could discuss enlightenment and salvation with shaven-headed Hare Krishna devotees and longhaired Jesus People, or art and imperialism with members of the Committee to Strengthen Canadian Culture. Pamphlets for these groups and others joined coupons and advertisements for Yonge Street businesses in the litter of paper that covered the street. The mall was Toronto's loudest, busiest, and most chaotic marketplace in ideas.

Fighting Traffic

Conspicuous by its absence, the automobile also played an important role in defining the Yonge Street mall. When the City of Toronto took over planning of the experiment from environmentalists GASP and Pollution Probe in 1970, it was quick to set the new initiative apart from the Leave the Car at Home Week. The mall, its planners emphasized, was not anti-car; it was about bringing people space, crowds, and life downtown. William Archer, the city councillor who spearheaded the project, saw no contradiction between the street closure and his continuing support for the Spadina Expressway; in his view, shared by many, making people space and facilitating metropolitan mobility were complementary responses to the challenge of the motor age.[56] But in the charged political context of the early 1970s, it was impossible to exclude conflict around automobility from the mall's newly created space. On a day-to-day basis, its image was that of a place provocatively separate from the motorized city. Local newspaper coverage tended to exploit the contrast between it and ordinary downtown streets in two ways. On the one hand, the dailies printed articles that treated the closure as a potential nightmare for drivers, warning of its role in creating "chaotic traffic jams" and questioning whether Toronto could afford the inconvenience. On the other hand – and this was the majority view – they exclaimed that an auto-free Yonge was a "miracle" respite for pedestrians worn out by the noise, smells, and dangers of downtown traffic.[57]

This distinct urban space seemed to lend itself to symbolic appropriation by anti-automobile activists. In 1971, Pollution Probe organized a mass bicycle parade that was timed to coincide with the opening ceremonies of the mall. Several hundred cyclists of all ages converged in front of the Ontario Legislature in Queen's Park, before riding eight-abreast down Yonge Street to the pedestrian mall, in a bellringing "cycle army" seven blocks long. As with similar events organized in Paris, Philadelphia, or New York the same year, Pollution Probe saw in the "pollutionless bicycle" a fun and accessible symbol of resistance to the domination of the cumbersome, chemical-spewing car.[58] The parade succeeded in attracting significant media attention, putting the issue of automobile pollution firmly back on the agenda at the mall.[59] It was also an important moment for the

In a city dominated by the car, opening a major street to pedestrians generated both excitement and conflict. View of the mall looking south from near College Street, 1971 or 1972. | City of Toronto Archives, series 1465, item 43

fledgling urban cycling movement in Toronto, beginning a decade in which it would organize as a lobby group and convince the municipal government to invest for the first time in cycling paths and other urban infrastructure.[60]

A few days later, despite the best efforts of the mall organizers, debate over the Spadina Expressway came to Yonge Street. On June 3, 1971, Premier William Davis announced the cancellation of provincial funding for the project, effectively overturning a decade of transportation planning in Toronto and giving a surprise victory to the citizen-led Stop Spadina coalition. Journalists followed along as jubilant placard-waving, dancing, and singing protesters took over the mall, shouting "We won!" and "You can beat City Hall!" They went on to explain for the benefit of less well-informed readers that the mall was an ideal place for the celebration, since it was a "symbol of pedestrian rights" and "the ban-the-car movement."[61] In subsequent years, other actors would return to the idea that pedestrianization was an anti-pollution, anti-automobile statement. For example, it was front-page news in 1973 – "Choke! Splutter! Gasp! Yonge St is hard on your lungs" – when researchers reported consistently high levels of automobile pollution on Yonge, only shrinking to tolerable levels for human health during the pedestrian mall.[62] Through these interventions, the mall came to symbolize not just people space, but the ongoing environmentalist fight against traffic and the possibility of taming the car's influence on the city.

"A Meeting Place for Youth from All across Canada"

The Yonge Street mall was a youthful place. The presence of student environmentalists, twenty-something buskers, and teenaged vendors was part of a larger appropriation of the street by youth from Toronto, the urban region, and beyond. Like other categories of mallgoer, young people came to Yonge to work, shop, or enjoy the spectacle. In a downtown landscape lacking in open spaces, the street closure provided a place to meet and linger that presented no barriers – physical or financial – to entry and no formal limits to the time one could spend there. Dozens of images taken by media, City officials, and street photographers testify to the large groups of young people who congregated on the mall, strolling up and down the strip, sitting in circles talking or singing, or simply milling around, seemingly waiting for something to happen. At times, and on specific sections of the street – particularly on the entertainment corridor north of Dundas – young people were the dominant age group. In summer 1974, researchers stopped two thousand people on Yonge to create a profile of the average mall user: nearly half were sixteen to twenty-five years old, as opposed to 18 percent in the city's overall population.[63]

A significant number of these youth were not locals. During the early 1970s, Toronto was a hub for the thousands of young people who crisscrossed the country or the continent on their way to and from school or work, or simply in search of adventure and experience through mobility.[64] These "transient youth" – as they were labelled by a 1969 national inquiry – naturally gravitated toward the Yonge pedestrian mall's central location in search of food, excitement, a bed, friends, job information, or even medical attention. Certain spaces became informal gathering points, including a long landscaped lawn near Yonge and Queen that one teenager referred to as "a meeting place for youth from all across Canada."[65] During the 1973 closure, police reported encountering "juveniles from as far away as Yellowknife, N.W.T." on the mall.[66] As the report attests, some were stopped and questioned by the police. But many more found their way to the Peoples' Information Service, a twenty-four-hour office staffed by young summer workers, set up adjacent to the mall in 1971 using a federal Opportunities for Youth grant. Like Toronto's new youth hostels and "tent cities" on the University of Toronto campus and in west-end High Park,

A meeting place for youth from across Canada. Making the scene on one of the pedestrian mall's landscaping features, summer 1973. | Ron Bull/ *Toronto Star* 1231457073 via Getty Images

this information bureau was part of a national network of government-funded and informal services whose purpose was to help Canadian cities cope with summer influxes of young travellers.[67]

A car-free Yonge was clearly attractive to young people; but unlike that of suburban families, their presence was often viewed as an obstacle to its success. To be young in North America during the 1960s and 1970s was to be under intense scrutiny. Urban spaces in Toronto where young people gathered in numbers also stirred up anxieties about misbehaviour and disorder that could rise to hyperbolic proportions, whether framed in terms of sexual promiscuity and rowdiness at fast food restaurants in suburban North York or acid dropping and venereal disease at the "dens" and coffee houses of Yorkville's hip village.[68] That last association was important, since as early as 1971 even straight media outlets such as the *Toronto Star* were reporting that Yorkville had lost its groove and that the new magnet for Toronto's youth counterculture was the Yonge Street strip.[69] Some disagreed: alternative monthly *Guerilla* disparaged the Yonge and Dundas intersection as Toronto's "arsehole" and dismissed the pedestrian mall as "drab and plastic," although it continued to sell its issues there.[70] But the idea that the mall was the new Yorkville had stuck in the public imagination. Most Yonge Street merchants saw little economic opportunity in the crowds of youth – longhaired or not – that gathered on the mall, where their very presence threatened to disrupt its family ambience and displace paying customers. Of course, negative representations of "hippies" and hitchhiking panhandlers tended to mask the varied ways in which young people participated in the mall experiment. They were just as likely to be shopping for records or hurrying to work as loitering in the manner that so irritated certain observers. Students on summer break were responsible for setting up the mall's decorations and street furniture, for selling ice cream and waiting tables, and for doing pedestrian counts and sweeping up at the end of the night.[71]

An "Orgy of Lawlessness"?

More damaging to the mall's reputation than youthful vendors and panhandlers were its associations with bad behaviour and urban disorder. From 1972 on, individual incidents of violence or rowdyism were profiled in the local press. For example, in June of that year, twenty-five-year-old Jim Davies wrote to the *Toronto Star* to complain of being attacked on Yonge: "Almost 200 people stood and watched early Sunday morning while I was punched and kicked to the pavement in the middle of downtown Toronto. Nobody thought of coming to my aid, nobody called a policeman, and nobody looked me in the eyes when I walked up to them afterward and through bloodied lips asked why they hadn't helped."[72]

A photo of the author's puffed, bruised face ran beside the letter in a prominent place on the editorial page. But the loudest and most widely credited criticisms came not from the street, but from a respected official in the municipal government. In October 1973, Toronto chief of police Harold Adamson submitted a long report to the City in which he censured the mall and recommended that it either be scaled down or halted the following year. Using arrest statistics and excerpts from officer reports, he portrayed the mall as a dysfunctional public space where police were only barely able to maintain order: "an 84-day orgy of lawlessness," as one *Toronto Star* reporter put it when the report was released publicly a month later.[73] Over the next year, Adamson would repeatedly depict the mall as a drain on police resources and a contributing factor to rising crime rates, a stance that fit into his larger agenda of lobbying Metro Toronto for budget increases and other levels of government for new police powers.[74]

Just how dangerous was Toronto's people place? The public was shocked, first of all, by Adamson's report of the number of arrests made on Yonge. In the summer of 1973, this amounted to 1,074, or an average of a dozen each day. However, the number was deceptive in that only 5 percent (51) were for violent offences; the majority were for drunkenness (528), followed by possession, use, or sale of marijuana and hashish (178), the fastest-growing category of offence in Canada at the time.[75] When compared to the non-mall years for which specific Yonge Street statistics are available – 1977 and 1978 – the numbers are similar, with the notable exception of alcohol-related offences, which were higher during the mall.[76] Of the fifty-six major incidents cited in Adamson's report, all but six occurred in the evening or at night; more than half took place between midnight and 4:00 a.m., mostly on Fridays and Saturdays. What this suggests is that Yonge Street, Toronto's busiest entertainment zone – with at least ten pubs and bars in the mid-mall strip alone – had recurrent problems with intoxicated, boisterous crowds on summer nights, with or without cars. During the closure, this was increased, as the mall's expansive public spaces made Yonge a natural place to congregate and continue the party.

The issue was exacerbated by aggressive police tactics. As Adamson's arrest figures suggest, the Toronto police were very active during the mall. By the summer of 1973, an average of twenty-five officers were walking the beat on Yonge during any given day; on weekends, the number was closer to fifty. Their strategy focused on minimizing or removing "control problems," which could refer to illegal or disruptive activities (vending, panhandling, drinking) or to the presence of perceived undesirables, including transient youth, hippies, and motorcycle types.[77] Notably, this form of policing included stopping, questioning, and "warning off" young people who fit a certain familiar description – men with long hair, anyone who dressed in a particular way – a profiling practice that had been at the root of tension between police and youth in Yorkville a few years earlier.[78] Unlike in previous years, however, 1972 revisions to the Canadian Criminal Code had removed three vagrancy offences that the police had widely used to control undesirable persons: wandering in public without means of support, being a common prostitute, and begging.[79] Consequently, it became much more difficult for police in Canadian cities to regulate crowds and their behaviour.

These factors contributed to a pattern that began with police on foot engaging with large crowds of revellers and spectators, attempting to disperse them. Unsurprisingly, both passersby and those who were being asked to move on perceived such demands as harassment. Officers were heckled or obstructed, prompting them to call for backup and make arrests; however, police vehicles had difficulty in accessing the mall, slowing response times and the removal of suspects. Excerpts from police reports on 1973's most significant incidents show how officer-crowd conflict produced a spiral of escalation:

> 2:45 a.m. At Yonge and Elm Streets a man was arrested in a crowd of two hundred disorderlies. During the arrest a large segment of this crowd pelted the officers with rocks, dirt clumps from the flower beds, and other handy missiles.

> 11:45 p.m. As the result of two men being arrested for robbery on Yonge Street a near riot developed. One youth jumped on an officer's back knocking him to the ground, and another officer was attacked by the crowd. This situation resulted in the arrest of twelve persons, for Assault Police, Obstruct Police, and Cause a Disturbance.[80]

Although police did not provide a breakdown of arrests by gender, their descriptions of major incidents suggest that those involved were primarily men, as were the vast majority of the officers who confronted and later arrested them. The mall was not a particularly dangerous place, but on hot summer nights a combination of rowdy masculinity, aggressive policing, and intoxicated crowds significantly amplified its capacity to produce disorder.

Disruption and Control

By 1973, police criticism had changed the tenor of public discussion of pedestrian malls in Toronto. The positive images of the mall that had predominated in previous years lost ground in the face of growing concerns that removing cars from Yonge had produced a disorderly space. The project still had many public defenders. In the wake of a series of highly critical articles in the *Toronto Star* building on Harold Adamson's comments, citizens wrote to the paper, chastising it for its "slanted, biased" take, which gave the impression that "people coming to the mall would be abused, insulted, robbed, and possibly molested."[81] William Archer similarly denounced police criticism as "grossly exaggerated," confidently asserting that the mall's "control problems" had technical solutions, including the continued reorganization of its public spaces to make them less conducive to loitering or the gathering of crowds and the passing of municipal bylaws to curb nuisance behaviours.[82] But these attempts to shift the discussion away from bad behaviour largely failed. Anti-mall lobbying reached its peak in summer 1974, when a York County grand jury described the street

'I'll be honest, I preferred carbon monoxide.'

By 1974, images of the pedestrian mall as a dysfunctional public space dominated discussion about its future. | "I'll Be Honest, I Preferred Carbon Monoxide," *Globe and Mail*, August 6, 1974.

closure as "a blot on Toronto ... a crime centre for drug pushing, prostitution, and a miriad [sic] of other illegal activities," and suggested that it be discontinued.[83] Even though this recommendation carried no legal force, and the grand jury's report did little more than repeat police testimony against the mall, its verdict was given widespread attention in the press.[84]

Just as significant were growing rifts among the Yonge Street business community regarding the mall. The leadership of the Downtown Council remained in favour of the project, but its efforts to consolidate support revealed growing dissatisfaction among its members. In 1972, a survey conducted by the group found that nearly one in three businesses on the mall were opposed to its continuation, citing competition from vendors, increased shoplifting, and expenses incurred for entertainment and extra staff. The following year, nearly half of those surveyed (44 percent) were opposed, highlighting in their comments their frustration that the financial benefits of pedestrianization were not evenly distributed along the strip, but mainly accrued by people who sold souvenirs and gifts, and by the owners of cafés and bars with outdoor terraces.[85] Meetings of the Downtown Council became heated as an anti-mall group emerged, criticizing the council's executive for having "bullied" it into participating in the traffic ban.[86] By the end of 1973, Yonge's independent businesses were no longer solidly behind the project they had so desperately lobbied for a decade earlier. Their day-to-day observations and the influence of the police anti-mall campaign produced fears that pedestrianization might in fact be an agent of decline, not revival. Youth and their conflictual relationship with police were a key element in this more pessimistic assessment of the mall. "No one wants this to turn into another Yorkville," explained Downtown Council president Peter Clark, when asked why he thought the 1974 closure should be shorter than that of the previous year.[87]

Downtown's larger corporate interests had never been in favour of pedestrianizing Yonge Street. Although Eaton's had participated in the early street closures, organizing special sales and promotions, its redevelopment agenda significantly undermined the mall's long-term viability. During the land assembly for the Eaton Centre, its subsidiaries bought up two dozen properties on the west side of Yonge Street north of its Queen Street store.[88] By the time the first Yonge pedestrian mall opened in 1971, these storefronts were mostly sitting empty, as Eaton's worked at reviving its plans for the superblock site. This created a commercial dead zone of more than a block long, which broke the continuity of the retail strip and attracted little pedestrian traffic; this effect was amplified after the winter of 1973–74, when Eaton's began to demolish these properties, confronting Yonge Street pedestrians with a blank wall of construction hoardings.[89] Not only did this effectively create a gap in the summer pedestrian malls, but it was a reminder that Eaton's plans to build a privately managed, climate-controlled alternative to the downtown shopping street threatened to make Toronto's people place obsolete.

Eaton's competitor Simpson's worked against the street closures more directly. From 1970, it established itself as the most vocal business opponent of a car-free Yonge Street. Like independent retailers, Simpson's leadership put enticing the well-to-do suburban consumer at the heart of business success; unlike its smaller neighbours, the store believed that the only way to achieve this goal was by maintaining open access to its private parking garage. Company president Edgar Burton summed up both his store's view and a decades-old analysis of metropolitan retail relationships when he explained that "the one thing that will turn Yonge St. off as a viable shopping street is if the ladies who drive downtown to shop have to face additional traffic obstacles."[90] From 1970, Simpson's executives made it clear that they were "unalterably opposed" to a pedestrian mall, refusing to send a representative to planning meetings and warning that the company would hold the City responsible for any business lost due to traffic restrictions.[91]

Municipal officials did not take these warnings lightly. Not only was Simpson's a major downtown employer and payer of municipal taxes, but the question it raised about liability for business losses would haunt Toronto's four-year pedestrianization experiment. Just a few years earlier, Ontario's Expropriations Act had been amended to include the idea of "injurious affection," opening the way for compensation claims not just for the expropriation of private property, but for other government actions causing financial loss.[92] Municipal legal staff warned the mall organizers early on that closing Yonge raised the possibility of civil suits, an analysis that was confirmed as growing dissatisfaction with the reconfiguration of the street prompted not just Simpson's, but several other businesses on the strip, to threaten legal action.[93] To protect itself from litigation, Toronto was forced each summer to ask the Ontario government for special indemnifying legislation, effectively making the mall dependent on the waning goodwill of the provincial legislature. In 1971, backing the green, citizen-oriented mall seemed a natural choice for Progressive Conservative premier William Davis, whose decision the same year to cancel the Spadina Expressway was part of a larger effort to rebrand himself as a "decisive, modern, ecologically-minded leader" and to capture the centre in Ontario politics.[94] A few years later, this was no longer the case, as press coverage of the mall became increasingly negative and Davis's cabinet raised objections to this continued provincial interference in municipal affairs. In 1974, Toronto officials were told that the Province would no longer act as guarantor for the mall.[95]

These accumulating objections to the mall stemmed from the same source as its popularity: its capacity to disrupt the street's existing balance of uses and the routines of urban life. Pedestrianization, in its own modest, small-scale way, was a radical intervention, not in its social or political goals, but in the extent to which it reconfigured how the street worked. Making Yonge into a people place meant converting a thoroughfare into a destination, a carefully regulated corridor for circulation into a flexible public space. Removing vehicles also meant neutralizing parking bylaws, traffic signals, the distinction between sidewalk and road, and the offence of jaywalking – all the habits, regulations, and infrastructure that together constituted the motor-age street, organized to separate users and to maintain orderly and unobstructed movement from point A to point B.[96] The mall had a few elements of purposeful organization – benches and street cafés, entertainment areas, crossings at major streets – but the euphoria of early accounts suggests that people experienced it most of all as an exciting, free, and even somewhat transgressive space.

That freedom through disruption, and in fact everything that was innovative about the mall, created challenges. There were no scripts, at least initially, for a busy car-free street in downtown Toronto: how much space merchants could occupy in front of their stores or how they would receive deliveries; how loud stereos could blare; how long teenagers could loiter or how quickly crowds should move on, if at all. These and other relationships between the mall's users – established and new – had to be renegotiated, a process that took place both within the municipal bureaucracy and every day on the street. The frustration of the police faced with disorderly crowds, of merchants dissatisfied with their sales, and of mallgoers forced to navigate a gauntlet of preachers, pamphleteers, and panhandlers was a product of this context of renegotiation. Other North American cities with pedestrian malls had grappled with these issues, but the Yonge Street mall's administrators found little inspiration in their communications with municipal officials in Kalamazoo, New York City, or Ottawa.[97] In fact, the daily conflicts and undesired uses referred to on Yonge as "control problems" were a ubiquitous feature of pedestrian streets across North America by the 1970s, contributing in many cases to their reorganization or removal.[98] By the summer of 1974, this was also the case in downtown Toronto. People who flocked to Yonge Street continued to appreciate the experience – a survey of two thousand mallgoers showed an 88 percent approval rate – but by that point the principal actors involved in organizing and sustaining Toronto's people place were tired of disruption and were seeking a return to the status quo.[99]

DOWNTOWN YONGE STREET was abruptly reclaimed by motorists on August 15, 1974, three days into a public transit strike that halted buses, streetcars, and subways across the city and jammed the streets with thousands of additional cars. The decision to shut down the mall just nine weeks into its fourteen-week run was made, Toronto Council argued, to stop it from being blamed for the resulting downtown traffic congestion. From the start of the strike, frustrated motorists had been edging their way honking onto Yonge, using its narrow, one-lane fire route as a shortcut to avoid gridlock. But the decision also reflected City authorities' frustration after four summers of managing debates over Toronto's most popular and disorderly public space. This became obvious when several councillors used the opportunity of debate over the project to present a motion banning any future pedestrianization experiments in Toronto.[100] Although the motion failed, the message was obvious: the Yonge pedestrian mall no longer seemed so much a symbol of the promise of the future as a reminder of the problems of the present. It was widely believed that banning cars had increased youth rowdyism, encouraged proselytizing and illegal vending, and damaged the street's reputation, while only selectively improving sales and the downtown experience.

No public space in Toronto, and probably few anywhere in the world, was so intensively visited, measured, or discussed as the Yonge Street pedestrian mall from 1971 through 1974. What emerges from the police and planning reports, photographs, letters, and press coverage is a picture of creative disorder, of a complex and contested space that was shaped by a wide cross-section of the urban population. Like the street it transformed – only more so – the mall was at once a spectacle, a workplace, a site of consumption, and a venue for political expression. Over four summers, these multiple identities coexisted, sustained and given meaning by the differing uses that people made of the street. Window shopping or reclining on a grassy lawn, hawking jewellery on the sidewalk or serving pints of beer on an improvised terrace, measuring air pollution or handing out coupons for discount jeans – few of these acts were understood by the people who engaged in them as political, but together they shaped the mall just as much as debates in the council chamber or the advocacy of organized pressure groups. Because of its centrality, because it was charged with meanings and conflicts, the Yonge Street mall provides us with a unique perspective on the streetlife of a major North American downtown.

Pedestrianizing Yonge Street failed, if success meant continued summer closures or, as many of its proponents hoped, a permanent car-free street. Toronto Council discussed the latter idea several times during the mid-1970s but with little result, despite a range of proposals for improving the formula tested in previous summers, including adding a dedicated police "mall patrol unit" or allowing a single lane of traffic on the mall to prevent the buildup of crowds and to facilitate emergency access.[101] As explored in the next two chapters, those conversations were overshadowed and eventually derailed by debate about the growth of the sexual entertainment industry and renewed plans to redevelop the street. In that respect, Toronto's experimental closures of downtown Yonge can be understood as part of the larger story of the rise and fall of the North American pedestrian mall, an intervention that seldom lived up to the expectations of the hundreds of cities that implemented them from the 1950s through the 1970s. As few as one in ten pedestrian malls in Canada and the United States have survived into the twenty-first century.[102]

Yet there was more to the history of the Yonge Street mall than frustrated hopes for revitalization. Supporters of the project relied on that dream, but also on a range of other ideas and influences, including popular ambivalence toward the automobile, growing environmental awareness, and calls to preserve Yonge's storied retail landscape from destruction. As the impacts of development, new planning trends, and citizen activism challenged the rebuilding consensus of the 1950s and 1960s, Torontonians seized on pedestrianization as the symbol of an alternative vision for downtown, one that encouraged sociability and civic belonging, and protected elements of the past while containing the impacts of redevelopment and the private car. In this context, the idea of downtown Yonge as a "people place," which permeated discussion of the mall, was more than mere rhetoric. It was the crystallization of these concerns into an agenda that united, for a while, diverse opponents of the rebuilding consensus. More than any other municipal initiative of the period, the Yonge Street pedestrian mall captured the excitement and creativity of this effort to work out an alternative downtown future. At the same time, it demonstrated the limited capacity of citizens and government to transform the street without the involvement of the corporate interests that controlled an increasing share of it.

4

Fighting Sin Strip

At the start of 1973, J.M., a father living in the middle-class west Toronto suburb of High Park, wrote to Toronto mayor David Crombie protesting changes he related to the spread of the sexual entertainment industry on Yonge Street:

> It is with great anxiety that I write this letter to you and beg you [to take] some drastic action to have the Downtown area of Yonge Street cleaned up ... I and my family thoroughly enjoy shopping Downtown, it was really something to look forward to, but on our last Trip just before Christmas [it was] a tremendous relief to leave and get back Home to our house. It is sad that a beautiful city such as ours has to be dragged down [by] the so called "businesses" that have sprung up in the past few months. BODY RUB PARLOURS, STRIP HOUSES, FLESH MOVIE HOUSES ... I'm sure that if we do not [clean them up] we are going to have a Main Street such as BUFFALO has to-day. Stores that are all derelict, boarded up windows ... Blight ridden streets permeated by Bums, Addicts, Drunks, and all other sorts of Riff-Raff.[1]

That winter, his first in office, Crombie received more than three hundred such letters, the start of a five-year campaign that would mobilize thousands of Torontonians, causing him to remark that "in the whole history of the mayor's office there has never been so much mail."[2] Many of those who wrote based their accounts, like J.M., on personal experience; others mobilized through their faith communities or in response to lurid media coverage of Toronto's "Sin Strip." Roused by fears for the urban future, moral outrage, and claims of a democratic right to downtown, these individuals demanded that the mayor act to clean up sexual commerce and save the street. In doing so, they placed downtown Yonge at the centre of ongoing debates over pornography, censorship, and sex work in 1970s North America, and made it a key site for the emergence of new forms of sexual regulation at the municipal level.[3]

This chapter traces the brief life of Sin Strip, a product of changing sexual values, consumer demand, and Toronto's real estate development boom that disappeared amid a wave of public protest and police repression in the late 1970s. By the time the Yonge Street pedestrian mall was cancelled, the Yonge-Dundas intersection had become the epicentre of a highly visible sexual entertainment zone that overlapped and coexisted with the street's more established functions. A gendered space, it was constructed around women's labour, male entrepreneurship, and the profitable satisfaction of heterosexual male desire, a combination that reshaped downtowns across North America during the 1960s and 1970s. Musicians, filmmakers, and poets used Yonge's new incarnation as a backdrop for hard-luck stories and explorations of urban life, but Sin Strip was vilified more than it was celebrated. Citizens like J.M. were part of an unlikely coalition of suburban conservatives, downtown progressives, and populist media outlets that pressured the local state to dismantle the new sexual geography of the street. Achieving that goal proved a hollow victory, however. Breaking up Sin Strip accelerated the dispersion of sex shops throughout the city, while doing little to address concerns about decline, rooted as they were not in immorality but in changes spurred by the redevelopment boom and the continued economic marginalization of Yonge's Victorian shopscape.

The Sexual Revolution and the Postwar Sex District

Sex work and commercialized sexual desire have shaped urban lives and landscapes across North America for centuries, in contexts as different as the dance houses of colonial Victoria and the working-class red-light zones of early-twentieth-century Manhattan.[4] Sin Strip and the other sex districts that developed in American and Canadian cities during the 1960s and 1970s were rooted in this longer history. In many cases, they were situated in areas that were already associated with vice, while adapting or scaling up established business strategies: suggestive burlesque dancing evolved into fully nude striptease, brown paper-wrapped pornographic parcels into displays of row upon row of glossy magazines. Like previous concentrations of sexual services, they encountered opposition from citizens and religious authorities, and were subject to state regulation and repression. In other ways, however, there was no precedent for the postwar sex district.[5]

Emerging at the confluence of sexual revolution, loosening obscenity and prostitution laws, and urban development, it was bigger, more complex, and more brazen than anything that had come before.

First, the postwar sex district was public. Rather than consciously avoiding attention by occupying private homes or marginal neighbourhoods, sex-oriented businesses tended to locate on heavily trafficked downtown streets, often inserting themselves into existing shopping and entertainment areas where they coexisted with other uses. Emerging from the shadows to take over storefronts, marquees, and the sidewalk, they advertised aggressively. Brightly lit signs promised "topless girls," "sex aids," or "nude massages," and store windows openly displayed pornographic magazines, posters, and video loops. Touts patrolled in front of strip clubs, and female staff solicited prospective clients from the doorways of massage parlours. This conquest of downtown public space was most evident in a few of the largest, trendsetting metropolitan vice precincts, including New York City's Times Square, San Francisco's North Beach, or, in Canada, Toronto's Sin Strip and Montreal's Saint-Catherine Street. But it was not limited to these major cities; by the 1970s, visitors to downtowns across the continent were encountering "the sexual revolution writ large on the urban landscape," often in unmistakeable neon signage.[6]

Second, the sexual entertainment zone was deeply commercialized, imitating and integrating with the mainstream consumer economy in a range of ways. Nineteenth- and early-twentieth-century red-light areas were organized around the brothel and its offer of clandestine female companionship and private sex acts; commercial sex in other forms was a rarity and, when present, a sideline.[7] By the 1960s, this relationship had flipped. There was less actual sex being sold than before, but many more explicit performances and sex-related services and products, from strip-tease to sex aids, nude massages to coin-operated peep shows. Sexual entertainment became big business, increasingly mass produced, commoditized, and subject to market norms of content and price. Pornographic magazines such as *Playboy* and *Hustler* built national brands; hardcore films achieved international distribution; performers followed closely what their counterparts in other cities were doing – and exposing – and followed suit. Driving all of this was the sector's immense profitability, both at the level of the individual shop and on the production side. To give just one example, sales of adult magazines in Canada more than tripled between 1965 and 1975, reaching over 13 million copies annually.[8]

Finally, the sex districts of the 1960s and 1970s were, somewhat paradoxically, both more openly explicit and more legitimate than previous incarnations. They existed not in defiance of legal controls, but as one factor driving their weakening and obsolescence. Between 1965 and 1975, performers and sex shop operators were key defendants contesting obscenity law in Canadian and American courts, resulting in judicial interpretations that significantly narrowed its scope, at least regarding depictions of heterosexual sex between adults.[9] Full nudity in performance and portrayal of real sex acts in pornography became the norm, where just a few years before they had been vigorously censored and driven underground. Widely seen as trendsetting and boundary pushing, the postwar sex district became cool, at least for a while. As explicit sexuality spread into popular culture and the nude female form became a staple of countercultural iconography, a wider audience came downtown to explore it. The hardcore film *Deep Throat* was one of the top fifty grossing films in the United States for nearly two years after its 1972 release and was even reviewed in *Time* magazine, imparting the stamp of artistic acceptance, if not respectability. Theatrical screenings of softcore pornography attracted crowds of hundreds on Sin Strip and in other major Canadian cities, and other offerings from striptease to sex toys also developed an appeal well beyond the so-called raincoat brigade of single men.[10] Across the continent, young men and women, and curious older couples – people who would never have dreamt of patronizing past sex districts – flocked to see what one New York cultural critic called "porno chic."[11]

From the Strip to Sin Strip

By 1972, this trend had spread to Toronto, and sex work and sexual entertainment were emerging as key sectors in downtown Yonge Street's marketplace. This represented a continuity with its history as Toronto's centre for consumer culture and as one of Canada's largest popular entertainment districts. From the music halls of the nineteenth century to the cocktail bars and jazz clubs of the postwar decades, entrepreneurs on Yonge had long been able to leverage changes in the law, artistic modes, and technologies to produce successful businesses.[12] North American and global trends were tested and exploited commercially on Yonge, after which they radiated outward to the rest of the city and region. The street played host to a long list of entertainment firsts – Canada's first stacked theatres (1913) and Ontario's first cocktail lounge (1947), among others – and this continued with its centrality to the postwar development of sexual entertainment. By 1970, a dozen bars and taverns, eighteen restaurants, and six theatres, as well as an assortment of clubs, pool rooms, and other entertainment outlets crowded into just a few blocks of Yonge's neon-lit strip, widely understood as *the* place in Toronto to find "Saturday night action."[13] The sex shops, adult cinemas, and body rub parlours that opened over the next five years integrated into and benefited from this highly developed and densely used zone, taking over unused commercial spaces and changing the selling strategies of existing businesses. They arose in parallel with another manifestation of the sexual revolution: the clustering of some of Toronto's first openly gay and lesbian bars and nightclubs a few blocks north around the intersection of Yonge and Wellesley Streets.[14]

Sex-related businesses thrived on Yonge Street as a transitional use for its highly valued but deteriorating Victorian shopscape. By the late 1960s, the construction of the Yonge subway line and the Eaton Centre land assembly had dramatically increased the speculative value of property on the commercial strip. According to realtor A.E. LePage, in 1970 only the financial district had higher commercial land values; the value of many key parcels had increased several times over the course of the 1960s, even though the buildings that stood on them were in poor condition.[15] Eaton's property portfolio was unmatched in size, but it was not the only corporate interest investing in the street. By the early 1970s, banks, investment groups, anonymous holding companies, and other entities owned a growing portion of the strip: one investigation found that the 233 separate properties between the waterfront and College Street were owned by just sixty-eight individuals and companies, with the latter predominating.[16] Not only were large sections of the strip in the hands of absentee landlords – rather than the business people who operated there, as was the case in the late nineteenth and early twentieth centuries – but the prospect of sale for redevelopment provided a powerful disincentive to maintaining or improving those buildings. Sex shops were among the few categories of businesses that would willingly lease this pool of aging, uncertain, but relatively high-rent properties, and particularly their cramped and poorly maintained second- and third-floor commercial spaces. As small retailers, offices, and service establishments left Yonge Street, landlords who were eager to maintain their flow of investment income welcomed body rub parlours and adult bookstores in their place, especially when their new tenants offered above-market rents.[17]

Sexual entertainment as it appeared on Sin Strip was a labour-intensive industry that required little capital to set up or operate. Unlike the arrival of the department store in the late nineteenth century, or the profusion of cinemas and theatres in the early twentieth, the emergence of Sin Strip was not marked by major investments in Yonge's physical transformation. Signs

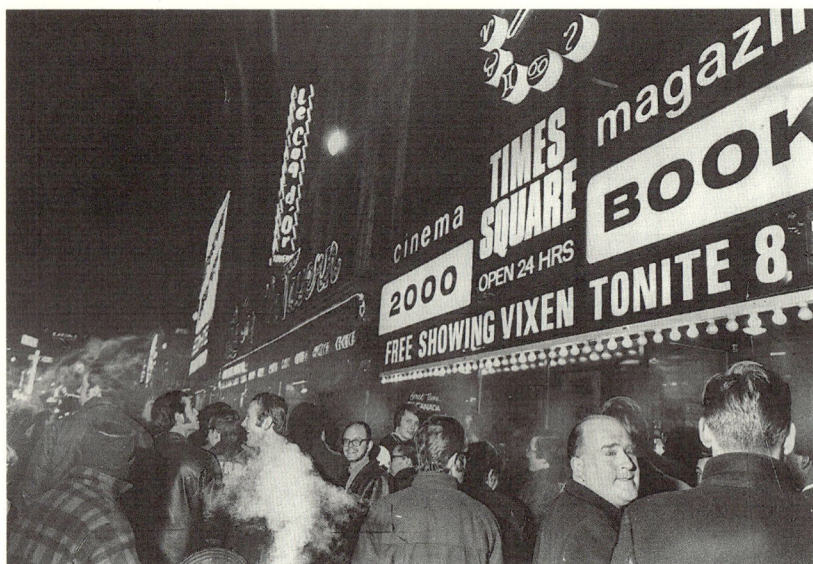

A gendered space. Men jam the sidewalks in front of Cinema 2000, March 1970. A free screening of softcore film *Vixen*, intended to make a statement about censorship, was stopped halfway through by police. | Jeff Goode/*Toronto Star* 502842465 via Getty Images

and window displays changed, and storefront interiors were renovated, but the material imprint was otherwise light. The social and cultural impacts were substantial, however. As explored in the first chapter of this book, Yonge Street played a central role in the changing gender dynamics of downtown during the late nineteenth and early twentieth centuries, developing as a site for feminized consumption and mixed-gender amusement. Sin Strip's rapid advent did not erase the street's existing and evolving gender relations, but selectively reconfigured them, whether at the level of the sidewalk, the city block, or even the individual building housing both sex-related and other businesses.[18] The result was that by night the Yonge strip became a playground for heterosexual men, a space profoundly shaped by the interactions between women's labour and male desire.

Three distinct groups participated in remaking Yonge Street as a gendered space. A small number of entrepreneurs, almost exclusively men, imported business strategies already tested in United States cities and adapted them to Toronto's economic and legal context. Sex shops tended to offer several types of services and to open, close, and change their names on a regular basis, causing consternation for the Toronto police in the

1970s and a frustration for the historian attempting to count and classify them today. A snapshot of Sin Strip at its peak in 1974–75 shows forty-eight sex-oriented businesses clustered on the Yonge Street strip and side streets in the immediate vicinity: seven sex cinemas, eight adult bookstores and peep shows, three strip clubs, and thirty-one body rub parlours.[19] Multiple businesses were often operated by the same person or organization, commonly in premises rented from the property portfolio of a single landlord. Most kept a low profile, but several cultivated notoriety, crafting their brands and boasting in media interviews about the profitability of their businesses.[20] The most visible member of this cohort was Arnold "Mr. Arnold" Linetsky, the disco-suited owner of Starvin' Marvin's strip club and three massage parlours. He ceaselessly lobbied the Downtown Council and the City of Toronto for recognition as a legitimate member of the business community, going so far as to challenge – without success – the reformist candidate for neighbouring Ward 6 in the 1976 municipal election.[21]

The second group comprised the hundreds of workers whose labour sustained the sex district. A small number were men, including clerks in adult bookstores and security guards in adult cinemas, body rub parlours, and strip clubs. But in an industry built around the appeal of "Girls! Girls! Girls!" it was women's labour that really mattered. Their work on Sin Strip came in diverse forms, encompassing the public and the private, the commodified and the intimate.[22] For the women who danced in the bars and strip clubs, it meant theatrical nudity. Released from the arcane codes of behaviour that governed mid-century burlesque, the industry standard by the mid-1970s was for fully nude, frankly sexual performances in establishments serving alcohol, a development that enormously increased the profitability of striptease.[23] "Look but don't touch" was the mantra of the strip club, but for other sex workers on Yonge, carefully regulated – and priced – physical contact with clients was the raison d'être of their routine. In the body rub parlours, young female staff met clients in private rooms where they negotiated services ranging from topless massages, nude dancing, and photography sessions to "extras" such as masturbation or intercourse.[24] Nude masseuses, whether they engaged in sex acts or not, did not see themselves as prostitutes. The safety and predictability of their indoor work set them apart from the smaller number of women who worked outdoors on Yonge or in the neighbourhoods east of the strip.[25] Finally, in the age of video and magazine, much of the labour that sustained Sin Strip was disembodied. Its cinemas, adult bookstores, and video peep shows thrived by selling images of the female body and portrayals of sex, the commodified labour of women in an industry that spanned Canada, the United States, Europe, and beyond.

The third and largest population that participated in making Sin Strip was its clientele. Whereas bars with striptease performances and larger adult cinemas attracted mixed weekend crowds, the industry mainly catered to straight male desire. The men who bought pornography, visited body rub parlours, and masturbated in peep show cubicles on Yonge were often portrayed in the media as lonely, somewhat pathetic outsiders, but in reality they were a varied group that included regulars and out-of-towners, professionals and immigrant labourers, students and over-sixties.[26] One key demographic was the convention crowd; downtown Yonge lay within walking distance of thousands of hotel rooms, and until the mid-1970s its bars and music venues were highly recommended by the tourist board. Places such as the Drawing Room, a restaurant offering a weekday lunch with topless waitresses, designed their services to appeal to groups of businessmen.[27] Photographs and film from the period also highlight the presence of inebriated, thrill-seeking groups of young men, whose journey up and down the strip might start in a bar and end in a private room of a body rub parlour.[28] This kind of trajectory from traditional to sexual forms of entertainment was common and easily viewed as a normal element of masculine behaviour. The handful of Sin Strip clients who spoke up to defend the scene in the 1970s emphasized just that normality, arguing that Yonge's sex shops were patronized "not by sexual deviants, but by the average guy who may be spending the night downtown with his buddies or by visiting businessmen who may want to let their hair down a bit."[29]

From Curiosity to Concern

This ongoing transformation of downtown Yonge Street was intensely scrutinized. Prior to 1972, media portrayals of Sin Strip were generally positive, integrating early manifestations of the sex industry into the existing popular narrative of Yonge as a big-city entertainment destination. Male journalists from the local dailies made regular pilgrimages to the strip, including visits to strip shows, erotic film screenings, and adult bookstores, and their articles presented it to the public as an exciting and cosmopolitan urban space. This version of Sin Strip held no dangers for the male flâneur. A 1969 front-page article in the *Toronto Star* urged readers to check out the "Saturday night action" on Yonge, where "hordes of people swarm up and down the street through a carnival atmosphere of neon and noise." In 1971, a *Globe and Mail* reporter explained that "the strip ha[d] a pastime to suit every preference," situating sexual entertainment as a natural element of the downtown ecology.[30] Not long after, however, this libertine curiosity began to fade, increasingly replaced by exposés of the sex industry's negative impacts on the street. The appearance of large numbers of body rub parlours from summer 1972 was one cause of this, a development that added a new stop to journalists' itineraries, while also introducing the public to body rub attendants and the tawdry upstairs commercial spaces where they worked.[31] Another reason was the emergence of Sin Strip as an issue in that year's municipal election.

Promoting Toronto's sexual entertainment district, 1974. Nude body rub parlours and their aggressive advertising tactics were singled out by critics of Sin Strip. | Ron Bull/*Toronto Star* 515076195 via Getty Images

The idea that downtown Yonge required a "cleanup" was a surprise addition to a mayoral campaign focused largely on how the city would balance urban development with concerns for citizen participation and neighbourhood protection.[32] Over two months in fall 1972, the question of municipal action on Sin Strip migrated from the political fringe – where it was first raised by far-right candidate Don Andrews – to be incorporated into the platforms of the two front-runners, centrist Tony O'Donohue and moderate reformer David Crombie.[33] Astute politicians who were experienced in working with and through citizen groups, both men saw in the issue a chance to connect with voters on a subject of concern. Crombie in particular embraced the rhetoric of participatory democracy that was so prevalent in the neighbourhood activism of the time, and he ran a winning campaign promising to make City Hall more responsive to citizen input and concerns.[34]

Campaign issues do not always maintain a place on the agendas of incoming governments. Following David Crombie's victory in December 1972, Sin Strip might have disappeared from city politics; instead, it was kept alive by the lobbying of the Downtown Council. In a brief entitled "Problems of Downtown Yonge Street" sent to the press and the newly elected municipal government in mid-December, the group's members voiced for the first time their anxieties about their new neighbours on the strip.[35] They argued that there was a clear difference between their own "established businesses" – which paid taxes, obeyed municipal regulations, and had an abiding interest in the street's future – and the new sex shops, which accepted short-term leases, did not maintain their premises, and alienated mainstream consumers with aggressive, sometimes explicit advertising. Framing the stakes as both economic and civic, the council warned that unless the City acted, the sex industry would undermine both the viability of downtown Yonge as a marketplace and Toronto's reputation as one of the safest and best functioning of large North American cities.

Further pressure came from a new voice in Toronto's shifting media landscape. The *Toronto Sun,* a tabloid launched in late 1971 from the ashes of the *Telegram,* seized on Sin Strip as an issue that would help it build its readership and voice as the "people's newspaper."[36] On its way to capturing a fifth of the city's newspaper market, the *Sun* provided lurid coverage of the sex district and regular editorial appeals for a municipal "crackdown" on commercialized vice.[37] By 1975, the other two major papers were converging on the same editorial line, but in 1972 the *Toronto Sun* presented itself as the lone outlet speaking in the name of ordinary Torontonians, a strategy that proved remarkably effective in rallying citizen discontent.

The paper prolonged and amplified the discussion of Sin Strip that had begun during that year's election, while shifting the terms of the debate to conservative populist grounds. Even before taking office, David Crombie had agreed to meet with the Downtown Council to discuss its concerns about the street. In media interviews, he also mentioned his interest in further citizen input.[38] The *Toronto Sun* sought to hold him to this promise. Its first Sin Strip exposé, published on December 29, 1972, was accompanied by a message that invited people to write to the mayor about "the present state of the Strip." After that, the tabloid followed up with editorials calling on Crombie to respond with definite action.[39]

Citizen Mobilization

In this way, a reformist mayor eager to bring new voices into City Hall, a merchant group frustrated by the sex industry's impacts on its businesses, and a populist tabloid seeking readership together contributed to labelling Toronto's sex district as an issue of public concern and a field for municipal action. This created space for a process of citizen mobilization against Sin Strip that began with a small core of *Toronto Sun* readers before expanding to include thousands of individuals and groups across the urban region. The virtually exclusive target of this campaign was Toronto mayor David Crombie. Only a handful of letters reached other elected representatives or municipal officials at this time, highlighting both the influence of Crombie's public statements calling for input and, more broadly, the dual role of the mayor of Toronto as chief municipal legislator and symbolic head of the urban community. By the end of March 1973, Crombie had heard from over 1,000 concerned citizens, 360 of whom sent individual missives. Thousands more would sign petitions over the next two years. Reading their communications and mapping and analyzing the personal information that they supplied gives a unique insight into this process of political mobilization and the understandings of citizenship and the city that lay behind it.[40]

The citizen campaign against Sin Strip was geographically dispersed, reflecting downtown Yonge's particular resonance as a reference point for people in the widening urban region. More than one hundred people wrote from outside the jurisdiction, primarily from the five suburban boroughs of Metro Toronto. They often justified their intervention by establishing abiding connections with, and a sense of ownership of, downtown. "Despite the Mississauga address, I consider Toronto as my city," explained one typical letter.[41] Within the city itself, solidly middle-class suburbs such as High Park and David Crombie's former municipal ward in North Toronto, both with higher incomes and lower proportions of non-English-speaking immigrants than the city average, were particularly active. But other concentrations of letter-writers broke with this trend. For example, residents in the lower-income apartment zone near Sherbourne and Wellesley Streets, just northeast of the Yonge strip, also wrote to the mayor, underlining that opposition to Sin Strip was a cross-class movement. Mapping also reveals mechanisms of mobilization. Personal letters to the mayor tend to be dispersed dots on the map, representing people who wrote individually in response to their morning newspaper or the evening news; clustered dots, on the other hand, track the work of door-to-door campaigners and people organizing in communities of faith. For example, the Centennial United Church on Dovercourt Road in west Toronto was the locus for a petition signed by forty-three people, many of whom lived within a few blocks of the church itself.[42]

Citizens who wrote to the mayor sometimes provided personal information about themselves, which helps to flesh out the picture. They described themselves as concerned citizens, parents, Christians, and taxpayers, identities that reflected not only their social backgrounds, but the rhetorical positions they adopted in their letters. For instance, individuals and couples who identified themselves as parents placed their children's welfare – and that of children in general – at the centre of their appeal. This anti–Sin Strip mobilization was distinctly feminine, with women representing nearly 60 percent of those who wrote, and married adults with children significantly outnumbering youth or single people. Anglo-Celtic surnames predominated. Although the 1970s was a key era for the political maturation of Toronto's immigrant and ethnic communities around certain key issues, they did not become a major part of the sex industry campaign until later in the decade.[43] Finally, the style and content of the letters clearly indicate that many people who involved themselves in this debate were educated and accustomed to expressing themselves in writing, though a significant minority wrote with more difficulty, crossing out words and making frequent spelling mistakes.

Opponents of Sin Strip often wrote from personal experience and commonly wove their objections into narratives of discovery, dramatizing the moment when they realized that Yonge Street had changed for the worse. These accounts usually began with a journey: "It has been some time since I was downtown," wrote west-end woman R.B., "but Saturday the opportunity availed itself." Downtown businessman R.D. wrote, "My wife and family met me downtown for a dinner out and to look at the Christmas windows." In presenting their intentions to shop, dine out, or

take in a show, these writers positioned themselves – consciously or un-
consciously – as exactly the kind of middle-class, suburban consumers
that Yonge's established businesses were so desperate to attract. However,
their encounter with Sin Strip disrupted their enjoyment of the excursion.
R.B. continued: "I did not find the walk along the 'Strip' the pleasure it
once was. I found signs of nudes on the sidewalk advertising 'skin' shows
(much to the embarrassment of my 12-year old son) and loudspeakers
blaring music in most store doorways much to my aural discomfort."
Similarly, M.B. from North Toronto wrote that "I was down to have supper
one night and could not believe my eyes ... with all the weired [sic] people
and one did not feel safe at no time."[44] The result of this uncomfortable
encounter was a ruined afternoon or evening and a decision not to repeat
the experience. Businessman R.D. echoed many of his fellow activists when
he wrote that "we decided not to take our family downtown on Yonge St
in the future."[45]

As these letters suggest, most citizen opponents of Sin Strip had never
set foot inside any of its sex shops: they wrote from the sidewalk. There
were exceptions, of course, such as W.W., who wrote to the mayor from
the nearby Salvation Army men's hostel on Sherbourne Street, enclosing
a ticket stub for a strip show and a list of twenty-one specific businesses
he had visited and felt should be shut down. But the vast majority of those
who related personal experiences of the strip did so as shoppers and pedestrians who came to the street for other reasons. Their focus was most of
all on the visible, outdoor aspects of the sexual entertainment sector, especially its dominance in Yonge's public realm. They complained of the
"Midway" atmosphere celebrated in earlier media coverage of the strip,
offended by the assault of bright lights and noise that assailed pedestrians
as they passed through the area, the invasion of the sidewalk by touts and
body rub attendants, or the distribution of explicit coupons and the resulting piles of litter. A few women focused on the question of street harassment. S.M., for example, described being intimidated by the catcalls
of "crowds of men cackling and passing ridiculous comments, huddled
around the outdoor television sets outside the strip joints," where they
could watch poor-quality live feeds from inside. Likewise, twenty-two-
year-old D.B. from North York wrote an account of an evening out on the
strip that ended with her crying in the back of a taxi, after being propos-
itioned for sex while waiting for the bus home.[46]

Many who wrote fit their own experiences into a larger argument
about public space and the right to downtown. Citizens felt that with Sin
Strip's emergence, people like them – the public, the majority, the average

person – had lost control and use of downtown Yonge Street, which was increasingly appropriated by a fringe minority for its own purposes. They established a distinction between activities that were public, legitimate, and accessible to all, including shopping, strolling, and conventional mass entertainment, and those associated with the sex industry, which they understood as private, illegitimate, and impinging on their enjoyment of the street. In a letter to the *Toronto Star* that also crossed the mayor's desk, planning consultant Leon Kumove suggested that the fundamental question was "to whom does Yonge St. belong?" As he explained,

> In recent years we have come to think of it as a street that belongs to all the people. It was a street upon which people of all ages, walks and life [sic] were given to promenading ... All of this is threatened with a major change in which the storefronts along Yonge St. are turning into a few types of enterprise catering only to certain groups of people.[47]

This perceived narrowing of Yonge's use and appeal by Sin Strip users was cast as abrupt and undemocratic. "The swinger set has taken over," complained S.P. from Scarborough. "The majority of people who live here are not in that category, and we resent the imposition of their ways on ours." In this populist interpretation, the municipal government's role was above all to respond to the will of the majority and return the street to its control. Or, as S.P. succinctly closed her letter, "Give us back our downtown."[48]

That "us" was often specifically female. Although they did not identify as feminists – and a few explicitly rejected the label – many writers described Sin Strip as a women's issue with gendered stakes. In doing so, they anticipated the mixing of feminist and moralizing discourses that would become commonplace in 1980s anti-pornography campaigns.[49] "We have yet to see the woman's side presented in this male-dominated issue," wrote one of many correspondents who believed that women had a specific and valuable understanding of Sin Strip and its social impacts. One common area of focus was the sex industry's undermining of marriage and the family. "It seems whatever the 'men' want these days they get," wrote P., a mother whose letter concentrated on the phenomenon of married men spending their evenings in strip clubs and massage parlours, while leaving their wives at home to raise their children. "Imagine how a lot of women feel," she continued, "exploited to the very end." Others feared that Sin Strip's catering to male desire and treatment of women as sex objects were incitements to sexual violence. "The end result of this mass stimuli usually takes place elsewhere," continued S.P. "How often have we read of women being attacked on their way home at night?"[50] Alongside these individual voices was more organized activism. A two-year petition drive launched by Toronto's Local Council of Women culminated in spring 1975 with the presentation of a phonebook-sized, 8,500-signature petition to Metro and Toronto Councils. This was one of the largest campaigns in the group's history, an echo of its prominence as a Protestant, maternal feminist voice in late-nineteenth- and early-twentieth-century social welfare debates.[51] Gender solidarity had its limits, however. As much as they sought to present the "woman's side" of the issue, citizen campaigners systematically restricted that category to wives and mothers, ignoring the possibility that their analysis might also include the largest group of women concerned by Sin Strip: those who worked there.

Anti–Sin Strip activists wrote the changes they observed on Yonge Street into narratives of decline, a framing, as Alan Hunt observes, that is common to projects of moral regulation.[52] They claimed to possess roots in the city going back decades or generations, as well as shared memories tinted with nostalgia for the strip *before* – before the 1960s, before the sex industry – when "the shops were interesting, the street was quiet and the sidewalks were clean." Explicitly or implicitly, they compared the present condition of the strip with its past incarnations and stressed what had been lost. "I have watched the heart of Toronto grow [since] about 5 years old when my Dad had a little cigar store on Queen and Church [and the city was] alive and magical" recalled D.B. from North York, one of many letter-writers whose understanding of downtown was shaped by a postwar migration from centre to suburb. "Now I am unable to feel relaxed on the main street [of] the city of my birth."[53] In many cases, this deterioration was projected into the future. Letter-writers made anxious comparisons between Yonge's transformation and the decay, criminality, and social conflict they associated with the American city, revealing how permeable the border was to the postwar discourse of urban decline.[54] Sin Strip risked "degenerating into another Times Square" warned one letter; others referenced the hollowed-out centres of deindustrializing cities such as nearby Buffalo, Rochester, and Detroit. In this analysis, Americanization and decline were virtually synonymous. Indeed, to some observers, Sin Strip's transnational vocabulary and product line – Times Square Books, *Playboy* magazine – were evidence that the sex industry itself was a manifestation of cultural imperialism, "an insidious thing ... creeping in steadily" from south of the border.[55]

Bound up with the spectre of American-style urban decay was a social critique fuelled by Christian morality. Of the more than one thousand citizens who spoke out against Sin Strip in 1972–73, nearly half did so on religious grounds, self-identifying as "God-fearing citizens" or "concerned Christians" and forming a distinct group within the larger campaign. Rather than acting individually, these Christian campaigners mobilized as part of their church congregations, typically during and after Sunday services. And instead of offering personalized and often very personal reflections on Yonge Street – although some did – they lent their support to a crusade whose tactics and message were directed by a small group of ministers and lay activists. The evangelical Christian and Missionary Alliance played a key role in sparking this effort, which began in the group's ten affiliated Toronto-area congregations, before spreading outward to mainline Protestant churches across the city.[56] Although some Alliance sermons preached in January 1973 were full of fiery rhetoric and denunciations of "Toronto's sin-lane to ruin," the group was also skilled at adopting the language of civic activism and moderating its message to appeal to a wider Christian public. Its pragmatic strategy was summarized in a set of instructions on effective letter writing sent to dozens of Toronto churches in early January: "1. The more letters, the more influence. 2. avoid using unfounded statements. 3. be concise."[57]

Over the next three months, twenty-one churches across Metro Toronto heeded this call for action and added their voices to the Alliance campaign. A letter from the pastor of the Toronto Japanese United Church bore eighty signatures from the congregation; the women's Bible circle at Parkdale Baptist Church wrote representing fifteen voices. St. Michael's Choir School, a semi-private Catholic institution just a few blocks away from the strip, sent a letter home with students urging parents to write to the mayor, and dozens did. Many churches distributed a form letter provided by the Christian and Missionary Alliance, and three hundred such letters, often retyped or handwritten on church or personal stationery, made their way to the mayor's desk that winter.[58] All conveyed the same message: that commercial sexual entertainment was both a sign of and a contributing factor to a more generalized moral and social decline in North American society. This was a familiar discourse, one that had been rehearsed in Toronto and across the continent for nearly a decade in relation to other social and cultural changes of the era, including rising recreational drug use, the decriminalization of homosexuality, and the perceived decline of civility.[59] A.K. from the northern suburb of Don Mills captured this sense of a long 1960s decline when he wrote that "the liberal element has had full sway for about ten years now and we've only gone downhill."[60]

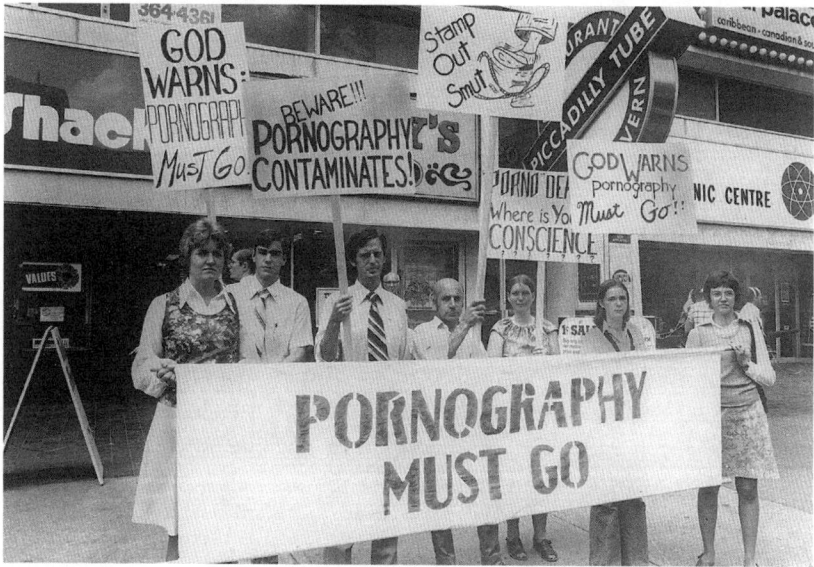

Small group demonstrations like this one by members of the International Family Association were a regular feature of the citizen campaign against the sex industry. Yonge and Dundas Streets, July 1975. | Harold Barkley/*Toronto Star* 502842695 via Getty Images

What was new, however, was the key role played by Toronto's evangelical churches and a core of young Christian activists in defining and propagating this message in relation to Sin Strip. In the 1970s, social conservative reaction to the permissive society in Canada was invigorated by a surge in the popularity of evangelical churches and Christian movement activism, following the American trend that prompted *Newsweek* to declare 1976 "the year of the evangelicals."[61] This shift was visible not just in the tone and scale of the letter-writing campaign, but also in Yonge's streetlife. Long a key site for religious proselytizing and pamphleteering, from early 1973 downtown Yonge's sidewalks also played host to small, regular demonstrations against Sin Strip. These included more general protests, such as the parade of bearded young men from Christian service group Emmaus who condemned the city's "worldly ways," as well as groups that targeted specific strip clubs and sex shops, such as the conservatively dressed men and women from the International Family Association who picketed Zanzibar Tavern and other sex businesses with a banner reading "Pornography must go."[62]

Citizens seeking a cleanup of Yonge Street were numerous and insistent, but they were not alone in weighing in on the issue. A few letters defended Sin Strip's existence, naturalizing it as a part of the metropolitan experience and defending the right of Torontonians to choose how they were entertained. "A big city needs its Strip," argued downtown man G.G., one of several individuals for whom Yonge's "character and colour" were a normal development for a larger North American city, offsetting the blandness and conservatism of the residential suburbs.[63] However, rights-based arguments that condemned the cleanup campaign as censorship were more common, and it was in this vein that Toronto-area writers and prominent public intellectuals Barry Callaghan and Pierre Berton intervened in the debate starting in late 1972. In a series of media interviews, Berton in particular attacked what he saw as a morality crusade by David Crombie and the *Toronto Sun*. This public involvement was in line with his outspoken denunciation of film censorship and police harassment of countercultural youth since the late 1960s.[64] However, these statements had the unintended effect of bolstering the populist sentiments that underpinned the citizen campaign against Sin Strip.[65] In their wake, dozens of people wrote to the Toronto papers and the mayor, denouncing Berton and Callaghan as out-of-touch liberal elites, angrily asserting that "we have some civil rights too, and one of them surely is to be able to shop on our favourite street with our children, without having our senses assailed by filth."[66]

Policing, Zoning, and Licensing the Postwar Sex District

Just what would it mean for Toronto's municipal government to "clean up" or "crack down" on Sin Strip? From early 1973, both Toronto and Metro Toronto responded to the citizen mobilization against the sex industry by investigating what was currently being done to regulate Yonge's body rub parlours and sex shops, and what new tools could be deployed to make that regulation more effective. Following a path taken by countless municipalities in the United States and Canada during the 1960s and 1970s, they sought to use the limited powers available to them to contain, control, or even eliminate the sex district. This process, like the grassroots campaign that sparked it, was intensely scrutinized. Each new proposal was accompanied by newspaper articles, letters to the editor, radio call-in segments, and TV news reports, further establishing the legitimacy of municipal action on the issue.[67] Pressure to act was maintained through this media exposure and through continued citizen lobbying that echoed the main themes of the 1972–73 campaign.

The municipal agency with the most resources committed to Sin Strip was the Metro Toronto police. In addition to 52 Division's daily patrols on foot and by scout car, Yonge Street between Gerrard and Queen was a site of concentrated activity for the three dozen officers of the city's Morality Bureau.[68] Established in the late nineteenth century with a broad remit to police vice, the morality squad remained the largest special unit of the Toronto police in the 1970s, although it was no longer the paternalist social service – arbiter of domestic abuse, gambling, contravention of the Sabbath, and unlicensed drinking, among other offences – it had been in earlier decades.[69] Instead, it was an investigative unit chiefly concerned with obscenity and prostitution, a role that led its officers to regularly visit Yonge's adult cinemas, bookstores, and other sex-related concerns, documenting their opening and closing, the services offered, and any possible contraventions of the law. Within this larger sphere of activity, six members of the bureau were specifically tasked with investigating what was widely understood as the most flagrantly illegal type of business on Sin Strip: the body rub parlour.

With the regular presence of these two units and periodic interventions by others, downtown Yonge was the most heavily policed section of Toronto. But policing was not the panacea that opponents of the sex industry imagined. By 1973, raids of adult bookstores, a common feature a few years earlier, had become increasingly infrequent as the list of chargeable pornographic materials became shorter and convictions more difficult to obtain. Strip shows were largely self-regulating, and smaller sex cinemas were circumventing censorship with alternative film formats and private viewing booths. Massage parlours posed their own specific enforcement problems. Patrols had to get past warning buzzers, peepholes, and other delaying measures; undercover officers were subject to a series of tests designed to identify them. As one officer described in 1977,

> the female attendants will not discuss services until a $20.00 fee has been paid and the customer is in the session room. The customer is asked to strip, and in some cases, take a shower. He also has to produce identification ... If she is satisfied the customer is not a police officer, she will then discuss "extras" (offers of sex).[70]

The alternative was to raid these parlours, but this required significant manpower and held little promise of success. In fact, the police force's ability to secure convictions of any kind on Sin Strip plummeted from the early 1970s onward. For example, police reports indicate that in 1976 officers laid 106 charges on Yonge's sex businesses: 43 for showing obscene films and 63 bawdy house charges for massage parlour operators and attendants. However, only a handful of meaningful convictions resulted from this activity, as nearly all of the accused had their cases dropped before prosecution or received small fines and suspended sentences.[71] Police brass argued that without noteworthy changes in the law, they were "powerless" to rein in Sin Strip.[72]

The outsized presence and diminished enforcement authority of the police fed into a de facto policy of containment that prevailed on Sin Strip until 1977. Officers remained visible on the strip and engaged in day-to-day surveillance of sex-related businesses, on terms that were often negotiated with their owners and employees. In certain cases, they documented the operations of those businesses, preparing detailed reports that might be used in future prosecutions. However, their primary concern was the maintenance of order. Filmmaker Janis Cole, who observed and filmed the daily life of body rub parlours on Yonge in the mid-1970s, recalls that the police regularly visited parlours, not to make arrests, but to determine that there were no difficult customers, incidents of violence toward attendants, or problems spilling out onto the street.[73] Through this process, the force effectively sanctioned the existence of Sin Strip, just as police in the nineteenth and early twentieth centuries had helped to create informal red-light districts across the continent by applying similar strategies of toleration and control.[74]

Another policy tool proposed by the municipal government for a Yonge Street cleanup was zoning. As in other North American cities, the City of Toronto's ability to impose public controls on private building and land use had long been a powerful tool for shaping the spatial and social organization of the city. Employed in previous eras to contain polluting industry, to separate commercial and residential functions, and to discourage apartment construction in middle-class districts, by the early 1970s zoning was a key weapon in the arsenal of community activists and reformist politicians in central Toronto. This was especially the case in the battle to maintain the character – and property values – of gentrifying neighbourhoods where single-family Victorian homes were still the norm.[75] City councillors and municipal bureaucrats also saw it as a tool for reconfiguring Yonge Street's sexual geography, following the recent example set by cities in the United States. Two zoning strategies for sexual commerce were raised in Toronto Council and by the municipal bureaucracy. The first was dispersal, as pioneered by Detroit with its 1972 "Anti-Skid Row Ordinance," which dictated that no new sex business could open within a thousand feet of an existing one or without permission from nearby residents. The second was containment, exemplified by Boston's official designation in 1974 of a downtown "adult entertainment zone" – often referred to as the "Combat Zone" – as the only locale where sex-related concerns could operate.[76] Both sought, in very different ways, to use limited municipal powers to disrupt sexual commerce.

Discussion of zoning for sex in Toronto oscillated unproductively between these strategies of dispersal and containment. A 1974 staff report favoured the latter, arguing that "massive use prohibitions throughout the City except within a limited 'exempt' area" would be the most effective response to the spread of sex-related businesses.[77] In subsequent discussions, Toronto Council unanimously approved altering the city's zoning bylaw to reflect this change, but its members were unable to agree on the new geography of sexual commerce they wanted to establish. It was understood that the "exempt" area, as defined by the bylaw, would not be downtown Yonge, which meant two things: first, the necessary dispersal of existing sex businesses from Sin Strip – for which there was no immediate policy tool – and second, the designation of a new district to receive them. No elected official was willing to seriously entertain the idea of placing a de facto red-light district in his or her ward, resulting in proposals that ranged from the impractical to the far-fetched, including moving sexual commerce "offshore" to the park and amusement area of the Toronto Islands.[78] In a way, all of this was academic. Although Toronto's zoning bylaw was eventually modified in 1977 to limit "adult physical culture establishments" to two industrial zones far from downtown, under provincial law this prohibition could not be enforced retroactively, restricting its usefulness on Yonge Street.[79]

With policing viewed as an incomplete solution and zoning a blind alley, Metro Toronto's licensing powers became the focus of municipal efforts to regulate or eliminate Sin Strip. By the summer of 1973, nude massage parlours were suburbanizing, moving north along Yonge to the city limits and discreetly opening their doors on east-west commercial streets.[80] Very quickly, the regulation of sexual entertainment became a metropolitan issue, although cleaning up Yonge remained the central theme. North York mayor Mel Lastman vowed to "declare war" on the estimated twenty parlours in his borough, and other suburban politicians followed suit, creating a broad consensus in Metro Council in favour of action.[81] Here, as elsewhere, opponents of Sin Strip quickly ran into the modest limits of municipal power. Initial efforts to entirely prohibit non-therapeutic massage parlours were supported by the lobbying of professional health studios and the Ontario College of Massage, but they fell apart in 1974, when it was determined that such a ban was beyond municipal jurisdiction. Instead, Metro adopted a new strategy, seeking to bring Toronto's body rub parlours under a municipal licensing and inspection regime that already regulated taxis, restaurants, and dozens of other types of business across the city.

Giving Metro power to license and regulate massage parlours required changes to Ontario's Municipal Act, bringing the provincial government into the debate over Sin Strip for the first time. Bill Davis's Progressive Conservative government was initially unreceptive to lobbying for an amendment to the act; in May 1974, the Ontario attorney-general maintained that the municipality's efforts to prohibit body rubs were a thinly veiled attempt to legislate morality, and the licensing proposal was seen as a continuation of this logic.[82] But by summer 1975, the Davis cabinet had changed its mind, its decision coming just weeks after the public submission of the Toronto Council of Women's petition, with its 8,500 signatures. That intervention and other citizen actions had clearly had an effect. Explaining his decision to the press, the premier described the new powers given to Metro as his response to citizen concerns about the sex industry on Yonge, arguing that "there is a growing public interest in this area [and people] expect the government to show some leadership." As critics noted at the time, his backing of Metro Council's agenda could also be seen, like previous interventions in city politics, as a calculated strategy for shoring up electoral support in the most populous region of the province.[83] The decision was applauded in Toronto, where Mayor David Crombie optimistically predicted effective municipal action on Yonge Street within a year.[84]

The result was Bylaw 137-75, passed by Metro Council in August 1975.[85] Under the pretence of assuring health and safety standards and preventing exploitation of employees and clients, it subjected body rub parlours to twenty-four pages of regulations designed to hamper their operations, discourage their clients, humiliate their staff, and ultimately drive them out of business. Metro massage parlours – there were approximately one hundred by summer 1975 – had three weeks to apply for twenty-five annual licences, with fees of $3,000 for owners and $50 to be paid by each attendant, well in excess of the $15 charged to registered therapeutic masseurs. Once under the municipal licensing regime, they were obliged, to keep their licence, to strictly limit advertising, close their doors by 1:00 a.m., regularly clean common areas, and remove locking doors or other hindrances to entry, this last measure designed to facilitate access by police and municipal inspectors. In terms reminiscent of the Victorian Contagious Diseases Act, the bylaw further mandated that women who worked as attendants must provide certificates showing them to be "free from communicable diseases and medically fit." In theory, it also made them subject to snap medical inspections "at any time" by the municipal medical officer of health.[86]

This illiberal bylaw, sarcastically dubbed Toronto's "War Measures Act" by the *Globe and Mail,* was only partially enforceable, as Metro officials well knew.[87] Most Sin Strip locations chose to circumvent the law by rebranding as nude encounter studios, topless photography parlours, and other businesses outside of the regulated body rub parlour category. Only twenty-one parlours applied for licences in 1975–76, and within that group several larger, high-profile parlours banded together to launch a legal challenge to the bylaw.[88] Their appeal, spearheaded by owner Arnold Linetsky as president of the newly formed Yonge Street Adult Entertainment Association, contended that although municipal regulation was desirable, the bylaw's provisions were "punitive" and intended to drive them out of business. Not only did this campaign allow Linetsky and other Sin Strip entrepreneurs to publicly position themselves as "legitimate, law-abiding businesses" unfairly treated by government, but it more importantly hamstrung enforcement of the new bylaw. Twenty-five cases prepared by Metro legal staff for violations of the body rub regulations sat in limbo for eighteen months while the appeal made its way to the Supreme Court of Ontario, before being withdrawn in early 1977.[89]

The Summer of '77

In this way, three layers of government – municipal, metropolitan, and provincial – were drawn into the drive to clean up downtown Yonge Street. The City of Toronto and Metro Toronto systematically mobilized their civic bureaucracies and, in consultation with legal counsel, pushed the limits of municipal power in their efforts to uproot sex cinemas and body rub parlours. By early 1977, the first concrete results of this process were apparent. First of all, now that the legal challenge brought by Sin Strip entrepreneurs had been resolved, the initial prosecutions under Metro's licensing bylaw could begin, leading to nine convictions for "body rub owner – no license" by July. In parallel, Metro Council passed, pending provincial approval, a new bylaw that would expand this licensing regime to regulate any and all "places of amusement offering nude services," including parlours that had rebranded to avoid the law.[90] Finally, legal staff continued to pursue other creative methods of interfering with the income of Sin Strip businesses, including requesting court injunctions to close any sex shop that was convicted of violating the Criminal Code or Metro's licensing regime.

In many significant municipal issues of the 1970s, including development regulation and transportation planning, political support tended to split along urban-suburban or reformist-booster lines. Such was not the case for a Yonge Street cleanup. Measures such as Toronto's new zoning regulations or Metro's body rub bylaw had strong support among elected officials, continuing the trend of unexpected – and often uneasy – alliances that had begun in winter 1972–73 between reformist mayor David Crombie and the populist conservative *Toronto Sun*. There was a substantial distance between the discourses and political styles of suburban social conservatives such as East York reeve True Davidson, who embraced the illiberal, moralizing tone of the citizen campaign against Sin Strip, and downtown community activist and Toronto councillor Alan Sparrow, who rejected it. But by summer 1977, both were in favour of municipal intervention against the sex industry. This was underlined by the June publication of a scathing report on the industry by three reformist city councillors, including Sparrow, presenting in detail the terms of downtown progressives' opposition to Sin Strip.

The report of the Special Committee on Places of Amusement offered a research-based critique of sexual commerce, including analyses of ownership patterns and business activities on Sin Strip, policies deployed in other cities, and a rudimentary sociological analysis of sex work in the city.[91] Explicitly rejecting prohibition, censorship, or other government intervention that interfered with civil liberties, it called for understanding Sin Strip as an urban – rather than a moral – problem. Despite this distinction, the report did not tack toward a new accommodation with the sex industry; in fact, its main themes did not differ substantially from the existing consensus in Metro and Toronto Councils. It recommended generally that the City act "firmly and decisively" to address the industry, which it referred to as a "public nuisance" and a "catalyst to the degeneration of Yonge Street and surrounding neighbourhoods."[92] More specifically, it endorsed the strengthening of zoning and licensing regulations, increased provincial-municipal cooperation, stricter enforcement of laws, and an end to police fraternization with sex workers. Other elements of the report were familiar to those who had followed the citizen campaign since 1972, including its latent anti-Americanism and claims that the sex industry nourished other forms of criminal activity. The two were neatly linked in the recurrent unproven assertion that American organized crime was a key player in the development of Toronto's sex district.[93]

The public release of the Places of Amusement Report in June 1977 renewed citizen activism against Sin Strip and began the first stages of a coordinated crackdown on its sex-related businesses. Not only did a new wave of letters and phone calls reach Mayor Crombie's office – four hundred in June and July 1977 – but new segments of the urban population began to mobilize in response to the report's recommendations. Most significant was the intervention of the Confederation of Residents' and Ratepayers' Associations (CORRA), an umbrella organization that represented dozens of mostly middle-class neighbourhood groups across Toronto. Formed in 1968, CORRA became an important voice in city politics in the wake of the fight over the Spadina Expressway and the 1972 election, and a key force in keeping moderate reformist councillors in power.[94] Its public support for the Places of Amusement Report, and that of other individual ratepayers' and residents' groups, sent a clear signal that the cleanup campaign was engaging a more varied and better-organized constituency than in the past – and one directly implicated in the electoral fortunes of the reformist majority on Toronto Council.[95]

Building on this momentum, Metro and Toronto officials established new structures to coordinate the offensive against Sin Strip and renewed their lobbying of the provincial government for additional resources. Toronto Council set up a special committee to implement the Places of Amusement Report, and in early July the mayor and members of council met with the Ontario attorney-general to discuss "fast-tracking" prosecutions of and court orders closing Yonge Street sex businesses. When provincial support was not forthcoming, David Crombie worked to bring public pressure to bear on Premier Bill Davis, publicly criticizing him for ignoring the "yawning cesspool on Yonge."[96] Meanwhile, on July 6, the police established a task force to coordinate enforcement on downtown Yonge, bringing officers from 52 Division and the Morality Bureau under the same command for the first time. This Sin Strip task force had a new mandate, replacing toleration and fraternization with a policy of "rigorous enforcement" of the law. The results of this approach were quickly visible. In July 1977 alone, officers investigating sex-related businesses made 62 arrests and laid 120 prostitution and obscenity charges on Sin Strip, nearly equalling their totals for the previous six months.[97] Although a few letters to the mayor or local newspapers responded negatively to this police action and to Crombie's dramatic rhetoric – one warned that his campaign "smack[ed] of totalitarian dictatorship" – they were outnumbered by those who approved of the municipal government finally taking action on downtown Yonge.[98]

This deployment of municipal powers was given a new sense of urgency on August 1, 1977, when police found the body of twelve-year-old shoeshine boy Emanuel Jaques on the roof of Charlie's Angels, a Yonge Street body rub parlour. Missing for four days, Jaques had been lured away from his shoeshine stand on the strip with the promise of extra cash, before being sexually assaulted and murdered by four men. Three of his killers were casual employees of Charlie's Angels, performing odd jobs for its operator in exchange for rooms in the building. They were arrested the same day the body was discovered – one gave himself up at nearby 51 Division – and their gruesome crime was front-page news across Canada.[99] The *Toronto Star* and *Toronto Sun* provided daily coverage of the "shoeshine boy murder" for a week, interviewing the boy's grieving family and citizens who expressed outrage at his senseless death. More than any other event of the summer of 1977, this crime galvanized public support and new state resources for a prolonged crackdown on the sex industry.

The news of Emanuel Jaques's murder provoked public expressions of rage and grief – in telephone calls, letters, and street demonstrations – that gave the campaign against Sin Strip a powerful affective charge. Emotions, historian Barbara Rosenwein reminds us, are social phenomena. They arise within the self but are felt and expressed in communities that they in turn contribute to shaping and governing.[100] As people in Toronto tried to make sense of and articulate their individual responses to the Jaques murder, they naturally drew on shared vocabularies of feeling, and their collective emotional experience became a basis for a significant new political mobilization. The day after the boy's body was discovered, staff at Toronto City Hall scrambled to record messages as hundreds of citizens telephoned the mayor. Their notes highlight that "most callers were deeply distressed" and emphasize their common repertoire of emotions: "*outrage* at tragedy which many feel could have been prevented ... *grief* for the loss of a young child ... *anger* at why the gov'ts haven't taken action before this."[101] Rage and grief also ran through the new stream of letters demanding action on Yonge – more than eight hundred, in all – that began to pour into the mayor's office that week. "I've been angry and depressed for two days," wrote a woman from North York, forty-eight hours after the Jaques murder was made public; others described being "shocked," "sickened," or "nauseated" by the news.[102] Crucially, these calls and letters not only communicated citizens' emotional and physical states, but demanded that they be given political weight.

The emotionally charged mobilization that followed the Jaques murder drew in individuals and communities that had been absent from earlier phases of the anti–Sin Strip campaign. Many explicitly mentioned that the brutality and immediacy of the crime, and its location in the heart of the city, had impelled them to call or write to a public official for the first time in their lives. Others felt a personal connection to Jaques and his family that inspired them to action. A young female employee of Wendy's Hamburgers at the intersection of Yonge and Dundas wrote an eloquent letter to the mayor describing the crime as an emotional blow to the community on the strip:

> Anybody who has anything to do with the corner of Yonge and Dundas (that is, lives there, works there or just hangs around there) loved that little boy and is heartbroken ... Nobody smiles, and the past few days have been spent with people crying and walking around with red eyes ... So many people have been promising for so long to do something about that "Sin Strip." But now it's too late.[103]

In the Regent Park area, two kilometres east of the strip, dozens of the Jaques family's neighbours signed a petition that they hand-delivered to City Hall during a rally to demand that something be done. This type of local action was reproduced throughout the city in August and September 1977, as more than three thousand people signed dozens of petitions circulated among neighbours, in workplaces – from clients and employees of a women's hair salon, for example – and at other gathering places.[104] This dynamic of mobilization differed from earlier phases of the campaign against Sin Strip in its smallness of scale and relative disorganization; there was nothing along the lines of the Christian and Missionary Alliance's centrally coordinated form-letter campaign of 1973 or the petition drive launched that same year by the Toronto Council of Women.

Ethnic solidarities and shared migration experiences shaped how the city responded to the murder of this child of working-class immigrants from the Azores Islands. If the urban population was accustomed to seeing European immigrants cast as perpetrators of crime – as media coverage of several murders in postwar Toronto attests – in the case of Emanuel Jaques, they were unequivocally viewed as its aggrieved victims.[105] Historian Gilberto Fernandes has explored how the summer of 1977 was a key moment in the larger trajectory of political maturation of Portuguese immigrants in Toronto, goading thousands to engage in local activism and forcing recognition of the community's potential influence in electoral politics. As captured in Anthony De Sa's semi-autobiographical novel *Kicking the Sky* (2013), the Jaques murder brought home the dangers of

On August 8, 1977, a week after the murder of Emanuel Jaques, thousands of Portuguese Canadians rallied at City Hall. Some held signs demanding the death penalty for his murderers. | Domingos Marques/Clara Thomas Archives ASC17414

urban life to a population that was largely of rural origin and tapped into feelings of alienation from mainstream Canadian society that arose from their working-class diasporic lives.[106] At the public funeral held at St. Agnes Catholic Church on Grace Street – in the heart of Portuguese Toronto – thousands of community members gathered in an expression of grief, joined by the mayor, the local councillor, and other Torontonians. A few days later, a crowd of between ten and fifteen thousand people, carrying banners and signs in Portuguese and English, marched downtown to rally in front of City Hall and Queen's Park, where they expressed their anger and demanded severe penalties for Jaques's killers.[107] Members of other ethnic communities identified with this retributive anger and more broadly with the frustrations of the immigrant experience in a major North American city. Mobilizing through Greek Orthodox and Catholic churches and secular ethnic organizations such as the Italian Canadian Congress, they lobbied the mayor and other elected officials to recognize their claims, as citizens and workers, to a civic voice.[108]

Mariana Valverde calls our attention to the "slippage" between categories and targets that occurs when societies work to define and regulate perceived moral and social problems.[109] In the case of the Jaques murder, the anger and fear of Portuguese Torontonians and the population at large were initially focused on the killers, but they subsequently shifted to the people and businesses that made up Sin Strip and to Toronto's gay community. The first of these displacements was immediate, and it encountered few challenges in the media or political discourse, apart from a few ill-timed statements by Yonge Street's sex entrepreneurs. From the day Jaques's body was found on the roof of Charlie's Angels, media coverage of the crime placed the blame squarely on Sin Strip, calling the boy "a victim of Yonge St." and demanding that the City act immediately to "purge" the area.[110] It was widely accepted that by providing the physical setting for the boy's death, employment for his killers, and more broadly by encouraging sexual perversion and objectification, the sex industry was as guilty as the men who actually murdered him. This slippage from the individual to the general, and from investigation of a crime to regulation of consensual sex acts and sexual entertainment, lay behind the acceleration of the Yonge cleanup campaign in the summer and fall of 1977.

The second displacement of blame for the Jaques murder was more contested, although it had significant impacts in the long term. From early August, gay men in Toronto pushed back against persistent assertions that they were responsible, as individuals and as a group, for the murder. Jaques was victim of a brutal sexual assault by men, one of whom had turned to well-known queer activist George Hislop for advice before giving himself up to police. Building on these facts and on prevalent homophobic discourses, police and media persistently described the boy's assault as a "homosexual orgy" and his death as "homosexual murder," suggesting that such crimes were a normal part of sexual relations between men and that the entire gay community bore the blame for them. This slippage was actively resisted by civil liberties associations and by local activists, including the Coalition for Gay Rights in Ontario, who argued that "the gay community cannot be held responsible for some of its members just as all heterosexuals cannot be held responsible for the actions of some."[111] Nevertheless, the association persisted. In the short term, gay men were subject to verbal and physical attacks, and forced to travel in groups to and from gay clubs and other queer social spaces on and around Yonge Street. In the longer term, the Jaques case was one of several incidents – another was the 1978 publication in a gay community newspaper, the *Body Politic*, of an article entitled "Men Loving Boys Loving Men" – that served to justify the Toronto police raids on gay bathhouses that began in the late 1970s and peaked in 1981 with the mass arrests of Operation Soap.[112]

Dispersing Sin Strip

Intense local and national interest in the Jaques murder and renewed, expanded citizen mobilization against Sin Strip created a political opportunity for pro-cleanup actors in Toronto's municipal government.[113] As David Crombie's chief advisor explained in a candid media interview on August 13, 1977, the mayor and allies in both the Toronto and Metro governments had been waiting months for an approach that could broaden and clarify public support for a crackdown on body rub parlours and sex shops: "Ironically, we didn't have to develop one. The murder accomplished that. Three weeks ago Crombie was a fascist for trying to clean up the street: now he's ineffectual for not doing it sooner."[114] Following the Jaques murder, all three levels of government concerned with the Sin Strip issue came under sustained criticism in the media and from constituents for their delay in responding to calls for a cleanup. Metro Toronto and the Ontario government in particular were eager to demonstrate to the public that they were vigorously pursuing action against the sex industry. In the words of Metro's legal department, they also wished to "refute the allegation that [they] were guilty of delay" before the murder occurred.[115] They agreed to devote considerable new resources to concerted action to permanently break up Toronto's downtown sex district.

Public pressure and this rush to display engagement turned the imperfect policy tools put together by Toronto and Metro since 1973 into a formidable arsenal. Police were the most active City agency during the crackdown, further intensifying the policy of coordinated "rigorous enforcement" already in place before the murder.[116] Significant police hours were allocated to targeted raids on body rub parlours and other sex shops by Morality Bureau and 52 Division officers, resulting in 107 arrests leading to 182 charges, mostly for bawdy house and other prostitution offences but also for obscenity and drug possession. Officers also increased the attention they paid to minors congregating on the strip. Sidewalk patrols were increased, and hundreds of teenagers were questioned and warned by police not to frequent the area. Police reported paying particular attention to boys seen near or in the company of "suspected homosexuals," a practice that underlines the extent to which they interpreted the Jaques killing as an example of homosexual predation.[117] Overall, in the wake of the murder the Toronto police were more active on Yonge Street than they had been at any time since the Second World War.

Other City agencies also devoted considerable resources to frustrating Sin Strip's operations. Both Toronto and Metro sent staff to inspect Yonge's sex-related businesses in an effort to accumulate bylaw infractions and fines and to uncover grounds for violations of the places of amusement bylaw. In the first two weeks after Jaques's death, Fire Department officials carried out eighteen inspections, and the Toronto medical officer of health reported that his staff had inspected twenty-one massage parlours and found sixty-six infractions, ranging from lack of a first-aid kit to unsanitary floors. By far the most effective branch of the municipal government was Metro's Licensing Department, which detailed twenty licensing inspectors to go over Yonge's sex businesses with a fine-toothed comb. These inspectors accompanied police on raids – entering thirty-three businesses and helping lay a total of fifty-four charges in August – but they also visited massage parlours in plainclothes, posing as clients.[118] Unlike police officers, they were not immediately recognizable by their haircuts or familiar faces, and they were not barred by their superiors from removing their clothing during inspections, making them more effective at gathering evidence for bawdy house charges. Over the next few months, staff would conduct more than two hundred such inspections.[119]

The final element of the crackdown was the expediting of the prosecutions and injunctions that resulted from these raids and inspections. Proponents of a cleanup had long viewed the glacial pace of proceedings in provincial courts as a major obstacle to enforcing the law on Sin Strip. This situation changed quickly after the Jaques murder, with the provincial government dedicating a judge and a courtroom at Old City Hall – just a block from Yonge – to hearing Sin Strip criminal cases and nominating a special prosecutor to pursue them.[120] Equally important was Metro Toronto's hiring of special counsel Morris Manning, formerly of the provincial attorney-general's office, to use any and all legal tools to shut down sex shops and prevent their reopening. During the next few months, Manning would concurrently pursue "four methods of attack" in fulfilling his mandate. These included the ninety-three cases he launched for violation of Metro's licensing bylaw but also three other approaches whose purpose was to create significant financial hardship for sex shop owners, whether through court-enforced penalties or legal costs. These were civil suits, applications for court injunctions to close individual businesses, and the use of the largely untested Disorderly Houses Act, a Second World War–era law that empowered judges to order the padlocking of convicted bawdy houses.[121]

Harassment through rigorous enforcement and the multiplication of criminal and civil proceedings had an immediate effect on Sin Strip. Repeated visits from police and inspectors created a hostile climate for body rubs and other sex-related concerns. There were fewer customers, and after numerous arrests and the threat of fines, female employees were wary of showing up for work. Lawyers who represented sex industry businessmen explained that "daily raids" of their premises had made it impossible to stay open. According to one letter to the chief of police, officers were "entering these premises refusing, despite requests, to identify themselves or to produce search warrants. On several such occasions, these officers have broken down doors and terrorized the occupants of these establishments ... Such police activity is commonplace in a 'police state' but should not be condoned in this locality."[122]

Closures began with Charlie's Angels, where Jaques's body was found, before expanding up and down Sin Strip as raids and summons continued. By mid-August, five other body rub parlours had shut their doors, and by the end of October 1977 only four of the forty sex-related businesses operating on Yonge just two months earlier remained open. Thirteen had been closed by court injunctions pending civil proceedings, and two had been padlocked under the Disorderly Houses Act following criminal convictions. Others folded voluntarily to avoid inspections and various forms of harassment or because their landlords, also facing the threat of legal consequences, had terminated their lease.[123] Several of Yonge's more mainstream and legitimate sex businesses – including nude dancing venues and adult bookstores – continued to function, and two body rub parlours would subsequently reopen after acquiring a license to operate from Metro. But 1977 marked the end of Sin Strip's time as Toronto's sex district.

OVER FIVE YEARS, from 1972 through 1977, thousands of Torontonians took part in a citizen campaign to remake downtown Yonge Street. Gathering in churches, neighbourhood associations, apartment corridors, hair salons, and suburban kitchens across the urban region, they decided individually and collectively to contest the emergence of Sin Strip. Their letters, phone calls, petition drives, and street demonstrations were structured around a series of common messages – rejection of the sexual revolution, fears for the urban future, nostalgia for an idealized past – but they were also idiosyncratic and individual, shaped by media discourses, communities of faith, ethnic solidarities, and personal experiences of the street. They made clear demands for state action. Anti–Sin Strip activists claimed political space in a moment of urban reform and citizen empowerment, and used it to pressure the municipal government into developing new tools and strategies for managing sexual commerce downtown. The regulatory regime assembled in response to this campaign was applied with devastating effect in the summer and fall of 1977, when the Emanuel Jaques murder fixated public attention and anger on Yonge Street and created a political opportunity for its transformation.

The breaking up of Sin Strip displaced sexual regulation debates from Yonge Street, but it did not end them. Sex work remained a feature of downtown life after 1977, although as scholar Deborah Brock suggests, it was spatially reorganized. The closing of Yonge's dozens of nude massage parlours and encounter studios contributed, along with changes in the law, to a significant increase in the number of women involved in street prostitution in the Jarvis Street area just east of the strip – by 1978 widely referred to as "the Track" – which rapidly become the focal point for sex work debates in Toronto.[124] Two new voices involved themselves in those debates. First, residents in the gentrifying neighbourhoods surrounding the Track became the key actors calling for regulation of sex work, which lost its capacity to mobilize citizens at a metropolitan scale when it left downtown Yonge Street behind. Second, sex workers themselves, almost entirely silenced in the 1970s conflict over Sin Strip, became active participants. The shared experience of police repression during the Yonge crackdown was a key factor in the advent of Canada's first organized sex worker advocacy group in Toronto, BEAVER (Better End All Vicious Erotic Repression), and its demands for the legitimization and decriminalization of prostitution.[125]

An unintended consequence of the demise of Sin Strip was the acceleration of the ongoing dispersal of sexual entertainment beyond the central city. As early as 1973, body rub operators had begun to leave downtown in large numbers, contributing to their regulation becoming a metropolitan political issue. However, the majority were still concentrated on Sin Strip until summer 1977. This situation changed with that year's shutdown, as new parlours overwhelmingly chose to locate on lower-rent and above all less scrutinized commercial strips and suburban shopping plazas. Similarly, bars and clubs across the urban region adopted, and by their ubiquity normalized, the business strategies that had proved so controversial on Yonge; by fall 1980, an estimated 186 premises in Metro Toronto were offering a combination of alcohol and adult entertainment, whether in the form of strip shows, wet T-shirt contests, or topless performances. As provincial MPP Jack Johnson explained in a Queen's Park debate on the subject, "Certainly, crackdowns have removed some of the more questionable establishments from Toronto's downtown core, but many of them have moved. Instead of heading into the city centre, one can bump and grind in every Metro borough."[126] Local reaction could be fierce: in 1979, a body rub that attempted to open near Yonge and Eglinton was destroyed by arson after a vigorous residents' campaign. But decentralization – ironically, in some cases under the auspices of Metro's licensing law – would become the defining characteristic of the new spatial organization of sexual commerce in Toronto. The same was true in other cities whose postwar sex districts had also been dispersed by combinations of citizen activism, policing, and real estate development.[127]

Citizen campaigners and their allies were successful in forcing sex shops off Yonge Street, but their larger concerns about urban decline and character could not be addressed so easily. In the short term, the clampdown on Sin Strip simply replaced commercialized vice with another, equally worrisome image of downtown decline: block after block dotted with empty rental spaces, boarded-up doors, and "For Lease" signs that created significant gaps in the street's retail and entertainment corridor. A spring 1978 planning survey of downtown Yonge found 350,000 square feet of empty, unleased commercial space, representing 8 percent of the total for the entire strip – excluding the Eaton's lands – and 14 percent of the entertainment area between Gerrard and Dundas.[128] "Will the people come back?" asked urban affairs columnist David Lewis Stein, in one of a series of columns that helped relaunch public discussion about the street's future in the wake of the suppression of one of its most lucrative types of business. Investigations produced mixed results. Some journalists and business people who observed the 1977 Christmas shopping rush saw a street "alive" with families returning to a restored downtown, but others saw only one path to a lasting revitalization. "Either we can let Yonge St. deteriorate further," argued a *Toronto Star* editorial, or "we can restore vitality to the street by means of major redevelopment ... Which will it be?"[129] In this context, a decade after the demise of the first Eaton Centre, Toronto was given a new chance to debate the project's transformative vision for its main street.

5

Malling Main Street

In spring and summer 1979, as construction of Canada's largest shopping centre crept down the west side of Yonge Street, city newspapers were full of reports on its progress. Much of the coverage was celebratory, the tone set by the confident messaging of developer Cadillac Fairview in a full-page advertorial spread in the *Toronto Star*:

> Eaton Centre has changed a somewhat declining, although sometimes colourful, retail area into an exciting new "city within a city" that shoppers and visitors can enjoy in comfort all year round, day and night. An ambitious five million square feet retail complex, a magnificent "place for people" in the heart of Toronto ... which will ensure the ongoing vitality of the city's downtown for many years to come.[1]

Somewhat unexpectedly, the mall also received a stamp of approval from one of North America's leading progressive urban critics. In a letter to the *Globe and Mail,* Jane Jacobs praised its attention to fostering civility and pedestrian amenities, and argued that its shopping galleria and downtown Yonge Street would "strengthen one another."[2] But where Jacobs saw mutual benefit, others saw competition and loss. In an article entitled "Death of a Main Drag," *Globe* journalist Stephen Godfrey articulated a persistent critique of the development: that it could succeed only by draining people and dollars away from an already struggling retail strip. The Eaton Centre, he explained, "is not the saviour Yonge Street and the downtown core was waiting for. It may, in fact, prove to be the critical blow."[3] Revitalization, support, or replacement? However participants in this debate understood the relationship between centre and street, all agreed that the project would have a transformative impact on downtown Yonge.

View south along Yonge Street at Dundas toward the newly completed first phase of the Eaton Centre, 1977. | Ron Bull/*Toronto Star* 502838963 via Getty Images

The public failure of the first Eaton Centre in 1967 marked the end of the postwar rebuilding consensus in Toronto but not of the drive to profitably repurpose the company's downtown land bank. In 1970, a new plan for the west side of Yonge Street was released, still bearing the Eaton name but now controlled by an outside developer, with the retailer reduced to the role of minority partner. The design was also profoundly different – the skyscrapers, plazas, and civic agenda of the city of tomorrow were replaced by an urban adaptation of one of North America's most successful architectural forms, the regional shopping centre. As these changes suggest, the second Eaton Centre (1970–79) came to life in a very different context from the first. The flagship project of Canada's largest development corporation, Cadillac Fairview, it was emblematic of a decade in which investment capital returned to downtown on a vast scale, with urban strategies influenced by two decades of suburban success. Passionately scrutinized and debated, it became a key site for critiques of the corporate city and for the emergence of redevelopment as the most contested municipal issue in 1970s Toronto. More than any other intervention of the period, the Eaton

Centre remade Yonge Street, integrating four blocks of the strip into a single modern megastructure and introducing new elements of centralization, privatization, and control that significantly changed how it operated as a marketplace and public space.

The Corporate Development Paradigm

Growth and consolidation in the development industry transformed how Canadian cities were built in the 1960s and 1970s, and who profited from that process.[4] Change began on the urban fringe. In his study of Canadian suburbanization, Richard Harris describes how stricter government regulation, new financing structures, and growing demand all contributed to a shift in the 1940s and 1950s from an entrepreneurial to a corporate model of building neighbourhoods.[5] Toronto's Don Mills (1952–60) suburb, with eight thousand dwelling units on a comprehensively planned, two thousand-acre site, was the most famous example of a national trend that favoured big developers with experience, in-house expertise, and easy access to credit and investment capital. Across the country, suburbs scaled up, multiplied, and began to look alike – and so did their builders. The rise of the planned and packaged corporate suburb marks the end of Harris's study but also the beginning of a new paradigm for urban land development. From the suburbs to the central city, by the 1970s investor-owned, professionally managed corporations would take a leading role in every aspect of city building in Canada.[6]

"The story of Cadillac Fairview," observes the author of the company's official history, "is the story of the transformation of urban Canada in the decades following the Second World War."[7] The claim is in some ways grandiose, but it makes sense to consider the builder of the Eaton Centre as an exemplar of the new arrangements of capital produced through postwar urban growth. The first of these was concentration. Cadillac Fairview was created by the 1974 merger of three businesses – Canadian Equity and Development, Cadillac Development, and Fairview – that collectively owned $1 billion in real estate throughout Canada.[8] The resulting development corporation was Canada's biggest in terms of assets, but it was by no means unique. By the mid-1970s, five national development giants had holdings valued at over $300 million each, and a few large companies materialized to dominate in every city, such that in the early 1970s 10 percent of firms were responsible for as much as 75 percent of urban development activity.[9] Consolidation created economies of scale and boosted investor confidence, increasing the profitability of complex, longer-term projects. It also made monopoly growth a major issue of public concern in what had historically been a fragmented industry. Studies commissioned by the Canada Housing and Mortgage Company and the Royal Commission on Corporate Concentration in the mid-1970s both concluded that the industry's "deep-seated concentrated structure" had not led to price manipulation; at the same time, they documented the extent to which building Canadian cities had become the work of a small pool of powerful businesses.[10]

The second innovation of the period was integration. Major developers expanded their operations up and down the supply chain and across sectors, changing how they made their money and becoming considerably more complex and diversified. With vertical integration, virtually the whole development process was brought in-house, from land assembly to design, construction to marketing. Increasingly, developers' involvement did not end with the completion of a project; as apartment and commercial construction caught up to house building, companies became property managers and landlords, creating valuable long-term revenue streams. By the early 1970s, apartment builder Cadillac Development and retail and office specialist Fairview each employed upward of five hundred staff to do this work, and through subcontractors they managed the work of thousands more.[11] Their merger with Canadian Equity and Development, the builder of suburban Don Mills, was a dramatic illustration of the industry's trend toward horizontal integration, spanning previously separate real estate markets. In 1975, newly formed Cadillac Fairview owned and managed sixteen thousand apartments, fifteen office buildings, and thirty-three shopping centres; rental income on those properties accounted for two-thirds of its $160 million in revenue, but the company also owned six thousand suburban acres on which it was building four thousand homes for sale.[12] The same expansion strategies were, on a smaller scale, transforming the work of developers across Canada.

These two trends depended on a third: financialization. The corporate development industry grew as the conduit for massive capital flows from other areas of the economy into real estate, and so into producing the fabric of the city.[13] Developers built, as an axiom, with other people's cash. As Cadillac principal Ephraim Diamond put it, success in the field depended on "the ability to raise gobs of money" – and the postwar decades saw key innovations in that process. The first was access to government-backed institutional finance. By the late 1950s, most homes in Canada were being built with mortgage financing under the National Housing Act (1938), a federal program that was the glue for close business relationships between residential developers like Cadillac and big, conservative lenders: insurance companies, trusts, and banks. Those mutually profitable relationships would persist and expand into other areas of construction in subsequent decades.[14] Just as important was large-scale "switching" of surplus industrial capital into real estate. Canadian Equity was incorporated in 1953 by industrial financier E.P. Taylor to buy up and develop land in suburban Toronto; Montreal's Bronfman dynasty created Fairview in 1959 as a vehicle for reinvesting the profits from distilling giant Seagram's.[15] Finally, from the late 1960s the biggest corporate developers – including Cadillac and Fairview – went public, raising millions in equity from shareholders while significantly changing their governance structures. These innovations reorganized Canadian urban development into a financial services industry whose product was the city and gave a widening circle of institutions, groups, and individuals a stake in its future success.

New Partnerships, New Models

In the mid-1950s, municipal and business elites began to promote redevelopment of the Eaton's lands as a catalyst for downtown transformation, a corporate stimulus package for the ailing heart of an otherwise booming metropolis. This discourse of revitalization continued to be associated with the project after its cancellation in 1967, but it was increasingly disconnected from economic realities in Toronto and other Canadian cities. By the late 1960s, downtown was already being transformed. Across Canada, urban real estate markets and development activity repeatedly set new records – realty firm A.E. LePage's annual survey breathlessly announced "the greatest year in history" for the industry in 1969 (and then in 1971, 1972, and 1973) – and capital poured back into the centres of major cities, especially in Toronto.[16] Beginning with the opening of the first fifty-six-storey tower of the TD Centre in 1967, partnerships between corporate developers and major financial institutions rebuilt Toronto's financial district into the largest in Canada, nearly doubling its office space, adding thousands of white-collar jobs, and establishing a new skyline in soaring glass and steel.[17] High-rise apartment towers mushroomed in neighbourhoods adjoining the core, and dense commercial development followed the Yonge subway line north to the new interchange at Bloor Street and beyond. By the early 1970s, hundreds of millions of dollars were being invested each year in rebuilding Toronto's core, leaving the Yonge Street retail strip looking less like a potential leader in that process than the exception in an otherwise rapidly changing city.[18]

Within the Eaton's organization, the accelerating pace of change became a key argument for returning to the Eaton Centre idea. Since publicly renouncing its leadership role in 1967, the company had done little to follow up on the inquiries of a series of major developers – at least nine, including Fairview – interested in taking over the project.[19] An April 1969 report by Eaton's development department to company leadership argued that this inertia was no longer tenable. "The hazards of inaction are real," it warned, since "the moving forces in Toronto today will not wait to follow our lead. They will, instead, build around and above us, [or] relocate the downtown core around a nucleus other than an aging Eaton retail complex."[20] In this last scenario, the Yonge and Bloor area, which in a few years had emerged as the second-largest retail concentration in Toronto, was envisioned as the most likely competitor.[21] Could downtown Yonge, and by extension Eaton's, be replaced as the heart of the city? To the fear of being left behind by growth was added Eaton's long-standing desire to consolidate its downtown operations: to merge two aging stores into one and to reduce the carrying charges in property taxes and mortgage payments on its twenty-three acres of Yonge Street property between College and Queen, which in 1968 alone amounted to $5.6 million.

By the end of 1969, Eaton's leadership was convinced that large-scale downtown redevelopment in Toronto was a fact, with or without its participation, and that the company must leverage the boom to modernize, shed unused properties, and secure its corporate future. This meant partnership, not with municipal government as envisioned a decade earlier, but with a developer who was able to provide the expertise and capital necessary to succeed where the retailer alone had failed. Fairview was the obvious choice. The Bronfman family's investment vehicle was one of the biggest shopping centre and office developers in Canada, and its head office was located just blocks away from Eaton's in its flagship project, the recently completed TD Centre. Furthermore, by the late 1960s the two companies were already enmeshed in mutually profitable business relationships. Eaton's pivot to the suburbs had made it a key tenant in several of Fairview's largest regional malls, and the pair were finalizing a three-way partnership with Toronto-Dominion Bank to build an integrated office tower, Eaton's store, and retail centre on a two-block site partly owned by the retailer in downtown Vancouver. Pacific Centre, announced in 1968 and built from 1971 to 1973, would serve as a trial run for the business arrangements that produced the much larger and costlier Eaton Centre.[22]

Partnership came at a cost. From the start of negotiations with Fairview, it became clear that Eaton's would have to abandon major elements of its 1966 plan.[23] Fairview brought to the table a history of mall building across Canada and a strong preference for the proven profitability of that form. At least a dozen new designs were presented to the retailer, and with each mock-up office towers evaporated, public plazas shrank, trees were uprooted, and pedestrian tunnels filled in. Not just the contentious Old City Hall block but the whole west side of the land assembly was left out of the development, effectively ending the centre's planned architectural and functional integration with New City Hall and Nathan Phillips Square, as envisioned in Project Viking and the 1966 plan. Instead, the complex would hug Yonge Street to the east and focus almost entirely on what Fairview considered the best and most profitable use of Eaton's properties: modern retail. This was acceptable to Eaton's leadership, who after 1967 had abandoned the dream, always far-fetched, of building a Canadian Rockefeller Center in downtown Toronto. The sticking point in negotiations proved not to be the shedding of office skyscrapers or civic obligations, but Fairview's requirement that the retailer abandon the Yonge and Queen corner, where it had faced off with competitor Simpson's for nearly a century, and move north to the intersection with Dundas Street.

This concession mattered because what Fairview envisioned for Yonge was not a civic centre or the hub of a new downtown, but something much more familiar to Canadian consumers: a regional shopping centre. At the top of the retail food chain in the suburbs, regional malls such as Toronto's Yorkdale (1964) and Montreal's Galeries d'Anjou (1968) relied on size, buy-in from major retailers, and location near expressways to attract shoppers from the metropolitan area and beyond. Referred to by their builders as "machines for making money" and "the best investment known to man," these big centres were carefully planned to provide large, consistent returns on the massive outlays of capital needed for their construction.[24] Their design was standardized across the continent – and then around the world – through the circulation of ideas and experts and the work of groups such as the International Council of Shopping Centers.[25] By the mid-1960s, virtually all regional malls in North America were variations on the "dumbbell," a shopping corridor bookended by two major department stores that drew foot traffic back and forth along its length.[26] Fairview had no intention of departing from that profitable script in downtown Toronto, where Eaton's and Simpson's would act as the north and south anchors of the mall. If the Eaton family initially resisted this arrangement, it was not because of the prospect of cooperating with Simpson's – the two were already highly successful as partners in Yorkdale mall – or for fears of lost sales. Instead, it was because leaving the perch at Yonge and Queen meant abandoning the symbolic capital accrued in a century of occupying Toronto's busiest intersection and subordinating a key piece of the company's corporate identity to the new spatial logic of modern retailing.[27]

First the planned shopping centre had conquered the suburbs; now it would help remake downtown. By the 1970s, the idea of transposing the highly profitable model of the shopping mall into the central city was gaining purchase throughout North America, promising a new, corporate-led paradigm for rebuilding in an era of dwindling public investment.[28] Nearly every large or midsized Canadian city installed a downtown shopping mall in the 1970s and early 1980s, as did dozens of cities in the United States. Rather than aiming for the civic grandeur of earlier rebuilding projects, these centres embraced the private-sector virtues of functionality, efficiency, and profitability. All required negotiation with local governments, and a few benefited from government financing, but they were most of all the work of partnerships between developers, investors, and big retailers.[29] The Toronto Eaton Centre was an outsized example of this trend. Fairview (Cadillac Fairview after 1974) agreed to buy and develop Eaton's properties, in the final agreement splitting ownership of the future development 60-20-20 with the retailer and the Toronto-Dominion Bank, the latter a crucial source of outside capital for construction.[30] As this significant investment by a large, conservative lender suggests, the second Eaton Centre was viewed as a more viable financial proposition than the first. As Fairview worked through the problems posed by moving its business model from periphery to centre, it helped lead a larger trend that made a shopping mall the central item on the downtown agenda in cities across North America.[31]

The Church of the Holy Trinity

Suburban shopping malls were built on greenfield land, but the Toronto Eaton Centre had to be slotted into an urban landscape complicated by a century of small-scale development and property transactions. To complete its land assembly, Fairview was required to negotiate with the owners of a series of holdout properties dotted throughout the project area. These included the Salvation Army, whose national headquarters was eventually omitted from the plans, and the University of Toronto, willed a Yonge Street shopfront in 1922 by its owner with the stipulation – voided after three years of negotiations and legal gymnastics – that it never be sold to her expansionist neighbour Eaton's.[32] By far the most important holdout was the Church of the Holy Trinity, a small, Gothic Revival Anglican church that sat on a key lot in the centre of the project site, hemmed in by Eaton's towering factory buildings. Torontonians could be forgiven a sense of déjà vu when, in May 1970, they read in their morning newspaper that the demolition of this historic nineteenth-century building was deemed by Fairview to be essential to the success of the Eaton Centre redevelopment, much like Old City Hall half a decade earlier.[33]

Built in 1847 as "the Parochial Church of the Poor of Toronto," endowed by an English visitor who deplored the city's lack of rent-free pews, Holy Trinity had found a new vocation as a downtown church by the mid-twentieth century.[34] Long separated by redevelopment and suburban migration from the working-class Anglo-Canadian population that had once surrounded it, the church maintained its relevance by developing a social mission based on inclusivity and service to marginalized communities. During the Great Depression, it fed and housed the unemployed and homeless, in the postwar decades it lent its premises to new congregations – Coptic Christian and Japanese Canadian, among others – and in the 1970s, it operated a twenty-four-hour distress centre, drop-in services for youth, and a free school. Holy Trinity was an early ally to many of the rights-based social movements of the long 1960s and a key site in a network of youth- and counterculture-friendly alternative social spaces clustered on and around Yonge Street, giving it a rebellious identity that more than once threatened it with disestablishment by the Anglican Diocese of Toronto.[35] In 1968, newly arrived Vietnam war resisters were billeted in the basement; in the early 1970s, the church hosted fundraisers for the Stop Spadina campaign, as well as meetings and dances for gay rights advocates of the Community Homophile Association of Toronto.[36]

Fairview initially viewed this small church much in the way that Eaton's had seen Old City Hall: as an obstacle to progress. Throughout 1970, it aggressively pursued Holy Trinity's land, making several offers to buy the church and its outbuildings and unsuccessfully lobbying the City of Toronto to expropriate them and thirteen other holdouts in the land assembly, should negotiations fail.[37] Eaton's public relations staff urged their development partner to be more cautious, noting that the church, like Old City Hall, could be "a rallying point for professional protesters or political opportunists or Eaton-baiters" and suggesting that the company earn credit with the public by moving it brick by brick to another location.[38] Both approaches were based on a fundamental misunderstanding of who Holy Trinity's congregants were, to some extent nourished by local journalism that portrayed them as hippie activists "who fly ecology flags on the front porch of their houses, and sign anti-Viet Nam war petitions ... and play guitars and recorders and use the word 'community' a lot."[39] In fact, the church's parishioners were an organized citizen group with

Holy Trinity and Trinity Square from one of the Eaton's warehouses, 1972. The Yonge Street strip is at the top of the photo. | Bob Olsen/*Toronto Star* 502807187 via Getty Images

significant social capital, expertise, and political influence. Among their numbers were lawyers, university professors, and two downtown councillors, including William Archer, chair of Toronto's public works committee and the planner of the Yonge Street pedestrian mall.[40]

Trinity responded to Fairview by proposing its own redevelopment scheme, underpinned by a vision for the heart of the city that brought together Christian humanism, the trend of "people planning," and the techniques of urban design. Congregant Gerald Robinson, an architect and member of the city's Planning Board, was the principal author of the venture, announced in January 1971.[41] It envisioned the closure of Trinity Square – the street encircling Holy Trinity, which by the 1970s essentially functioned as a parking lot – to create a pedestrianized public space reminiscent of European town squares, with the church at its centre. Tree-lined promenades would connect the square to surrounding streets. This plan had pragmatic goals, including renting part of the church's lands for commercial development to ensure its future solvency. But Holy Trinity made it clear that it also saw this $3 million project as an opportunity to realize a different model of urban development: to work through expertise to create a downtown "haven" accessible to rich and poor, a space dedicated to "man and his spirit" in a sector of the city otherwise devoted to "man as customer."[42] The church's redevelopment committee explicitly framed its planned Trinity Square as a critique of the unthinking materialism of projects like the Eaton Centre. As outlined in the committee's objectives, such developments "take a whole city block, clear off all the buildings and people, dig a big hole, put all the pedestrians in the hole and call it an underground concourse ... They want to maximize the return on their commercial investment; we're trying to create a people place that will bring together a number of human values."[43]

There were obvious parallels between this citizen mobilization and the Friends of Old City Hall's 1966 campaign. Both were firmly anchored in Toronto's educated elite and in a strong attachment to built heritage and the history of community – civic or religious – it embodied. In their own ways, both campaigns took a moral stance on the urban development process and its tendency to destroy such continuities through the short-sighted pursuit of profit. A key difference, however, was that Holy Trinity "argued from property," as a religious institution that possessed a clear, long-standing title to its land.[44] On that basis, and by offering a credible counterproposal to demolition, its congregation made a negotiated compromise the only politically viable option for continuing with the Eaton Centre project. From May 1971, when it became obvious that expropriating the church to turn it over to Fairview was politically unpalatable to both the municipal and provincial governments, the developer and the church entered into talks. Toronto Council made its own approval of the project contingent on the two parties reaching a deal, which put

Holy Trinity in a position of considerable strength.[45] These negotiations allowed the church's articulate and politically astute congregation to pursue its own interests by aligning them, temporarily at least, with those of the developer. They also had the unintended effect of stalling municipal approval of the new Eaton Centre by more than a year, opening the political process to other voices that were eager to assert their own interpretation of the public interest.

Contesting the Corporate City

A new politics of development was emerging in Toronto. Citizen resistance to undesirable construction – mostly apartment buildings and industrial uses in residential areas – had been a feature of Toronto life since the early twentieth century, but in the past such battles had been mostly local and uncoordinated.[46] That changed rapidly in the late 1960s, as the redevelopment boom encroached for the first time on middle-class and gentrifying neighbourhoods surrounding downtown. Between 1966 and 1971 alone, twenty thousand apartments, or about one hundred large residential towers, were built in the city, the response of big residential developers such as Cadillac to spiking demand for rental accommodation, the City's densification policy, and the attractive profits available in replacing brick houses with concrete high-rises.[47] Grassroots opposition by residents and property owners to what they saw as a physically destructive and socially disruptive trend reinvigorated moribund local associations and spurred them to band together in 1968 to form the Confederation of Residents' and Ratepayers' Associations (CORRA) as their unified voice at City Hall. There was no countervailing political organization of apartment residents *for* densification, although Cadillac and other large developers tried, inexpertly, to spark one.[48]

For most people in Toronto, anti-development activism was a conservative, localist strategy aimed at protecting the status quo in their neighbourhoods. As they broadcast loudly in their deputations and at public meetings, ratepayers' and residents' associations "merely wanted to be left alone."[49] But by the early 1970s, a network of journalists, researchers, and activists was publicly drawing links between these individual fights and integrating them into a systemic critique of the development industry and the capitalist urban process. One cluster emerged around activist Marilyn Cox of the environmental group Pollution Probe, who set up an "Urban Team" to tackle development issues in 1971; the same year, the student-led Downtown Action project received a federal Opportunities for Youth grant and set up shop in a small upstairs office in the parsonage of Metropolitan United Church, just steps from the intersection of Yonge and Queen.[50] Others, including publisher James Lorimer and journalist David Lewis Stein, became public explainers of the mechanics of real estate transactions, investment structures, and planning procedures, while newly elected city councillor John Sewell spent his first years in office exposing what he saw as the corrupting influence of the development industry at City Hall.

These activists and writers placed power relations in the foreground of their analysis. In 1971, a "Developers Series" in alternative newspaper *Guerilla* laid out a framework for understanding the urban development industry as a product of capital accumulation, urbanization, and state policy, an early example of the Marxist approach that informed most big-picture research on the topic.[51] Meanwhile, Downtown Action and Pollution Probe mined the public record to track land assemblies, construction permits, and planning approvals, revealing how the industry pursued its goals on a local level. Original and thorough, this research was intended not just to describe how developers wielded power, but to empower their citizen opponents to fight back.[52] Activists saw the development process as a struggle between two rival visions for the urban future. On the one hand was what James Lorimer memorably labelled the "corporate city," an assemblage of mass-produced forms – high-rises, shopping malls, ticky-tacky suburbs – that produced profits for their builders but did little to accommodate community or human potential. On the other hand was the democratic city, whose forms and pace of change would be determined by the people who lived and worked in it.[53] There were variations on this narrative, but nearly all shared its basic oppositions between citizen and developer, community and profit, good and bad planning.

Contestation of the corporate city began in academic reports and alternative media, but it also made significant inroads into mainstream public discourse. Primed by the politicization of apartment construction and the popularization of ideas of "people planning," Torontonians proved receptive to a counter-narrative of development – even a sometimes radical one – that aligned with their own concerns about the pace and direction of change.[54] In the mid-1960s, *Star* columnist Ron Haggart seemed a lone voice in the wilderness when he used the first Eaton Centre to criticize the City of Toronto's pro-growth boosterism. In contrast, by 1972 there was a thriving new genre of critical writing about urban development in Toronto. It appeared in smaller publications such as Pollution Probe's *Whose City?* newsletter, the Toronto reform caucus's *City Hall*, and community paper the *Toronto Citizen*, as well as in the major dailies, which began to regularly publish columns and editorials by David Lewis Stein and James Lorimer.[55] The focus was on Toronto projects and politics, but there was significant sharing of ideas between Toronto and other Canadian cities, contributing to a national conversation that would be institutionalized in urban research journal *City Magazine* from 1974.

Negotiating the Public Interest

Critics of the development industry and its perceived allies at City Hall found their voice in the public debates that accompanied the new Eaton Centre proposal. No other contemporary project fit so well with narratives of the corporate city and its citizen discontents than this giant suburban-style mall, planned by two of Canada's largest businesses and defied by a tiny church. From 1971 onward, a loose coalition of downtown activists, reformist councillors, and residents' groups mobilized in opposition to the centre. They called for changes to its plan and more broadly for a rethinking of the way that private development was handled in Toronto, insisting that citizen input must be given a decisive role in determining the public interest, whether in the neighbourhoods or downtown. At City Hall, John Sewell cited the project as an example of the way in which the public good – here protecting Yonge Street's existing balance of activities – was neglected as politicians and bureaucrats uncritically accepted developers' plans.[56] In summer 1971, Downtown Action began its own campaign, distributing leaflets on Yonge stating that the strip faced "imminent death" if the mall were built and asking shoppers to boycott Eaton's until the plans were changed in a "people-oriented way." Other citizen and activist groups joined the fray, including powerful ratepayer organization CORRA, and the *Toronto Citizen* warned that unless the Eaton Centre plans were opened up to public input, the project would become "the target of a citizen campaign on the scale of the Stop Spadina movement."[57]

These citizen voices erupted into the downtown development process at a time when it was in flux. By the early 1970s, key elements of the boosterist municipal regime cobbled together by Mayor Nathan Phillips and his successors in the 1950s and 1960s were being jettisoned or fading away. The City of Toronto's Development Department, created in 1962 as a sort of "anti-planning" unit tasked with expediting private development, was increasingly irrelevant. Frustrated by his limited power within the municipal bureaucracy, the department's founding commissioner, Walter Manthorpe, left in 1967 to work for Meridian, one of the city's biggest apartment builders; under his successors, the department's influence declined farther, and it was absorbed by the Planning Department in the late

1970s.[58] The Redevelopment Advisory Council was also sidelined. In an episode that perfectly captured the spirit of the moment, it lost its special status as an advisory group in 1971, after ratepayer associations complained that its members were too closely linked to developers. In the public hearings organized on Fairview's Eaton Centre the following summer, the City's corporate brain trust found itself relegated to the same place in the political process as the Annex Ratepayers' Association and the other civil society groups who sent deputations.[59]

The Eaton Centre came to the City of Toronto for approval at the start of a municipal election campaign that promised further changes. When centrist reformer David Crombie announced his mayoral candidacy in July 1972, he shared the front page of the *Toronto Star* with photos of families forcibly evicted in "the battle for Bleecker Street," as developer Meridian attempted to clear an inner-city block of Victorian houses to expand its St. Jamestown apartment complex.[60] Development and citizen empowerment emerged early on as the central, linked issues in that year's contest, with campaign literature, debate questions, and media analysis all focusing on placing candidates on the spectrum between pro-development and pro-citizen. "Let's change the development rules," opened a pamphlet for Crombie's campaign, and though that promise remained vague, it was clear that victory for the CORRA-endorsed reformists would mean a significant change in the way the City handled contentious projects.[61] The threat seemed real enough for the Urban Development Institute industry group, which normally avoided public comment on municipal politics, to launch a counter-campaign. Throughout 1972, it used mailouts to its captive audience – the tenants in the hundreds of apartment towers belonging to its members across the city – urging them to vote against the "anti-development pressure groups" who were trying to hijack the democratic process.[62]

Fairview did everything in its power to obtain municipal approval for the Eaton Centre before the December election, which seemed increasingly likely to bring a reformist victory. In 1966, Eaton's financial insecurities and reputational concerns had left it almost incapable of altering its plans; in contrast, in 1972 negotiating the public interest with the Holy Trinity congregation and Toronto Council became Fairview's strategy for avoiding a more broad-based negotiation that would be dominated by CORRA and other citizen groups. Two public meetings at City Hall in July gave a taste of what that might look like: each lasted over four hours, and because virtually all of the deputations were opposed to the centre, they resembled nothing so much as marathon criticism sessions targeting

Fairview, the project, and development industry practices more generally.[63] By mid-November, Fairview had agreed to build around and partially finance a pedestrianized Trinity Square at the heart of the complex as well as public rights-of-way to reach it, and to impose height limits on surrounding buildings.[64] The developer also conceded to a series of detailed proposals by City planners that focused on protecting Yonge Street's mix of activities and life as a public space, qualities recently rediscovered and assigned new value in the wake of the highly popular pedestrian malls of 1971 and 1972. These measures, supported by the Downtown Council, included replacing demolished shops and restaurants on Yonge with similar uses – not parking or office towers – providing at least twenty pedestrian entrances to the sidewalk, and not allowing construction to interfere with future plans for a permanently pedestrianized Yonge Street.[65]

These concessions and the land exchanges that would produce the superblock were written into a development agreement that was rushed to approval by Toronto Council just ten days before the municipal ballot. At more than 170 pages, this contract between the differing public and private entities implicated in the project was unprecedented in its length and complexity.[66] Critics called it "lax," pointing out that the City had grossly undervalued the streets transferred to Fairview and that the development guidelines for the west side of the complex were largely undefined. On the other hand, the agreement was exceptional in the ad hoc restrictions it placed on the disposition of private property, limits that the City solicitor, one of its authors, considered a heavy-handed, "awkward" tool for achieving the City's goals for the Eaton's lands.[67] A bundle of good intentions, partially enforceable restrictions, and political expediency, the document exemplified the messiness of redevelopment policy in a moment of political transition. Somewhat ironically, its approval would be the last political victory of William Dennison's mandate as mayor of Toronto, which was launched by his opposition to the demolition of Old City Hall. It was a measure of how much city politics had shifted – and of the toll of their day-to-day frustrations – that former people's champion Dennison ended his career raging against the obstructionism of civic activists and citizen groups and their inability to see the wider public interest in redevelopment.[68]

People Planning and Profit

Elected in the last days of 1972, the new mayor and council did not fulfill the Urban Development Institute's gloomy predictions of "stop[ping] Toronto's progress," but they did significantly change how the City handled redevelopment.[69] In 1973 alone, David Crombie's administration doubled the City's planning staff, which he reorganized into neighbourhood offices, appointed a citizen-led task force to study the major issues facing the urban core, and passed a "holding bylaw" capping the height of new downtown buildings at forty-five feet for two years, until a new plan for the core with different priorities was put in place. The objective of these changes was not to halt private development – it barely slowed – but to give the municipal government new tools for controlling it in the public interest. City building was imagined as a question of negotiation of the necessarily different goals of people and capital, facilitated by municipal expertise. "The city's future," explained the new mayor in a speech to the building industry, "has to be decided not on the basis of what is most convenient for speculators or developers but on the basis of sound planning and what is in the best interest of the city's people."[70] It was the start of a transformation of Toronto's planning system that would, by the decade's end, institutionalize the shift toward localism, neighbourhood preservation, and citizen consultation that underpinned reformist electoral success.[71]

With the questions of Holy Trinity and the land exchange settled, the key battleground became the complex itself. Malling downtown meant solving problems of land supply, urban complexity, parking, and access; but it also meant finding ways to urbanize suburban design. Until 1973, Fairview's planning process had focused almost entirely on the first, more technical set of problems, underestimating the political weight of the second. The centre's conceptual plan was roundly criticized for showing a complex that was as boxy, inward facing, and as disconnected from its environment as the era's large suburban shopping malls. Suspicions that Yonge Street was on track to becoming a "downtown suburbia" were aggravated by the fact that slides of the developer's most recent project, North York's Fairview Mall, were used at public presentations to convey the look and feel of the centre's interior.[72] In 1973 and again in 1974, newly empowered opponents of the project pressured Toronto Council to apply the holding bylaw retroactively or to refuse building permits until Fairview reworked the project to better integrate it, functionally and aesthetically, with the surrounding area.[73] Their campaign ultimately failed, but it reinforced for Fairview the importance of producing a new design that not only fulfilled the terms of the development agreement, but also pleased critics enough to forestall further challenges.

In this context, the Eaton Centre became an early exemplar of the architectural borrowings and adaptations that characterized urban shopping malls in North America. From the 1970s on, downtown retail centres recycled historic structures, built around existing street grids, and added eclectic, artistic facades in an effort to meet planning standards and public expectations that were higher than on the urban fringe.[74] In the case of the Eaton Centre, a change of architect launched the process. In 1973, Fairview hired Bauhaus-trained Eberhard Zeidler to redesign the centre, bringing both new ideas and the imprimatur of cutting-edge architectural practice to the project. Zeidler, best known for the high-tech pods, pavilions, and bridges of Ontario Place, Toronto's waterfront response to Expo 67, was well connected in urbanist circles in the city. He was also a friend and collaborator of Jane Jacobs, who participated in early planning sessions and helped develop the new design concept for the Eaton Centre.[75] Although inexperienced in commercial development, Zeidler proved very capable of addressing the project's double imperative of creating a place that people would want to visit and a quarter-billion-dollar development that satisfied a mall builder's standard of profitability. The two not only proved compatible, but in many ways mutually reinforcing. Under Zeidler's direction, futuristic materials and progressive urban design were placed in the service of commerce.

The showpiece of the new Eaton Centre design was an 860-foot-long, 120-foot-tall shopping arcade that stretched north along the west side of Yonge from Queen Street to the new Eaton's store at Dundas. This three-level enclosed mall would be roofed in glass, and bracketed by two curved-cornered glass-and-steel office towers thirty storeys in height. At its north end, a large atrium combined the entrances to Eaton's and Trinity Square. At the south end, a glass wall was pierced by a covered skywalk that spanned Queen Street and connected the centre to the second floor of Simpson's. In his memoirs, Zeidler explains that his skylit shopping "galleria," which would become the hallmark of the centre, was inspired by Milan's elegant, glass-vaulted Galleria Vittorio Emanuele II (1877).[76] He was not alone in his fascination with what urban critic Lewis Mumford called Europe's "most magnificent" shopping arcade. References to Milan's Galleria permeated the discourse of mall building in North America, as developers searched for historical prototypes for enclosed commercial streets and borrowed elements from Old World architecture and urbanism that would distinguish them from the competition. The roofs of most malls were limited to strategically placed skylights, but prestige projects such as Houston's Galleria (1970) integrated full-length glass vaults; in this respect, Zeidler's design owed as much to recent developments in the competitive world of shopping centre construction as to nineteenth-century European antecedents.[77]

Along with the shopping galleria, the most striking difference from earlier plans was the complex's integration with Trinity Square and Yonge Street. It was the only regional shopping centre in North America to be built around a functioning church. For those on foot, Holy Trinity effectively became the heart of the complex, one of just a few pedestrianized open spaces on or near the densely built Yonge strip. The sections of the mall that encompassed the church were stepped back and lowered to provide sunlight year-round, a major improvement for a church that had spent half a century fenced in on three sides by factory buildings twice its height.[78] Trinity Square was also the crossroads for four public pathways that divided the superblock into sections and connected to nearby streets. One of those pathways ran past the church and through the atrium of the shopping mall to Yonge Street, and there were changes on that side of the complex, too. At Dundas, the entrance to the Eaton's store was surrounded on three sides by a public plaza, and from that point south the east side of the mall was set back ten feet from the property line and fronted by a widened sidewalk with trees, benches, and thirty stores opening onto both Yonge and the mall. The combination of the galleria and these street-oriented features earned Zeidler's design a more enthusiastic reception than any earlier iteration of the Eaton Centre, most tellingly in Toronto Council, where it swayed several politicians who had previously cast votes against the project.[79]

Retail Pasts and Futures

Wary after its brush with controversy in 1966–67, Eaton's studiously avoided the spotlight while the fate of the new centre hung in the balance. In fact, at the retailer's request, its partnership with Fairview stipulated that the project be clearly identified as Fairview's initiative and the developer's staff as its "exclusive spokesmen."[80] That changed in May 1974, when Eaton's returned to the public eye to put its stamp of approval on the complex that would bear its name. A special issue of *Eaton News* trumpeted that "at last it's go ... after years of on again, off again bargaining," as company executives and Eaton family members posed for photos while they turned the first spadeful of earth for the mall's immense foundations.[81] In fact, it had been "go" for six months, since the start of the demolition of the former premises of Pollock's Shoes, the Honey Dew Restaurant, and thirty-two other small businesses. There was little nostalgia as they disappeared, at the tail end of a year in which Yonge's public image had been defined by discourses of decline, whether connected to the sex industry or to disorder on the summer pedestrian mall. Media attention was consequently upbeat about the transformation, suggesting that it was about time that these negative changes were countered and that a tired strip "renew[ed] its youth."[82] Shopfronts were replaced by a wall of construction hoardings, behind which Eberhard Zeidler's design slowly took shape, culminating in the opening of the Eaton's store and the first phase of the galleria in February 1977.

The Eaton Centre's opening was a major event that brought together its corporate backers with public dignitaries – including the mayor of Toronto and Ontario's premier and lieutenant-governor – accompanied by the pomp and ceremony of a civic celebration, including pipes, trumpets, and an honour guard in colonial-era costume.[83] Four thousand people packed the glass atrium, where they patiently listened to speeches and watched a ribbon-cutting ceremony before surging up escalators and through doors to explore Eaton's and the 160 other new stores of the mall's first phase. They were amply primed with information. Some press materials incorporated elements of the project's original story, that of retail-led downtown revitalization. Eaton's presented the mall as a major act of corporate citizenship, the linchpin of a nation-wide "comprehensive urban redevelopment program" that included Pacific Centre and London's Wellington Square. More novel, however, was its rebranding as a collaboratively designed, human-oriented place. Press releases emphasized that its striking design was the product of a new, more democratic way of re-building downtown: "Toronto Eaton Centre combines the ideals of government, religious institutions and the people of Toronto in an age when the democratic process is extending right down to the drawing boards."[84] In this telling, features such as the glassed-in galleria and pedestrian rights-of-way that had essentially been forced on Cadillac Fairview by the conflictual development process were embraced as reflections of its core function as "a people place" for Torontonians. In one stroke, the centre's decade-long history of citizen engagement was appropriated as a positive part of its image, rather than the frustrating obstacle it had often seemed to the project's corporate planners.

Never shy about celebrating its long history in downtown Toronto, Eaton's worked to connect the future promised by the centre with traditions anchored in the past. This was symbolized in late 1976 by the relocation of the statue of company founder Timothy Eaton which had sat in the Queen Street store since 1919. Journalists followed the three-thousand-pound bronze as it was shunted laboriously up Yonge to the rotunda of the new store, where it would fix its paternal gaze on a new generation of shoppers and employees. Soon after, the company launched a three-week closing sale at its two older stores, resurrecting the "Eaton

A new kind of public space. People crowd the Eaton Centre's atrium on opening day, February 11, 1977. Yonge Street is visible in the background. | Dick Loek/*Toronto Star* 502839267 via Getty Images

Special," a pre-subway shuttle bus running up and down Yonge Street, at the original price of five cents a ride.[85] Many Torontonians responded to these appeals to memory. City official and essayist George Heron was prompted to "mourn the loss of an old friend," the Queen Street store where as a child he escaped from the "drabness of the Depression years" by riding escalators, staring at window displays, and enjoying ten-cent milkshakes. A few long-time employees – "Old Eatonians" – spoke fondly about working for a company that treated them like family or about the prewar shopping district perpetually pulsing with life.[86] On closing day, Timothy Eaton's great-grandsons shook hands and kissed babies as thousands of Torontonians left their stores for the last time, hands full of discounted products and mementos such as mannequins and merchandising signs.[87]

References to tradition helped smooth over a break with past business models and ideas, one that Eaton's leadership hoped would help as it struggled to keep its place in an increasingly competitive retail market.[88] The opening of the Eaton Centre underpinned a larger corporate restructuring, emphasizing that for the retailer, downtown modernization had always been as much about shedding obligations – unprofitable property, staff, and divisions – as about building something new. Investment in the new flagship store, "the model for all department stores to be built in the next 20 years," according to chairman John Craig Eaton, was offset by the sale of both the College and Queen locations, the former to a consortium of developers planning a residential-commercial complex and the latter to Cadillac Fairview for the southward expansion of the mall.[89] Consolidating in one store pooled resources and staff, allowing the company to lay off more than three hundred "Eatonians," including clerks, merchandisers, and buyers, over the course of 1977. To that number were added two thousand more workers in the Toronto suburbs and thousands more across Canada who lost their jobs when Eaton's ended its century-old mail-order catalogue service.[90] These deep changes to Eaton's business model seemed effective, at least in the short term. Eight months after the opening of the new store, John Craig Eaton reported a 38 percent rise in downtown sales, boasting in a speech to the city's business elite at the Canadian Club that the centre was a "gamble that paid off."[91]

Building the centre was equally transformative for Cadillac Fairview. It validated the developer's own gamble, which was that downtown's locational, cultural, and social advantages would make mall building uniquely profitable there. Widely accepted as common sense in the development industry from the late 1970s, this strategy was untested at such a large scale when planning for the centre began. Spokespeople for Cadillac Fairview projected an air of unflappable calm, but internally coming to grips with Yonge Street's dense urban landscape, high property values, and an increasingly politicized development process was viewed as a significant financial risk.[92] The land assembly was costlier and more complicated than for any previous Canadian project, and three years of fraught negotiations with Eaton's, Holy Trinity, and the City of Toronto brought additional financial uncertainty. Managing this risk and building the Eaton Centre contributed to making Cadillac Fairview. The 1974 merger of Fairview, Cadillac, and Canadian Equity was completed just as construction began on the centre, putting the $250 million project on surer financial footing and making it the crown jewel of the new development giant, which subsequently installed its corporate headquarters on-site in the complex's southernmost tower. From that vantage point, staff looked directly down into Canada's most profitable shopping mall. By 1979, more than half a million people were visiting the galleria each week, yielding sales per square foot that nearly doubled those of a successful suburban mall. A major portion went into Cadillac Fairview's coffers in percentage rents – essentially a tax on tenants' sales – helping to finance its expansion into the largest publicly traded development corporation in North America.[93]

The opening of the Eaton Centre also wrought a larger transformation on the retail ecology of downtown Yonge Street. The mall effectively doubled the number of businesses in the area – by 1979, the galleria had three hundred and the strip slightly fewer – while at the same time dividing it into two distinct marketplaces, outdoor and indoor.[94] The former continued to be organized, as it had been for a century, by Yonge's mostly nineteenth-century shopscape. The property speculation of the 1950s and 1960s had put an end to the dominance of the independent owner-operator, but ownership of the Yonge Street strip remained fragmented among an assortment of investors, small landlords, and businesses. It was defined by a wide variety of small- and medium-scale private uses, including storefronts and upstairs services and offices, that depended for their livelihoods on their connection to the public street. Some were functionally interlinked, such as the concentration of bars, food outlets, and other entertainment venues on the east side of the strip between Dundas and Gerrard. But there was no organizing principle to this commercial corridor, ultimately produced and constrained by the individual, uncoordinated decisions of its owners and occupants, much to the frustration of those seeking to improve it, whether by refashioning the public realm or suppressing specific categories of activity, most recently sexual entertainment.

The Eaton Centre operated according to a different model. The galleria was planned, the product of two decades of experimentation and refinement of the science of malling in suburbs and cities across Canada and the United States. Little was left to chance in a design that used architectural, engineering, marketing, interior design, and other forms of specialized expertise to maximize the profit-making potential of each square foot of selling space. Cadillac Fairview focused, like other mall builders, on transforming shopping from an errand into a "unique experience" defined by the enjoyment of a comfortable, festive, controlled environment. Spectacular features, including striking works of public art by Canadian artists and a fountain whose waterspouts projected one hundred feet in the air, combined with more subtle touches of lighting, music, and design to encourage people to stroll, linger, and spend in the galleria's "interior urban streetscape."[95] Rather than an idiosyncratic mix of individual businesses, this indoor street was highly curated, with tenants arranged in functional groupings, as in the food court, or according to their target market segment, with the highest-rent spaces located on the upper floors of the galleria and smaller, lower-rent spaces below ground. This hierarchization in space was possible because the Eaton Centre had just one landlord, Cadillac Fairview, and one type of leasing arrangement that gave the developer not only a share of sales, but considerable control over what shops sold and how they marketed their goods.[96]

This sorting of businesses by profitability and fit reinforced key differences between Yonge Street's indoor and outdoor marketplaces. Like other successful mall managers, Cadillac Fairview aggressively pursued big domestic and international retailing chains – Pennington's, Foot Locker, Harry Rosen – with proven selling records and brand recognition, creating a tenant list that strongly resembled that of regional shopping centres throughout the country. Only a few existing Yonge Street businesses made the jump to the centre, where rents were among the highest in North America, up to twice the cost of an already expensive street-level location on the strip.[97] Even for those who could afford it, corporate leasing policies limited movement between the two marketplaces. There was no place in the family-oriented galleria for Yonge's pinball arcades, discounters, or record and poster shops, although from 1979 the complex boasted an eighteen-screen Cineplex movie theatre.[98] Not only were the galleria and the street functionally different, but their tenants had different interests. The mall's opening weakened the Downtown Council's claim to speak for the area, since from 1977 there was also a Toronto Eaton Centre Merchants' Association, with its own agenda and spokespeople. Whereas the former group continued to lobby the City for wider sidewalks and other improvements to the outdoor public realm, the latter focused on protecting vehicle access to the centre and discouraging the strip's "unacceptable social environment" from spreading indoors.[99]

Some contemporary commentators saw the relationship between Yonge Street's two commercial worlds as a zero-sum competition. They returned to the argument, first articulated in the early 1970s, that far from revitalizing Yonge, the Eaton Centre would "kill" the strip as a viable consumer marketplace.[100] However, reports from street level pointed to a more complex relationship. Although the centre and the strip relied on different business models, Eberhard Zeidler's design ensured that they were physically interlinked, sharing the flow of foot traffic that moved in and out of the mall and along Yonge's busy sidewalks. Rather than siphoning people away from the strip, the complex's regional pull brought them to it in increased numbers, including many of the suburban, female, and out-of-town consumers most prized by downtown businesses. Planning and market research studies in 1978 and 1979 found that 80 percent of adult women across Metro Toronto – and the same proportion of suburban mallgoers of both genders – had visited the centre since its opening; the galleria had

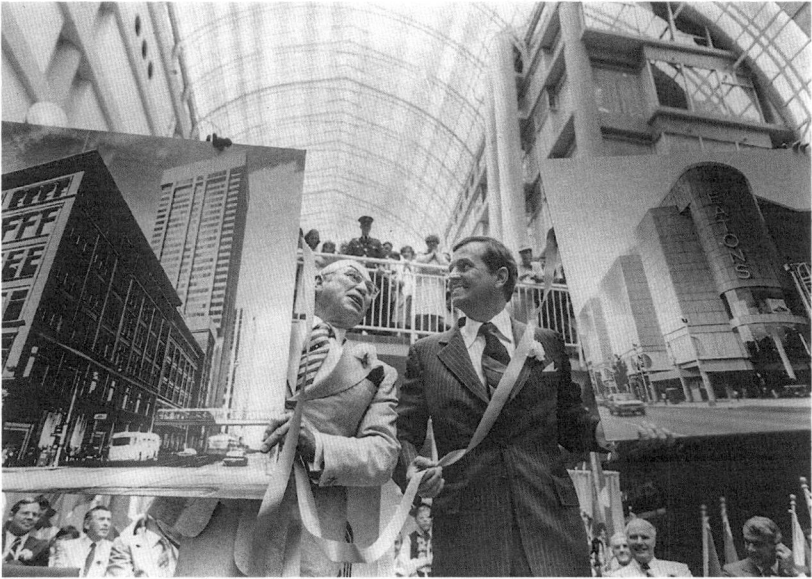

From rivals to partners. John Craig Eaton (right) and Simpson's chairman
G. Allan Burton celebrate the opening of the Eaton Centre's second phase,
including a footbridge across Queen Street to Simpson's, 1979. | Reg
Innell/*Toronto Star* 502323681 via Getty Images

eclipsed Ontario Place to become the city's most visited attraction, and
one-quarter of spending was in American dollars.[101] The impact on Yonge's
streetlife was most visible at the intersection with Dundas, which, with the
relocation of Eaton's and the new pedestrian plaza, would soon displace
Yonge and Queen as the city's busiest.[102]

Of course, more people on the street did not necessarily translate to
more money in the till; that was one lesson taught by the summer pedestrian mall. But Yonge's existing businesses seemed confident that they could
convert the crowds and positive attention brought downtown by the Eaton
Centre into value, consistently rejecting portrayals of them – and the strip
itself – as victims of redevelopment. In early 1979, as the expansion of the
galleria neared completion, reformist councillor and long-time centre critic
Alan Sparrow was booed at a meeting of the Downtown Council when he
announced that Cadillac Fairview's development was responsible for "the
destruction of Yonge Street." Continuing the exchange in a letter published
in the *Globe and Mail,* the council's president, David Walsh, reported
that the street was far from dead. On the contrary, he asserted, "the Eaton
Centre has given our downtown renewed life and confidence." As proof,

he listed a series of benefits felt on the strip during the previous two years, including new tourist traffic, busier evening shopping, and reduced rents due to the new abundance of retail space.[103] Walsh glossed over other less encouraging changes, the most visible of which was the loss of several of Yonge's few remaining mainstream retailers to the galleria. Clark Shoes, owned by long-time Downtown Council president Peter Clark, was among them, and his decision to move indoors marked not only a changing of the guard in the group, but the culmination of the strip's slow shift from mainstream shopping to entertainment and youth culture that began in the mid-twentieth century.[104]

The Private Street

Malling Yonge brought its shopping culture and public life indoors, where they flourished, but always within the limits of corporate control. Overnight, the Eaton Centre became one of downtown Toronto's busiest shared spaces, drawing people from the urban region and beyond to shop, eat and drink, socialize, rest, gawk, and stroll. It was a private building that functioned like a city street, and, as on the street outside, it was impossible to disentangle consumption from these other activities. Cadillac Fairview did not try, positioning the centre as both a marketplace and a public space. From its opening, promotion of the complex presented its enclosed streetscape as Toronto's new "Main Street," containing under its roof all the exciting and varied activities associated with downtown life.[105] The image of the mall as a space not just for shopping but *for living* was omnipresent in the print, radio, and television advertising campaigns that crafted its image in the public eye. "Life in the city starts at the centre," went the official jingle, commissioned in 1977 and later adapted into a series of television spots that showed well-dressed urbanites meeting, reading, sipping coffee, and falling in love – everything but shopping – under the galleria's glass roof.[106] This identity was reinforced by the complex's late opening hours and connections to the street, public transit, and Trinity Square.

The idea of a regional mall as an urban microcosm was not new. Whether in the suburbs or the city, the North American shopping centre was always intended to offer customers "a more perfect downtown."[107] Mall builders constructed state-of-the-art retail environments and used technology and private police to filter out the weather, clamour, and unwanted encounters of traditional commercial thoroughfares. This was particularly visible in the case of the Eaton Centre and other downtown complexes, where the street being repackaged for consumption was just a few steps away. In the view of the centre's builders, private control would allow them to improve on every aspect of the sidewalk experience, liberating consumers from all of its annoyances, whether climatic or human in origin. "Yonge Street has become a little bit too much of a hassle," explained Cadillac Fairview president Neil Wood in 1976, as the first phase of the complex neared completion. He then contrasted the frustrations of outdoor shopping with the safety and liberty that would soon be available in the centre:

> We want any woman to be able to come into the mall and feel that she isn't going to be pressed for a handout or hassled by somebody who has a religious cause or whatever. We want them to feel they've got a somewhat protected environment here. They can walk out the door onto Yonge St. if they want to experience that different kind of excitement![108]

Interestingly, though the scale and technical sophistication of the Eaton Centre were unprecedented in Toronto, Wood's objectives and gendered imagery were not. Attractiveness to middle-class female consumers had long been a key measure of retail success on Yonge, and for nearly a century Simpson's and Eaton's, like big department stores the world over, had built their own "protected environments" to offer women an alternative to the unruly street.[109]

Fifteen years into the era of the regional mall, Torontonians were accustomed to this kind of artificial urban streetscape, and along with most North Americans, they liked it. In summer 1978, a survey of twelve hundred pedestrians on and around downtown Yonge Street found a strong preference for being in the mall, even among the substantial percentage who stated that they also enjoyed the character and bargains of the strip. The things people disliked about Yonge Street – traffic noise, litter, explicit advertising, and panhandlers topped the list, as they had since the early 1970s – contrasted neatly with the positive adjectives attached to the Eaton Centre's convenient, climate-controlled, and "pleasurable" environment, particularly for older people.[110] A *Toronto Star* columnist commented on the way that the mall's amenities and location facilitated the migration of public life indoors: "Torontonians wanting to meet a friend downtown used to say, 'I'll meet you on the steps of City Hall.' Now, more often than not, they say, 'I'll meet you at the fountain in the Eaton Centre.'"[111] This came as no surprise to urban observers who were critical of the pedestrian experience available on the street. "Obviously [Torontonians] like the environment of the Galleria," wrote Jane Jacobs in her rebuttal to journalist Stephen Godfrey's takedown of the mall, adding that "one of the genuine attractions of the Eaton Centre is its civility, which is nothing to sneer at."[112]

Private policing. An Eaton Centre guard monitors the complex's state-of-the-art surveillance system, 1980. | Dick Loek/*Toronto Star* 502839111 via Getty Images

The civility that Jacobs praised was not inherent to the Eaton Centre's design but produced daily by security staff and systems that regulated how its shared spaces were used, and by whom. By the late 1970s, malls in Canada and the United States were devoting considerable resources to those questions and to combatting the financial and reputational costs of theft, loitering, and vandalism. The Eaton Centre was on the leading edge of this trend, particularly when it came to professionalization of security and the adoption of new surveillance technologies.[113] In addition to Eaton's own store detectives, the mall was patrolled by forty uniformed and plainclothes guards, headed by a former staff sergeant in the Metro Toronto police. Other supervisory roles were filled by military and law enforcement veterans. At a time when closed-circuit television was rarely used on a large scale, the complex's public spaces were watched by thirty-two cameras, all feeding into a central control room where they were monitored twenty-four hours a day and recorded for use, if necessary, in the courtroom.[114] The vast majority of people who used the centre hardly noticed their entry into this private policing regime, which despite its pervasiveness and technological sophistication was designed to interfere as little as possible in their enjoyment of the mall.

Other users, however, became keenly aware of the difference between public and private policing when they found themselves refused entry to Toronto's new Main Street, or were ejected from it. Unlike Metro police, Eaton Centre security staff did not have special powers of detention or investigation. What they did have was an up-to-the-minute surveillance system and a robust right to exclude rooted in property law, which they used daily to sort out the people and activities that were not compatible with the mall's carefully tailored version of the downtown experience. As early as April 1977, just a few months after the opening of the galleria, the developer expanded its security team and signalled the importance of keeping "undesirables" out of the complex. Over the next few years, that objective evolved into a policy of systematic exclusion of homeless people, buskers, vendors, religious proselytizers, and political protesters, all of whom were accustomed to claiming space on the street outside. Large groups of teenagers, and especially Black teenagers, profiled by security as shoplifters and troublemakers, were also targeted.[115] By 1980, Eaton Centre security was ejecting three thousand people from the premises monthly, one hundred per day, a rate that remained constant into the mid-1980s. Most of these removals followed the same pattern, with the person concerned escorted to an exit, given a notice of exclusion, and left to continue along the street, but each month hundreds of repeat or uncooperative offenders were detained until police arrived to lay trespass charges.[116]

Private policing proved more effective than law enforcement at domesticating Yonge's disorderly streetlife. Eaton Centre security staff encountered the same populations and behaviours as police on the street or the irate citizens who wrote to Toronto newspapers. Testifying in a trespass case of the mid-1980s, the complex's manager described the principal problems that his staff dealt with on a daily basis:

> We have a lot of problems with just general youth hanging out in the centre with nothing better to do ... We have problems with drunks and derelicts who try to use the centre as a place of residence ... We have problems with people trying to deal drugs from time to time and we have problems with different groups who espouse a particular philosophy or a particular political point who would try to use the centre as their forum [and] we constantly have to remove these people and keep them removed.[117]

The key difference was the efficiency of the available legal tools. Police on Yonge Street relied on a mix of negotiation and intimidation to control panhandling, loitering, and other unwanted but essentially legal behaviours. Since the 1960s, and particularly after the 1972 reform of vagrancy law, their strategy had been by necessity one of mitigation, not elimination. In contrast, Eaton Centre security had a strong legal case for excluding people on the basis of their profile – age, style of dress, visible poverty, erratic behaviour – whether or not a criminal offence had been committed. Every ten days, they removed as many people as the Toronto police made arrests during the entire so-called orgy of lawlessness that was the 1973 summer pedestrian mall.[118]

Cadillac Fairview's right to exclude was not absolute. The mixing of public and private functions that made the Eaton Centre so successful could also frustrate the developer's attempts to assert control over how its spaces were used. Public access was a central element of the development agreement signed with the City of Toronto in 1972 and subsequently built into Eberhard Zeidler's design. The streets that had been closed to build the mall were replaced with pedestrian rights-of-way, two cutting east-west through the galleria atrium at Trinity Square and at Albert Street, and another running north-south to connect to the subway.[119] Those passages effectively made the complex available twenty-four hours a day, and the idea that people could roam its indoor street on their way to and from the subway and the square became an accepted part of its operation. In at least one case, it was a successful defence against a trespass charge. Similarly, legal historian Eric Tucker has explored how labour rights and the Charter right of expression were tested in the shopping mall during the mid-1980s, as a series of legal challenges vindicated the right of Eaton's employees and their allies to run a union organizing drive in the main atrium, seen by the courts in this case to stand in for the street.[120] These victories were individually significant, but they did not set the stage for larger changes in the management of the Eaton Centre. Rigorous enforcement of property rights would continue to protect – but also circumscribe – public use of this private downtown street.

THIS CHAPTER HAS traced how, a decade after the "city of tomorrow" and twenty years from the first sketches of Project Viking, rebuilding finally came to the heart of Toronto. The second Eaton Centre assembled a new configuration of actors around what was, by that point, an old idea: leveraging Eaton's land bank to build a modern commercial centre on Yonge Street. That the retailer's properties and brand were bound up in the success of the scheme was a basic continuity with past plans, but in other respects the new centre was very much a product of the 1970s. Planned at the height of a downtown construction boom, it exemplified the corporate partnerships and new arrangements of capital that were then transforming the land development industry in Canada. It was North America's largest and most successful urban shopping mall, a category of building that barely existed in 1970 but that had been duplicated in city after city by the end of the decade. Arriving at a tumultuous moment in Toronto politics, it both shaped and was shaped by citizen opposition to densification and by the emergence of a new politics of development rooted in participatory democracy and a critique of corporate power. Rather than the great civic unifier imagined in the 1950s and 1960s, rebuilding Yonge Street proved a contested, politically fractious process that put the differing agendas of citizens, capital, and the civic administration into sharp relief.

Malling was a radical project, in the sense that it sought to fundamentally transform the urban landscape and the activities that gave it life. Inserting a shopping centre into downtown meant reorganizing property rights, business functions, mobility patterns, and public and private infrastructure within a vast area, and many of the problems faced by the centre – including holdout property owners and huge construction costs – flowed from this basic fact. Others were specific to downtown Yonge and to the political context of 1970s Toronto. The congregation of Holy Trinity saw the redevelopment process as an opportunity to advance its own vision for downtown; urban activists and reformist politicians used debates over the centre's form and impact to develop their critiques of the corporate city and to publicly promote people-oriented alternatives. These challenges moulded negotiations between Cadillac Fairview and the City of Toronto, producing substantial changes in the design of the centre, including a public square and footpaths, a new interface with the street, and the sky-lit, perpetually open galleria. Selectively embracing architectural artistry and people planning, the developer found a novel strategy for attaining its principal objective: maximizing the Eaton Centre's profitability as a marketplace and investment vehicle.

In the late 1970s, Toronto struggled to understand how the newly built Eaton Centre would relate to the street outside its doors. Would it revitalize Yonge, inspire it to change, or accelerate its decline? The complex was one of the most dramatic urban interventions of the decade, in Toronto or any other North American city, and it is unsurprising that none of the interpretations that emerged from these debates fully captured its impact on the street and downtown. Physically, it drastically transformed the built environment. Its construction levelled nearly a quarter of the strip, replacing a complex urban landscape with a single corporate mega-structure, trading brick for glass and steel, and exchanging the sidewalk for an enclosed streetscape. This significantly expanded the Yonge shopping corridor, while at the same time splitting it into two commercial worlds, each offering its own version of the downtown experience. Prosperity was not evenly distributed between the two. With its all-weather galleria, direct subway entrances, and abundance of big brands and chains, the mall was able to retain most of the new activity brought to the area; still, its economic dynamic with the strip proved to be as much complementary as competitive. Finally, the Eaton Centre reconfigured Yonge Street's public life, providing new spaces for it to thrive while narrowing its possibilities in the interest of private profit and control. It offered a new model of downtown space, publicly used but privately controlled, limited in its liberties but secured from the unpredictability and unwanted encounters of the street.

Remaking Downtown Yonge Street

Through its explorations of people planning and public space, entertainment and moral regulation, and redevelopment and corporate ambition, this book relates the story of nearly three decades of change on Toronto's Yonge Street commercial strip. It provides a historical account of a period, beginning in the 1950s and extending to the end of the 1970s, when Yonge was at the heart of efforts to reinvent downtown to meet the challenges of the modern metropolis. Depending on the observer, those challenges included not just the decentralization of people and investment, but changing demographics, the reorientation of consumer tastes and habits, and the spread of new ideas about the city. A range of downtown actors – including department stores, independent businesses, municipal politicians, and citizen activists – invested time, capital, and hopes in Yonge's transformation, working out their responses to these large structural changes in ways that were profoundly shaped by the contingencies of time and place. At almost any given moment in the postwar period, in fact, people were imagining multiple futures for Yonge Street. As a result, its remaking was a contested, messy, and at times contradictory process – and it was always public. The working out of the debates and improvement agendas of the postwar decades helped create the street as we know it today.

Power to influence the remaking of Yonge was unevenly distributed between individuals and public and private institutions. One main theme of this study is the important role played by the local state in determining the street's future. In the postwar period, a new municipal regime took hold in Toronto, one that sought to move well beyond its established role of service provision – keeping the water flowing and the streets clean – to embrace interventionist, long-range planning. This was most obvious at the level of the new Municipality of Metropolitan Toronto, tasked with planning and connecting the expanding suburbs, but the City of Toronto also shouldered new roles and responsibilities. A permanent Planning Department was established, whose focus was very much on the downtown commercial core; tens of millions of dollars were invested in building a modern City Hall and civic square. Beginning with the idea of redevelopment areas and continuing on to private-public partnerships – including most notably the Eaton Centre – municipal experts and elected officials sought to carve out an unprecedented place for local government in shaping the urban future. Early on, many of these efforts were devoted to encouraging continued investment in the heart of the city, in an effort to keep up with the dynamic suburbs and to secure tax revenues to pay for an expanding repertoire of services.

Even as the prevailing tone of politics changed in the 1960s and 1970s, the basic assumption that this kind of state action was necessary never changed. By the early 1970s, in the context of a development boom and a surge in citizen activism, the City of Toronto's focus shifted to limiting growth, or at least managing it in a politically acceptable manner. Meanwhile, planners and downtown politicians began to explore ways of protecting elements of the city – including distinctive, older shopping areas such as Yonge Street – from becoming casualties of volatile real estate markets and rebuilding at scale. This was the context in which the Yonge Street pedestrian mall and other attempts at preserving downtown's distinct urban environment were proposed. At the centre of all these interventions was a belief that the private city required public oversight to develop according to its potential. Although capital and property investment would be the engines of growth, local government had a crucial role to play in guiding the resulting change. Whether it possessed the tools to do so was another matter. Another recurrent theme in this study is that of the municipal state testing the boundaries of its limited powers to craft the future: attempting to enlist private capital to grow the tax base through redevelopment; using targeted licensing bylaws and fire and health inspections to shut down businesses deemed immoral by citizen activists; trying and failing to create new public space by closing a major thoroughfare to cars.

The power of the state was influential in more mundane ways. The day-to-day procedural activities of the municipal government – police patrols, inspections, enforcement of zoning regulations – played their part in remaking the street. Pedestrianizing Yonge Street, for example, enjoyed a great deal of public support, but it was also obstructed by elements of the municipal bureaucracy that saw it as disruptive of a careful balance of established uses. In the end, the summer pedestrian mall was undone as much by the City's incapacity to manage the new public spaces it created as by citizen opposition to the street's boisterous or unsafe atmosphere. On the strip, the police regulated how street space was used, and by whom, each day. High-profile operations including morality squad raids and drug arrests captured the most press, but the daily negotiations of informal policing were equally important. In the early 1970s, even as City officials blustered about the undesirability of the sex industry on Yonge, patrol officers were reaching their own pragmatic agreements with the owners and employees of body rub parlours to ensure that they operated with a minimum of conflict or disturbance. This complicity, however, had clear limits, breaking down overnight when public scrutiny of police and their activities on the strip was highest.

Another theme is people power. In the context of the robust civil society engagement of the long 1960s, I find that debates over Yonge Street played a mobilizing role analogous to fights over expressways and tower construction, with the crucial difference that downtown it was not homes or communities that were at stake, so much as a vision of what the city could or should be. Young community activists, suburban churchgoers, working-class Portuguese Canadians – a range of Torontonians – made their first forays into local politics during the 1960s and 1970s with letters to the editor, demonstrations, and deputations on the future of Yonge Street. Many others spoke out on the subject as part of a larger process of political engagement that began with other contested urban issues. As a result, citizen perspectives, wherever they were on the political spectrum, had a significant impact on Yonge Street during the postwar decades. By no means did citizens always lead in downtown transformation; but at the same time, they were rarely followers, and never bystanders. They were, in the final analysis, not a cohesive public so much as a series of vocal minorities and interest groups wielding an influence well beyond their numbers.

People power could be reactive and obstructionist – citizens saying "No!" – but it could also be creative. The Yonge Street pedestrian mall, as much as it was inspired by the international circulation of planning ideas, was propelled into reality by the engagement of a diverse coalition of citizen groups, including small Yonge Street merchants, hip youth, and anti-pollution activists. Meanwhile, successive groups of citizens forced their way into negotiations between the City and Eaton's, halting the Eaton

Centre project twice, and each time significantly changing its form and impact. More broadly, ideas of urban citizenship and democracy permeated discussions of Yonge Street, often serving to justify, shape, or frustrate the various futures that people envisioned for it. People asserted ownership over downtown and a right to have a say in determining its future. The image of Yonge as an essentially democratic public space, "a street for all the people," was employed on all sides of the battle over sexual entertainment. Debates over the Eaton Centre project, Sin Strip, and the pedestrian mall led to invitations for citizen comment and some of Toronto's first public planning consultations. Polls and surveys became key tools as businesses, politicians, and other actors attempted to rally or capture public opinion to support their plans for transformation. But though a range of people subscribed to this local version of the North American downtown ideal – that downtown was for everyone – this did not flatten difference or erase existing power structures. Where people power could influence the process, it did; where it could not, it ceded place to other types of power.

Nowhere is this clearer than in the role played by businesses and capital in this account. The story of Eaton's brief career as a land developer cuts to the heart of the influence of corporate power on the development of Yonge Street and the postwar city more generally. As we look over three decades of change on Yonge Street, it is difficult to overstate the importance of investment decisions and corporate ambition in determining its fate. As much as Yonge was seen as a public space or thoroughfare, its principal function was commercial: it was a marketplace for goods and services second to none in the city, although it certainly had its challengers by the 1960s. The marketplace attracted the crowds, and the crowds created profits for those who owned or rented access to the street. This simple fact motivated the entrepreneurs who shifted the strip's focus to entertainment from the 1940s or to commercialized sex in the 1970s; it was this function that Eaton's, and later Cadillac Fairview, sought to exploit with the construction of the country's largest and most modern shopping complex. Throughout the period, the City set the parameters for urban development, and organized citizen groups sought to limit its excesses or democratize it, but the primary source of dynamism remained private investment and the capitalist urban process.

Even before its completion, the Eaton Centre was refashioning downtown Yonge. By the late 1960s, the centre and other redevelopment proposals had vastly increased real estate speculation on the street, contributing to a volatile market whose bouts of inertia and expansion had far-reaching impacts on this key urban space. Properties changed hands frequently, and new value was created seemingly from thin air as Eaton's and its competitors snapped up Yonge Street's aging retail landscape piece by piece. This shift in ownership patterns helped create a pool of commercial buildings that were essentially held in stasis, without renovation or improvement, in anticipation of sale for redevelopment. These speculative properties proved well suited for short-term use as sex cinemas and body rub parlours. Their erasure was required to make space for downtown planning on a new scale. The creation of the Eaton Centre required the demolition of blocks of older buildings, unlocking the potential to install denser, more profitable constructions but also, for a crucial half-decade, further reducing the pool of premises suitable for viable independent businesses.

The Eaton Centre also cornered the market in ideas. Its long and fractious planning process gave its planners ample time to address critiques, and to capture what seemed best in the creative downtown politics of the time and incorporate it into the design. Once built, the centre not only duplicated many functions of the historic strip's businesses – retail, cinema, dining – but also appeared to provide a better, more controlled version of the street itself. The sex industry, discount stores, diners, and grindhouse cinemas might populate Yonge, but they could not afford to relocate to the new mall. Nor would they have been accepted as tenants if they could. Like the Yonge Street pedestrian mall of the early 1970s, the Eaton Centre's multi-level shopping concourse was free to enter: it included people-friendly benches and fountains, and it offered entertainment ranging from fashion shows to music. Unlike the public mall, it was privately managed and secured with a state-of-the-art security system aimed at excluding undesirable users – including the young people who flocked to Yonge in summer. The Eaton Centre was the perfect embodiment of the commercial success that many observers had hoped to see in the pedestrian mall, but with only a nod to its public objectives, or to the hopes for the urban future that a broad public had invested in the experiment. The unruly downtown shopping street had been perfected – at least from the perspective of a secured return on capital – through being privatized and domesticated.

Finally, Yonge Street emerges in this account as an actor in its own right. Its aging built landscape, its diversity, and its essential intractability inspired the improvement agendas explored here, but could also frustrate them. Change always proved more difficult than imagined, less controllable, more chaotic. Interventions were adjusted to circumstances, and actions had unintended consequences. Modernist hopes for aesthetic and functional coherence were long thwarted by the street's small lots and complex pattern of property ownership. The final configuration of the Eaton Centre, hugging Holy Trinity and its square and wrapping around the hulking mass of Old City Hall, is a testimony to the inability of advocates of comprehensive planning to fully realize their modernizing goals. Schemes to widen the street or to remove traffic from it were complicated by the delicate balance of uses that had developed on pavement and sidewalk over a century of crowds and commerce. And visions of a moral "clean sweep" of the sex industry, though powerful in motivating legal action, were more destructive than restorative – and never fully implemented. In this study of a contested urban space, Yonge Street emerges as the changing product of layers of ideas, networks, and different forms of power, and in that respect a microcosm of the modern city.

The Street Today

This book introduced Yonge Street with a short flâneur's tour on foot. A similar trip down its sidewalks today reveals much that is new but also continuities, as patterns from the past resurface to shape its transformation. Like the city around it, Yonge has never experienced stasis. If in the postwar decades it arose from the industrial landscape of Toronto's harbour, in the twenty-first century its beginnings are both more refined and more self-conscious. Its foot at the lakeshore is now marked by a brass plaque declaring it the "longest street in the world," a legacy of the flurry of imaginative promotion and celebration that accompanied 180 Years Yonge Week in 1975. Surrounding that marker is a landscape in transition, acre after acre now being repurposed for residential and commercial development. Proponents of Pier 27 and other projects slated for this area imagine a "minicity" that is a far cry from the parking lots and industry that made this area such an unprepossessing start for our postwar tour of the street.[1]

North of these newly inhabited spaces, the tour takes our stroller underneath two major metropolitan infrastructure projects dating from the postwar era. First are the somewhat forbidding spaces under the now crumbling Gardiner Expressway, completed at great expense in 1964 as a key element in Metro Toronto's urban expressway plan. This east-west commuter corridor is one of the most visible legacies of auto-centric infrastructure planning in the densely built core. It also, however, testifies to paths not taken: a connection to the southern tip of the unbuilt Spadina Expressway and an eastern extension of the route were left uncompleted, symbolizing by their absence the 1970s move away from expressway building that coincided with the Yonge Street pedestrianization experiments. Just beyond the Gardiner, the city's railyards, substantially adapted since the 1960s to house the GO commuter rail and bus system, offer another point of entry into the city from its fringes. Both the expressway and the GO hub speak to the reality of Toronto in the twenty-first century: that of a sprawling, polycentric region of 6 million inhabitants – 2.7 million in the city itself – in which the old downtown remains a major hub for work, transportation, and consumption.

The rebuilding of downtown has continued apace since the 1970s and the Eaton Centre's massive impact on Yonge's form and function. The street has experienced significant redevelopment over the last forty years, particularly in the zones bookending the main commercial strip. Today, the absorption of the southern stretch of the street into the office and financial services district, begun in the 1950s, is virtually complete. With a few exceptions – several stately nineteenth-century buildings and a few incongruous patches of low-rise retail – most of Yonge Street south of Queen is now a concrete and glass canyon flanked by some of the most valuable office space in the city. Meanwhile, at the north end of the strip, a residential development boom is remaking the College Street intersection and environs. The College Park residential and commercial complex, built in the 1970s around the former Eaton's store, is now dwarfed by the seventy-eight storeys of Canada's largest condominium tower, located just to the south. Moving north, block after block of the strip's low-rise retail landscape is punctuated by new condominium towers, construction hoardings, or pits for tower footings. The fortunes of developers continue to be made on Yonge Street.

The idea that thousands of people would be living – or want to live – within spitting distance of downtown Yonge is itself very much a product of the era I focus on in this study. A natural outgrowth of the era of people planning was a revisioning of downtown not just as the centre of the metropolitan region and a place of business, but as a community. This idea, already evident in the debates regarding the Yonge mall, became a central tenet of the reform urban planning of the 1970s and was enshrined in the City's *Central Area Plan* in 1976. The ongoing return to the central city and planning policies that encouraged residential densification helped to effectively double the population of downtown to 200,000 residents between 1976 and 2016. The rising value of downtown land and the apparently insatiable demand for upmarket condominiums have only intensified this trend. With more than a thousand storeys of mostly luxury condominium residences proposed or in construction on the Yonge Street corridor from College north to Bloor Street, some observers argue that the process is moving too fast. In 2016, Toronto's chief planner suggested that it might be time to "hit the pause button" on redevelopment, and downtown politicians have periodically floated the idea of a construction moratorium very similar to that proposed for apartments and office towers by the newly elected reformist administration in 1973.[2]

Since the 1970s, the former Eaton's lands have been entirely rebuilt. The centralization of control achieved through the long and costly land assembly process not only paved the way for a shopping galleria and department store, but also primed the rest of the superblock for transformation according to market demand. Over several decades, the west side of the superblock has been filled in with a million-square-foot office complex (1983), a luxury hotel (1991), and a combined commercial and educational building connected to Ryerson University (2006). Many of these uses echo those set out in Project Viking and the 1966 Eaton Centre, although they lack the aesthetic coherence so central to those schemes. Meanwhile, Trinity Square was completed in the early 1980s and continues to provide a popular island of green space in the heart of downtown, surrounding the still vital Holy Trinity Church. In stark contrast, the other "people-friendly" features that activists fought to have included in Eberhard Zeidler's original design – benches and trees on Yonge, direct entry into retail stores from the street – are gone. Doors opening onto the street have been converted into window displays, and false facades down the length of the mall have cut the sidewalk width nearly in half, with the intent of channelling as much foot traffic as possible into the profitable galleria. Today's centre presents Yonge Street with a blank wall, reminiscent less of the "mall connected to the street grid" imagined by Zeidler and citizen activists than of an upscale version of the archetypal suburban shopping centre.[3]

The Eaton Centre's commercialized public-private space remains a runaway commercial success for tenants and Cadillac Fairview. However, little today connects it to the retailer that made its construction possible and was for decades its most significant tenant. In 1997, after years of speculation about its declining profitability and competitiveness, Canada's greatest retailer filed for bankruptcy. The positive corporate image that Eaton's had worked so hard to preserve could not stave off failure in the face of broadening competition and the constant drain of overexpansion. Stores across Canada were sold off, including the Toronto Eaton Centre flagship, permanently closed by its new owner in 2002. There was considerable pathos as the massive statue of a seated Timothy Eaton, which was transported with much pomp and ceremony to the new store in 1976, was removed from the Eaton Centre lobby to its new home in the Royal Ontario Museum. After years as a Sears department store, the former

Eaton's premises were taken over by Nordstrom in 2016, one of a small number of North American department store chains that have weathered difficult economic times by focusing on luxury fashion and accessories. Simpson's has similarly been replaced. Since the 1990s, its elegant main store has been occupied by its successor, the Hudson's Bay Company, and more recently by its higher-end affiliate Saks Fifth Avenue. Whereas Canada's last surviving major department store chain faces an uncertain future, the former Simpson's store and tower complex are now part of Cadillac Fairview's substantial downtown property portfolio, raising the possibility of further renovation and integration with the Eaton Centre across the street. In the twenty-first century, the department store giants, responsible for the demise of many a smaller competitor in their nineteenth- and twentieth-century heyday, have in their turn been edged out of the market by big box retailers and specialty stores, and their prime real estate converted to more profitable uses.

In fact, today's stroller would be hard pressed to find many familiar landmarks on Yonge's commercial strip. Music hotspot Friar's Tavern became a Hard Rock Cafe, before being converted into a Shopper's Drug Mart; Sam the Record Man has been replaced by a Ryerson University student centre; Clark Shoes by a Burger King. Of the watering holes and music venues of the 1960s and 1970s, Zanzibar Tavern is the last holdout, still eking out an existence with strip shows and the occasional star turn as a Hollywood movie set. As predicted forty years ago by the embattled Downtown Council, in the long run many of Yonge's independent retailers and service providers have disappeared or moved farther north up the strip, replaced by chain outlets better able to capitalize on the street's crowds and pay its sky-high retail rents. Most are big American or multinational brands, reflecting a Canadian retail sector more than ever dominated by corporations whose reach and economies of scale are truly global. Those national chains that have survived have done so by adopting the same marketing and production strategies as their foreign competitors, making them effectively indistinguishable.[4]

Structurally, certain elements of the strip remain intact. Many of the century-old buildings that housed Yonge's small shops and services for decades are still standing. Their persistence speaks to the cost and difficulty of land assembly on this stretch of Yonge, the more restrictive zoning regulations that followed the Eaton Centre development, and a wave of heritage designations since the 1980s. Today, forty Yonge Street buildings between King and College are listed as City heritage properties, a measure that makes them more difficult to tear down for new construction. This has not, however, prevented their interiors from being gutted and re-adapted through what one architect referred to as "urban taxidermy," offering a historic streetscape diorama that masks the stripped modern spaces within.[5] A Starbuck's café has taken over the ground floor of the Victorian Oddfellows Hall; a sober 1940s bank building is now home to a cellphone store. Meanwhile, buildings with less storied histories have been covered over with metal and glass facades and corporate branding. One side effect of this process has been that up and down Yonge Street, whole buildings have in many places been taken over by a single tenant, dramatically reducing the density of uses – offices, apartments, secondary businesses – that our visitor to the strip observed decades ago.

Consolidation of a modern corporate shopping area is most advanced around the intersection of Yonge and Dundas, now the busiest commercial crossroads in the city and the most visibly changed section of the strip. The north entrance to the Eaton Centre dominates the corner and is the main reason for the shift of shopping and pedestrian activity north from Queen and Yonge. Diagonally opposite but very much in alignment with the centre's modernist aesthetic, the northeast corner block was entirely rebuilt in the 2000s as an L-shaped theatre, commercial, and restaurant complex called, successively, Metropolis, Toronto Life Square, and 10 Dundas Street East. Like the centre whose style it mimics, this private redevelopment project was facilitated by extensive municipal action, in this case the expropriation of key land parcels by the City.[6] And like the Eaton Centre, it has been blasted by urbanists and architects for its uninventive industrial exterior – "horrorchitecture," according to one critic – yet it remains immensely popular.[7] The complex forms the central platform for an accumulation of gaudy billboards, gigantic television screens, and corporate logos that now covers three of the intersection's four corners, advertising Yonge's shopping and entertainment possibilities even more comprehensively – and inescapably – than the neon signage of a previous era. If in the 1970s comparisons to Times Square were used to identify Yonge with criminality and sleaze, today, more often than not, they refer to this miniature version of New York City's sanitized – but still crassly commercial – "electric pandemonium."[8]

On Yonge Street, the local has given way to the global. Those critics of the street's rebuilding who in the 1960s and 1970s saw it as a victory for the corporate city were in a way correct. The trend on the street, as described here, has been toward the centralization of control over the urban landscape in the hands of real estate giants such as Cadillac Fairview and Brookfield Properties, and the replacement of diversity with more profitable but also more homogeneous consumer opportunities. Yonge today provides *more* than ever before – more retailers, more entertainment, more sales – but few of its offerings are substantially different from those available in Chicago's Loop, London's Oxford Street, or a suburban shopping mall in any successful globalized city. In this respect, the street's story echoes those of other successful Main Street commercial areas across North America and the world. This change has not, however, dampened enthusiasm for downtown Yonge as a shopping destination. The many observers who from the late 1960s contended that redevelopment would curb its human vitality or even "kill" it – often imagining a windswept, empty street – have been proved wrong. Despite its new clothes, Yonge today is as much a vital marketplace and an exciting (or frustrating) pedestrian street as ever. The renovated Yonge and Dundas intersection is now Toronto's busiest, its sidewalks crowded with more than 100,000 visitors each day, and more in the summer.[9] People continue to frequent Yonge's modernized shopping core at all hours of the day, and in that sense it remains one of the most successful elements of Toronto's public realm.

It is a public realm whose boundaries have shifted. Another significant change is that from the public to the private, which can also be understood as the enclosure and commercialization of urban space. This study touches at several points on the history of the various regulatory regimes used to manage Yonge as a public space. It explores how ideas of the street and its economic, social, or civic functions collided with the reality of competing uses and expectations on the Yonge pedestrian mall, and how the Eaton Centre's privately managed, publicly accessible galleria was built to avoid those same conflicts. The lessons of that era have not been lost on today's planners. The final major addition to Yonge's streetscape since the 1970s is Dundas Square, an acre-sized plaza at the southeast corner of Yonge and Dundas. Completed in 2002 as part of the same downtown regeneration initiative that produced 10 Dundas East, it offers seating, washrooms, fountains, and wireless internet. The square is a natural meeting place, and in warm weather it hosts daily and nightly events ranging from protest marches to concerts to fairs.

Dundas Square, like the Eaton Centre two decades before, represents a new model for urban public space. It is a public-private partnership managed by an arm's-length board made up of City officials, citizens, and representatives of downtown institutions, a governance structure very similar to the committees that ran the 1970s pedestrian mall. Permissible and non-permissible uses – the latter category includes smoking, unlicensed vending, and artistic performance without a permit – are set out clearly in a dedicated municipal bylaw.[10] Private security and surveillance technologies, paid for through event fees, enforce those rules and in doing so create a much more circumscribed environment than the classic city street. The contrast with the other three corners of the intersection, often crowded with buskers, evangelists, and leafleteers, is noticeable. In her account of the square's genesis, sociologist Evelyn Ruppert describes it as a place that exemplifies the "secure, consumer, and aesthetic city" imagined by today's planning professionals; local activists have protested it as part of the creeping privatization of public space.[11] If this study is any guide, Dundas Square is also the product of the debates of an earlier era that established an obvious public desire for people space downtown and offered a new corporate model for creating and managing it.

Other themes from the past are inscribed within Yonge's ongoing transformation. One that recurs regularly is danger. Downtown Yonge remains a site where Toronto negotiates its fears about urban insecurity, where crimes that might occupy the spotlight only briefly in other parts of town become the focus of emotive media coverage and public soul searching. In 1977, the murder of shoeshine boy Emanuel Jaques riveted attention on Sin Strip, provoking political mobilization, a renewed citizen-led morality campaign, and repressive action by City authorities against sex shops and, soon after, Toronto's gay community. In the twenty-first century, it is gun violence that captures public attention and maintains Yonge's reputation as a danger zone. In the most widely publicized incident fifteen-year-old Jane Creba was shot and killed at the height of the street's 2005 Boxing Day sales, victim of crossfire that erupted after an argument between two groups of young men. Her tragic and pointless death triggered public anger and anxious calls for a police response, resulting in one of the largest murder investigations in the city's history, involving dozens of officers, undercover surveillance, and more than 250,000 wiretap intercepts.[12]

Once again, a tragic murder that promised to unify the city also revealed deep divisions. In 2005, as in 1977, a single crime with a young victim was seized upon as an example of a larger social problem – in this case, gang violence – and used to justify a massive police response. The rhetoric was much the same, too. The detective in charge of the Creba investigation proclaimed just a few days after her death that Toronto had "finally lost its innocence," echoing almost word for word similar pronouncements made in the Emanuel Jaques case.[13] The explicit homophobia of the 1970s was replaced with a subtler racism, in which attacks on gang members – Creba was white, her accused killers Black – were broadened to criticism of the city's large Jamaican Canadian community. Of course, Black Torontonians were already intensely aware of the costs of gun violence. Creba's murder came at the end of a year – media dubbed it the "Year of the Gun" – that saw a record 359 shootings and 52 gun-related homicides in Toronto. The victims of that year's violence were overwhelmingly African Canadian men, and most were shot well away from downtown crowds in the city's low-income inner suburbs.[14] None had provoked a similar outpouring of public grief or anywhere near the same commitment of police resources.

Another persistent theme is nostalgia. This book tracks how in the postwar decades Torontonians expressed attachment to an earlier version of the street, in many cases hearkening back to an idealized downtown (and a city) characterized by public propriety, social cohesion, and safety. They contrasted this image with unwelcome changes occurring at the time, including the development of youth culture, the mushrooming of sex shops, and Yonge's general orientation toward popular entertainment. Expressed in this way, and often anchored to particular structures or businesses, popular understandings of the past had a major influence on downtown politics. Over time, those understandings changed, without weakening the strength of the attachment. Today, the version of the street that people decried fifty years ago – the glitzy, loud, neon-lit strip – is itself widely nostalgized in the films, poems, and journalistic musings of later generations of Torontonians.[15] Photos of downtown Yonge in the postwar decades outnumber those of any other street or period on the popular Vintage Toronto Facebook group, where a community of 130,000 reflects on change and personal memories of the city's past. Among the many people who decry the takeover of Yonge and Dundas by big brands, condos, and billboards, the 1960s and 1970s in particular are held up as a period when the street was more exciting and freer – when it was "cool."[16] Even the strip's "marvellously sleazy" sex shops are singled out for fond remembrance, as in one recent memoir of Yonge's punk music scene, although in most narratives they continue to be portrayed as a principal cause of the street's decline.[17] These shifting patterns of nostalgia and commemoration highlight that there have always been multiple histories of Yonge Street and that they continue to influence how people see the city and their place in it today.

The power of these public attachments to the past was made plain in 2007 when, after more than forty years on the strip, music store Sam the Record Man closed its doors. Ryerson University's proposed redevelopment of the site was very nearly derailed by public outcry over the loss of this iconic business, which so many people in Toronto and the wider region remember as their point of entry into the world of pop music and record culture. A citizen campaign quickly emerged, calling for the university and the municipal government to preserve Sam's trademark sign, a two-storey pair of spinning records illuminated in red neon. Within a few days, more than ten thousand people had shown support for online "Save the Sign" petitions, in many cases justifying their participation with personal memories of the store. After years of debate and vacillation, this campaign led to the City mounting the iconic neon sign on a public building facing onto Dundas Square, where it adds a historical element to the clamour of advertising and television screens.[18] Once again, the old Yonge Street has resurfaced to add value and cultural continuity to the new. Similarly, as the sandblasted and otherwise restored Old City Hall nears the end of five decades as a provincial courthouse, a new public discussion has begun about its adaptive re-use. Citizen voices unmistakeably favour keeping the building whole and in the public realm, and proposals very similar to those advanced by the Friends of Old City Hall in the 1960s – museum and community centre, among others – have been making the rounds.[19]

The debates over planning, development, and public space that defined the period studied here have not been resolved; instead, they continue to reappear with new participants and updated stakes. Just as they did in 1955 or 1975, in the twenty-first century people view Yonge Street through the dual lens of problem and possibility. As I researched this book, the old refrain that "downtown Yonge isn't what it used to be" re-entered common use in Toronto, this time in reference not to diminished sales or sleazy entertainment, but to the loss of diversity and vitality created by the breakneck speed of redevelopment, and most of all the construction of condominium towers along the street.[20] In 2016 and 2017, City officials and property owners clashed over the designation of Yonge from College to Bloor Street as a Heritage Conservation District, a measure designed both to recognize its long history and to define the terms on which private redevelopment can reshape its future.[21] Meanwhile, the Downtown Yonge Business Improvement Association, successor to the 1970s Downtown Council, invited the people of Toronto to participate in reimagining the street and released a report calling for Toronto to "build a great Yonge Street" through investment in pedestrian improvements and cultural programming. In early 2021, the City of Toronto adopted "yongeTOmorrow," a post-pandemic street redesign that has revived many key features of the 1970s pedestrian mall debates, including hopes for retail revitalization, calls for fewer cars and more people space – and trenchant opposition from the strip's largest property owners.[22] Yonge today remains a street in transformation, a dynamic commercial corridor and public space whose story is intertwined with that of the larger city. It continues to fulfill its role as a connector, not just of people and livelihoods, but also of past, present, and imagined futures.

Notes

The Street and the City

1 "Week of Cakes, Drums for City's Birthday," *Toronto Star,* August 30, 1975; "Super Candle Planned," *Toronto Sun,* August 21, 1975; "180 Years Yonge," *Globe and Mail,* September 6, 1975.

2 "Downtown: 180 Years Yonge," *Toronto Star,* August 26, 1975.

3 "Retailers Use Past to Help Yonge St. Future," *Toronto Star,* August 4, 1975.

4 Scadding, *Toronto of Old,* 376–524; William Kilbourn, *Toronto Remembered: A Celebration of the City* (Toronto: Stoddart, 1984), 21.

5 "Recalling the Wolves ...," *Globe and Mail,* September 6, 1975.

6 "Sex Industry Not Invited to Yonge Party," *Toronto Star,* August 29, 1975.

7 There is a substantial historiography on the postwar remaking of downtowns in the United States. Key works include Isenberg, *Downtown America;* Cohen, *Saving America's Cities;* Teaford, *The Rough Road;* and Frieden and Sagalyn, *Downtown, Inc.* In contrast, there is little scholarly work on the trajectories of Canadian downtowns in the second half of the twentieth century. Poitras, "Downtowns, Past and Present," 3–5, provides a brief overview, and throughout this book I cite studies on related themes – urban renewal, planning, and citizen activism, among others – that have been helpful in framing my research.

8 The diversity of postwar suburban history is captured in Kruse and Sugrue, *The New Suburban History;* and Harris and Larkham, *Changing Suburbs.* On Canadian suburbanization, see Harris, *Creeping Conformity;* and on manufacturing and decentralization, see Walker and Lewis, "Beyond the Crabgrass Frontier," 3–19.

9 Lizabeth Cohen traces this shift in "From Town Center to Shopping Center," 1050–81. For a Canadian case study, see Bunting and Millward, "A Tale of Two CBDs I," 139–66.

10 Teaford, *The Metropolitan Revolution,* 3.

11 Tracy Neumann does an excellent job of situating this traffic between cities in the context of larger transatlantic planning networks in *Remaking the Rust Belt,* esp. 1–44. Also see Saulnier and Ewan, *Another Global City.*

12 On the discourse of urban decline in postwar America, see Beauregard, *Voices of Decline*.

13 "Keeping the Aging Heart of the City Beating," *Globe and Mail*, March 26, 1962.

14 Winter, *London's Teeming Streets*, 1. On the organism as an enduring image of the city, see Langer, "Sociology – Four Images of Urban Diversity," 97–118.

15 One work that set the postwar agenda for curing the heart of the city was Gruen, *The Heart of Our Cities: The Urban Crisis*. On the flexible language of blight and decay, see Fogelson, *Downtown*, 317–79.

16 See Filion, Charney, and Weber, "Downtowns That Work," 25–27.

17 On the challenges of "relocation," see Harris and Moore, "Planning Histories and Practices of Circulating Urban Knowledge," 1503.

18 The principal reference on this active definition of urban space remains Lefebvre, *The Production of Space*. Also see Gunn, "The Spatial Turn," 1–14.

19 An important study that moves beyond the downtown historiography's focus on political and corporate elites and regime politics is Isenberg, *Downtown America*.

20 Charles Tilly makes an argument for the value of this kind of approach in "What Good Is Urban History?," 702–19.

21 Subject clipping files compiled by the Toronto Public Library and the City of Toronto Archives were immensely helpful; so too was the availability of the *Toronto Star* and the *Globe and Mail* in word-searchable – if imperfect – digital databases. Other publications, including the *Telegram* and *Toronto Sun*, magazines, and the alternative press, were found on microform and in print. Television and radio news from the era is less accessible, although the Canadian Broadcasting Corporation's online digital archive and YouTube yielded a few gems.

22 Canadian Facts, "A Study of the Attitudes of Metropolitan Toronto Adults towards the Proposed Eaton Centre, 1966," Toronto Reference Library, 301.1543 C12. The changing postwar landscape for the press is set out in Royal Commission on Newspapers, *Report of the Royal Commission* (Ottawa: Ministry of Supply and Services, 1981), 63–85.

23 For example, Toronto newspaper circulation in 1974 was as follows: *Globe and Mail* 141,330; *Toronto Star* 403,505; and *Toronto Sun* 101,372. Audit Bureau of Circulations, *ABC Factbook 1975/76* (Toronto: ABC, 1976), 84.

24 Phillip Gordon Mackintosh makes this point in *Newspaper City*, esp. ch. 1.

25 For an excellent essay on Yonge Street and Toronto on film, see Pevere, "Flickering City," 19–66. On Yonge and Toronto in literature, see Lavender-Harris, *Imagining Toronto*.

Chapter 1: Making Downtown Yonge Street

1 On Sir George Yonge's patchy record as a colonial administrator and MP, see Nick Dall, "Dead End," *Globe and Mail*, February 27, 2021.

2 One example is "Yonge Street L. Ontario Shewing the Communications from York to Lake Simcoe with a Project for Settling the French Royalists, D.W. Smith, Act. Sur. Gen. (1797?)," Archives of Ontario (AO), A-15, AO 1406.

3 On the transition from imperial outposts to settler colonies, see Greer, *Property and Dispossession*, 5–11.

4 The apt term "government village" is from Careless, *Toronto to 1918*, 43–69.
5 See, for example, Ann Jameson, *Winter Studies and Summer Rambles in Canada* (London: Saunders and Oatley, 1838), 2.
6 Scadding, *Toronto of Old*, 376.
7 On retailing in Victorian Toronto, see Santink, *Timothy Eaton*, 39–57, 67.
8 "Saturday Night on Yonge Street," *Globe*, October 24, 1881.
9 "Sunday Night Promenades," *Globe*, October 20, 1879. This critique became much more pronounced in subsequent decades, as Carolyn Strange explores in *Toronto's Girl Problem*.
10 On the temperance debate then ongoing in Toronto, see Sendbuehler, "Battling 'the Bane of Our Cities,'" 30–48. On moral order, see Weaver, "'Tomorrow's Metropolis' Revisited," 456–77.
11 Fogelson, *Downtown*, 9–43.
12 A keyword search of Toronto newspapers helps to track the arrival of the concept. Mentions of "downtown" – and its counterparts "uptown" and "suburb" – rise from a handful in the 1860s to hundreds annually after 1905 and to thousands by the 1920s.
13 On the emergence of the business district, see Gad, Buchanan, and Holdsworth, "Commerce in the Core," 153–54.
14 Santink, *Timothy Eaton*, 78–117.
15 Belisle, *Retail Nation*, 15–30.
16 Santink, *Timothy Eaton*, 223.
17 "Getting on Yonge Street," *Globe*, March 19, 1910.
18 "A Yonge Street Landmark," *Globe*, July 23, 1908.
19 On this process, see especially Sewell, *Women and the Everyday City*.
20 Strange, *Toronto's Girl Problem*, 23–24, 117–43.
21 Moore, "Movie Palaces," 7.
22 See, for example, Pringle and Booth, "Yonge St., King to Queen Sts., Looking N. from Canadian Pacific Building (1912)," Toronto Reference Library, Baldwin Collection, X 65-201.
23 Brian Bellasis, "Yonge Street," *Globe*, November 2, 1912.
24 On this ideal, see Isenberg, *Downtown America*, 4–6.
25 "Christmas Shoppers," *Globe*, December 24, 1906.
26 "Swarming Christmas Crowds Transform Downtown Toronto," *Globe*, December 21, 1925; Bellasis, "Yonge Street."
27 Lorinc et al., *The Ward*.
28 Bellasis, "Yonge Street."
29 Penfold, "The Eaton's Santa Claus Parade," 1–28.
30 This is a constant theme in the discourse of political and business elites from the Victorian era onward. See, for example, "Montreal Looks at Toronto," *Toronto Star*, August 27, 1937.
31 Gad and Holdsworth, "Corporate Capitalism," 212–31; Gad and Holdsworth, "Large Office Buildings," 19–26.
32 "Downtown Toronto Is Now Experiencing a Wonderful Boom," *Globe*, December 3, 1927.
33 Lemon, "Plans for Early 20th-Century Toronto," 11–31.

34 "Says Yonge St. Shabby Has Mean Shop Fronts," *Toronto Star,* January 31, 1927.

35 Report of City Architect re: Arcading Yonge Street, Nov. 13, 1928, City of Toronto Archives (CTA), F200-1512-469; "A Great Problem for Yonge Street Merchants," *Globe,* April 6, 1909.

36 "Retail Merchants to Make Protest," *Globe,* October 1, 1912; "Yonge St. Men Put Up Fight," *Globe,* September 21, 1921; "Make Objection to Assessment," *Globe,* September 29, 1921.

37 On the city's political culture, see Lemon, *Toronto since 1918,* 31. On the "service city," see Monkkonen, *America Becomes Urban.*

38 Harris and Luymes, "The Growth of Toronto."

39 "Idea of Parade Is 'Shop at Home,'" *Globe,* May 15, 1922; "Definite Plan to Build Trade," *Globe,* September 16, 1921.

40 Davies, "Reckless Walking," 124; Lemon, *Toronto since 1918,* 45.

41 On this process, see Norton, *Fighting Traffic;* and Mackintosh, *Newspaper City.*

42 Lemon, "Plans for Early 20th-Century Toronto," 18.

43 "Police Chief Is Willing to Confer at Any Time on Parking Problem," *Globe,* December 10, 1928; Simpson's display ad, *Globe,* April 27, 1925.

44 CTPB (City of Toronto Planning Board), *Core Area Task Force,* 154.

45 F.H. Leacy, *Historical Statistics of Canada,* 2nd ed (Ottawa: Statistics Canada, 1983). On Toronto suburbanization, see Harris, *Creeping Conformity.*

46 Rose, *Governing Metropolitan Toronto,* remains the best account of the inception and functions of Metro Toronto in this period.

47 Larry Smith & Co., Toronto: Preliminary Report, Vol. I & II, Feb. 17, 1954, AO, F229-271-1, B381767 (Smith Report, AO); *Financial Post,* November 5, 1955, cited in Penfold, "'Are We to Go Literally?,'" 9.

48 See, for example, "Asks 1-Way Streets Businessman May Run for City Council," *Toronto Star,* October 4, 1953.

49 The best account of this process is Young, "Searching for a Better Way," 84–138.

50 "Main Drag Real Pitfall for Unwary," *Globe and Mail,* August 17, 1951; "Downtown Signs Out by Dec 31," *Globe and Mail,* November 1, 1951.

51 "Girls, Bands, Floats to Help Put 'Old Lady Yonge St.' on Her Feet," *Toronto Star,* October 15, 1954.

52 Data drawn from CTPB, *Core Area Task Force,* 97–119, 398.

53 Metropolitan Toronto Planning Board, *Shopping Centres and Strip Retail Areas: Metropolitan Toronto Planning Area, 1969* (Toronto: MTPB, 1970), 2–3; see also Metropolitan Toronto Planning Department, *Strip Retail Areas and Shopping Centres, 1976* (Toronto: MTPD, 1977).

54 Cohen, "From Town Center to Shopping Center," 1059.

55 "Now ... Explore Yorkdale," *Telegram,* February 25, 1964.

56 On falling market share, see CTPB, *Core Area Task Force,* 269; Smith Report, vol. I, AO; and "Downtown Advised to Stress Quality," *Globe and Mail,* February 7, 1959.

57 Edward Relph develops this idea in *Toronto,* esp. 55–61 and 105–22.

58 Scadding, *Toronto of Old;* Micallef, *Stroll.*

59 Gad, "Metropolitan Dominance," 163–64.

60 CTPB, *Core Area Task Force,* 68–75.

61 Smith Report, vol. II, AO.
62 City of Toronto Planning Board, *Downtown Toronto: Background Studies for the Plan* (Toronto: CTPB, 1963), 9.
63 See, for example, "A City in Need of a New 'Main Drag,'" *Toronto Star,* January 2, 1971.
64 Data drawn from *Might's Greater Toronto City Directory* (Toronto: Might's, various years); MTPB, *Shopping Centres.*
65 Jacobs, *The Death and Life,* 145.
66 "Honest Ed's Toronto: 'It's Where the Action Is,'" *Toronto Star,* December 13, 1969.
67 "Donnie the Bootblack Lets You Set the Price ... ," *Toronto Star,* May 21, 1969.

Chapter 2: The City of Tomorrow

1 "A New Heart for Old Toronto," *Toronto Star,* March 2, 1966.
2 Belisle, *Retail Nation,* esp. 3–12.
3 On comparable projects, see Frieden and Sagalyn, *Downtown, Inc.;* Rubin, *Insuring the City;* and Neumann, *Remaking the Rust Belt.*
4 On the significance of the unbuilt, see Peyton, *Unbuilt Environments,* 6–8; and Osbaldeston, *Unbuilt Toronto.*
5 On the urban renewal order, see Klemek, *The Transatlantic Collapse.* Sam Wetherell provides a brilliant reinterpretation of the mid-twentieth-century British built environment in *Foundations.*
6 On the "ethic of city rebuilding," see Zipp, "The Roots and Routes of Urban Renewal," esp. 367.
7 White, *Planning Toronto,* 16–27; Brushett, "'People and Government,'" 44–58.
8 Lemon, "Plans for Early 20th-Century Toronto," 11–31.
9 On the basis of keyword searches in the archives of the *Globe and Mail* and *Toronto Star,* "redevelopment" and "renewal" entered common parlance in Toronto not long after their use in the American Housing Acts of 1949 and 1954, respectively.
10 Neumann, *Remaking the Rust Belt,* 14–21.
11 On Toronto's oscillations between conservative populism and interventionism, see Kaplan, *Reform, Planning, and City Politics,* 604–46.
12 "How U.S. Government Leads in Civic Redevelopment," *Toronto Star,* January 7, 1956.
13 Richard White discusses this in *Financing the Golden Age,* 11–23. Other data are from City of Toronto, *Annual Report of the Commissioner of Finance* (Toronto: City of Toronto, various years); and Metro Toronto, *Annual Report of the Commissioner of Finance* (Toronto: Metro Toronto, various years).
14 White, *Financing the Golden Age,* 26–27.
15 City of Toronto Planning Board, *Third Report and Official Plan* (Toronto: CTPB, 1949), 23; CTPB, *Urban Renewal: A Study of the City of Toronto* (Toronto: CTPB, 1956).
16 Lewis and Hess, "Refashioning Urban Space," 563–84.
17 For example, "Phillips for Mayor," *Telegram,* December 4, 1954.
18 Fulford, *Accidental City,* is an example; the best history of the project is Armstrong, *Civic Symbol.*

19 Nathan Phillips, *Mayor of All the People* (Toronto: McClelland and Stewart, 1967), 149.

20 Terms of Reference: City of Toronto RAC, Jan. 20, 1960, CTA, F200-1512-23.

21 "Wants Other Groups to Aid Plan Council," *Globe and Mail*, January 30, 1960; "Keeping the Aging Heart of the City Beating," *Globe and Mail*, March 26, 1962.

22 Burton: Planning for Progress: The Heart of Toronto, Feb. 4, 1963, CTA, F200-1512-23.

23 Burton to Council, Feb. 27, 1962, CTA, F200-1512-23; Simon Chamberlain, "Walter Manthorpe, Commissioner of Development (1962–67)," *City Planning* 3, 2 (Fall-Winter 1985): 2–6.

24 RAC Programme of Studies, Feb. 27, 1962; 1965 RAC Tour Report, Oct. 29, 1965, both in CTA, F200-1512-23. On the renewal tour circuit, see Neumann, *Remaking the Rust Belt*, 2–3.

25 Belisle, *Retail Nation*, 52–54.

26 City for Tomorrow Attendance, Apr. 1945, AO, F229-69, B294488, Store Attractions; "Eaton's College Street: City for To-morrow," *Toronto Star*, March 21, 1945.

27 Property data are from Nirenstein's National Realty Map Company, *Business Section, City of Toronto* (Springfield, MA: Nirenstein's, 1956).

28 "T. Eaton Debentures Are Offered Today," *Globe and Mail*, March 11, 1929.

29 International Realty Co. Limited: Houses Only, Apr. 26, 1951 and Business Properties Limited: Land, Buildings, and Equipment, Jan. 11, 1951, both in AO, F229-271-1, B381769, International Realty Co. Ltd and Business Properties Ltd.

30 Lewis and Hess, "Refashioning Urban Space," 572–73.

31 "Wonder If John David Eaton ... ," *Hush*, June 14, 1958; Reports re: Structural Condition of Main Store, 1955–60, AO, F229-271-1, B381767.

32 For an evocative look at the Eaton factories, see Valpy, "Timothy Eaton's Stern Fortifications," 135–39; and Kopytek, *Eaton's*, 278.

33 One key argument deployed in favour of the Yonge Street subway was its potential to raise property values and spur redevelopment. See Young, "Searching for a Better Way," 90.

34 Smith Report, AO.

35 Main Store Re-construction Summary, 1959, AO, F 229-271-1, B381767-1.

36 White, *Planning Toronto*, 144–46.

37 Notes on Meeting, May 31, 1956, CTA, F2032-723-159. On Gordon Stephenson, see Grant and Paterson, "Scientific Cloak/Romantic Heart," 319–36; Lawson to Byam, Sep. 11, 1956, CTA, F2032-723-159.

38 Building Condition – University, College, Yonge, Queen, 1956; CTPB Memorandum – Project Viking, Jun. 9, 1958, both in CTA, F2032-723-159.

39 CTPB Memorandum – Project Viking, Jun. 9, 1958, CTA, F2032, series 723-159.

40 University College Yonge Queen Redevelopment Study #1 & #3, Jun. 1956, CTA, F2032, series 723-159.

41 Gold, *The Practice of Modernism*, ch. 6.

42 CTPB Memorandum – Project Viking, Jun. 9, 1958, CTA, F2032, series 723-159.

43 Shapely, "Civic Pride and Redevelopment," 310–28; Gruen, *The Heart of Our Cities*, 214–20.

44 Controller's Office, re: Toronto Downtown, Aug. 28, 1959, AO, F229-271-1, B381767-1-1.

45 "$125 Million Project for Montreal," *Globe and Mail*, October 13, 1956.

46 For example, "For a Modern Canada on the Move," *Toronto Star*, October 20, 1958.

47 Nerbas, "William Zeckendorf," 6, 10; see also Zeckendorf with McCreary, *The Autobiography of William Zeckendorf*, 142–43.

48 Notes on Meeting, May 31, 1956, CTA, F2032-723-15; "Redevelop Here, Zeckendorf Hints," *Globe and Mail*, April 10, 1958.

49 Re: Toronto CBD, Jan. 27, 1962, AO, F229-271-1, B381767-1.

50 Typical of Canadian media coverage of the man is "Bill Zeckendorf and His Big Plans for Canada," *Maclean's*, November 24, 1956, 10–11, 86–95.

51 The first column is "Unfinished Business," *Toronto Star*, August 26, 1962.

52 "The Lesson of Place Ville Marie 2," *Toronto Star*, September 26, 1962.

53 The plan referenced is W & K: Eaton's Downtown Toronto, Feb. 18, 1960, AO, F229-271-2, B381622.

54 "The Lesson of Place Ville Marie 4," *Toronto Star*, October 11, 1962; "The Lesson of Place Ville Marie 2," *Toronto Star*, September 26, 1962.

55 See, for example, "Progress Report: Private Development," *Globe and Mail*, November 6, 1963.

56 City of Toronto Planning Board, *Plan for Downtown Toronto* (Toronto: CTPB, 1963), 33.

57 "Facelift for Downtown Endorsed by Planners," *Toronto Star*, February 2, 1963.

58 Exec. Committee Memo re: Toronto CBD, Jan. 29, 1962, AO, F229-271-1, B381767.

59 Larry Bourne, *Private Redevelopment of the Central City* (Chicago: University of Chicago Press, 1967), 97–98.

60 City of Toronto Development Department, *Major Developments Completed* (Toronto: City of Toronto, 1971).

61 "Toronto to Get Tallest Skyscraper outside N.Y.," *Toronto Star*, April 10, 1964; Burton: Planning for Progress: The Heart of Toronto, Feb. 4, 1963, CTA, F200-1512-23.

62 "Simpson's Unveils Plans for 33-Storey Tower," *Globe and Mail*, October 10, 1964.

63 Zeckendorf with McCreary, *The Autobiography of William Zeckendorf*, 197–98; Head Office Summary: Toronto Downtown Redevelopment, 1964, AO, F229-271-2, B381806.

64 Letter of Termination, July 9, 1964, AO, F229-271-2, B381623.

65 "Biggest Project since Subway, Eaton's to Spark Citybuilding," *Toronto Star*, December 2, 1965.

66 Eaton Centre Presentation to Board, Etc., Oct. 6, 1964; The Eaton Centre: A Development Proposal by the T. Eaton Co., 1964, both in AO, F229-271-2, B381623.

67 Chronological History of Eaton Centre, 1967, AO, F229-501-135, B382473.

68 For example, "Building Plans to Top Rockefeller Centre," *Telegram*, September 15, 1965.

69 Eaton Centre Ltd.: History of Property Acquisitions, Feb. 15, 1966, AO, F229-501-135, B382473.

70 The Eaton Centre Ltd. – Formerly Sunjam Corp. Ltd., 1967, AO, F229-501-135, B382473.

71 Spohn re: Toronto CBD Properties, Jun. 7, 1965, AO, F229-271-2, B381623. On the TD Centre assembly, see Collier, *Contemporary Cathedrals*, 126–27.

72 Planning and Development Report: Toronto CBD, Dec. 14, 1964; Minutes of Oct. 13, 1965 Meeting, both in AO, F229-271-2, B381623.

73 For a profile of Owen, see "Design in the Sky Is for the Birds," *Executive Magazine*, September 1967; Smith to A.Y. Eaton re: CANTEC, May 30, 1964, AO, F229-271-2, B381623.

74 "This Man Breeds Skyscrapers," *Ottawa Citizen*, November 26, 1965.

75 "A New Look for Downtown Toronto," *Canadian Business*, July 1966; Organizational Chart – Eaton Centre Ltd., 1966, AO, F229-271-2, B381623.

76 "Phillip Givens the Go-Go Man," *Globe and Mail*, November 30, 1966.

77 History of Old City Hall Price Negotiations, 1967, AO, F229-501-135, B382473; Cockfield and Brown, Sep. 1965, AO, F229-271-2, B381622.

78 "Malls, Towers and Spaces in Eaton's Downtown Plan," *Toronto Star*, September 16, 1965; "Eaton's a Way of Life to City Shoppers," *Telegram*, December 2, 1965.

79 "Eaton's a Way of Life to City Shoppers," *Telegram*, December 2, 1965; for a more detailed assessment of the tax impacts of the Eaton Centre, see Manthorpe, the Eaton Centre, Jun. 10, 1966, CTA, F220-11-659.

80 James Lorimer, "The Mutation of William Dennison," *Globe and Mail*, January 10, 1972.

81 "Won't Sell City Hall, Controllers Emphasize," *Globe and Mail*, November 14, 1963; "Dennison Bid Rejected," *Telegram*, December 11, 1965.

82 Their initial letters to Metro appear in AO, F229-271-2, B381622.

83 Friends of the Old City Hall, Jan. 25, 1966, AO, F229-162-0-371-1, B253778.

84 "Toronto's Other City Hall," *Architectural Forum* 124, 1 (January-February 1966): 32.

85 "Odds and Ends," *Canadian Architect* 11, 2 (February 1966): 5–10, 16–17, 20, 74.

86 Arthur, *Toronto*, xv.

87 See, for example, Drouin, *Le combat du patrimoine à Montréal*.

88 "Save-the-Armories Petition Goes to Metro," *Toronto Star*, March 9, 1961.

89 "Toronto's Other City Hall," *Architectural Forum* 124, 1 (January-February 1966): 32.

90 "Don't Sell – Dalai Lama," *Globe and Mail*, January 31, 1966. A summary of a 1967 interview with Acland appears in the rich but apparently unpublished report The Eaton Centre, 1967, CTA, F1048-2151-91.

91 On the importance of appeals to expertise in this era, see Stephen Bocking, "Constructing Urban Expertise," 51–76.

92 Royal Architectural Institute Submission, Dec. 6, 1965, CTA, F1048-2151-91.

93 James Acland, "Toronto's Civic Square and the Eaton Centre – II," *Journal of Canadian Studies* 1, 1 (May 1966): 52; Extracts from Letter of New City Hall Jury of Architects, May 13, 1958, CTA, F220-11-653.

94 Old City Hall, Uses, Early 1966, CTA, F220-11-658.

95 F.C. to Allen and Metro Council, Feb. 28, 1966; J.N. to Allen and Metro, Feb. 26, 1966, both in CTA, F220-11-653.

96 Notes re: Friends of OCH, Feb. 22, 1966, AO, F229-162-0-371-1, B253778.

97 "Dennison Bid Rejected," *Telegram*, December 11, 1965; Planning Commissioner to Metro Exec, Dec. 9, 1965, CTA, F220-11-658.

98 Programme March 1, 1966, AO, F229-162-0-371-1, B253778.

99 "Unveiling Plans for the Eaton Centre," *Toronto File,* March 1, 1966, CBC Digital Archives, http://www.cbc.ca/archives/entry/unveiling-plans-for-the-eaton-centre; Memorandum re: Eaton Centre Presentation, Mar. 1, 1966, AO, F229-271-2, B381622.

100 Description drawn from the Conceptual Plan for Eaton Centre, Mar. 1, 1966, CTA, 445061-9; and Transcript of Mar. 1, 1966 Presentation, CTA, F220-11-660.

101 Kinnear Statement, Mar. 1, 1966, CTA, F220-11-660.

102 Objectives, Dec. 1, 1965, AO, F229-271-2, B381623.

103 Kinnear Statement, Mar. 1, 1966, CTA, F220-11-660.

104 Murray Statement, Mar. 1, 1966, CTA, F220-11-660.

105 Transcript of Mar. 1, 1966 Presentation, CTA, F220-11-660.

106 "The Lesson of Place Ville Marie 2," *Toronto Star,* September 28, 1962.

107 See Terranova, "Ultramodern Underground Dallas," 18–29.

108 Transcript of Mar. 1, 1966 Presentation, CTA, F220-11-660.

109 Owen Statement, Mar. 1, 1966, CTA, F220-11-660.

110 Transcript of Mar. 1, 1966 Presentation, CTA, F220-11-660.

111 McEachern Report on Historical Names, Feb. 17, 1966, AO, F229-162-0-371-1, B253778; The Eaton History, Mar. 1, 1966, CTA, F220-11-660.

112 See Belisle, *Retail Nation,* 234–40.

113 The Church of the Holy Trinity, Mar. 1, 1966, CTA, F220-11-660.

114 Transcript of Mar. 1, 1966 Presentation, CTA, F220-11-660.

115 "Now: City of the Future," *Telegram;* March 1, 1966.

116 "A New Heart for Old Toronto," *Toronto Star,* March 2, 1966; "Eloquent – and Spacious?," *Globe and Mail,* March 2, 1966.

117 Canadian Facts, "A Study of the Attitudes of Metropolitan Toronto Adults towards the Proposed Eaton Centre, 1966," Toronto Reference Library, 301.1543 C12.

118 Eaton Centre Press Distribution List, Feb. 1966, AO, F229-162-0-371-1, B253778; "Cities: Farewell to Hogtown," *Time* (Canadian ed.), March 4, 1966.

119 "Most Municipal Politicians Favour Development Plans," *Globe and Mail,* March 2, 1966.

120 BOTMT to Metro, Mar. 17, 1966; RAC to City, Mar. 11, 1966, both in CTA, F220-11-653.

121 "7 City Chiefs Say Yes," *Telegram,* April 5, 1966; Lawson to BOC, Mar. 29, 1966, CTA, F220-11-658.

122 Manthorpe: The Eaton Centre, Jun. 10, 1966, CTA, F220-11-659.

123 White, *Planning Toronto,* 194–95.

124 "Architects Divided on Eaton's Project," *Globe and Mail,* March 4, 1966.

125 "Friends of Old City Hall Gaining Strength, Planner Says," *Globe and Mail,* March 2, 1966; "600 Hoot, Laugh at Eaton's Project," *Globe and Mail,* March 10, 1966.

126 "Old City Hall Supporters Rally at Hearing," *Globe and Mail,* March 23, 1966.

127 "Would Timothy Approve This Purple Prose?," *Toronto Star,* March 3, 1966.

128 "Metro Wants Eaton's Guarantee or 'No Sale' on City Hall," *Toronto Star,* March 16, 1966.

129 History of Other City Developments, 1966, AO, F229-271-2, B381622-8. On urban renewal in Hamilton, see Rockwell, "The Facelift and the Wrecking Ball," 53–61.

130 Unfinished Civic Business for 1966, Summer-Fall 1966, AO, F229-162-0-371-1, B253778.

131 FOCH: List of Supporters by District, Summer-Fall 1966, CTA, F220-11-656.

132 Canadian Facts, "A Study of the Attitudes of Metropolitan Toronto Adults towards the Proposed Eaton Centre, 1966," Toronto Reference Library, 301.1543 C12.

133 Minutes of the Metropolitan Toronto Council, June 24, 1966, CTA; "A Day That Will Decide the Future of Toronto," *Toronto Star*, June 24, 1966; "Council Dooms Old City Hall," *Toronto Star*, June 25, 1966.

134 See, for example, "Eaton Centre Scrapped," *Telegram*, May 18, 1967.

135 J.D. Eaton to Metro, May 18, 1967, CTA, F220-11-657.

136 "A Barefoot Boy from Renfrew Who'll Be Our Next Mayor," *Toronto Star*, December 6, 1966.

137 "The Three Major Candidates for Mayor and Their Visions of the City," *Globe and Mail*, December 1, 1966.

138 "Mayor Pushes Fight to Save Old City Hall from Wreckers," *Toronto Star*, January 12, 1967.

139 "When Eaton's Called, No One Was Home," *Telegram*, May 19, 1967; "Vital for Toronto," *Telegram*, May 20, 1967; "The Incredible Bungling That Costs Us Millions," *Toronto Life*, October 1967.

140 Eaton Centre Ltd. Balance Sheet, July 31, 1966; Report of Vice-President Finance/Administration, Dec. 1965, both in AO, F229-271-2, B381623.

141 Eaton's Future in Downtown Toronto, Apr. 1969, AO, F229-271-2, B381623-4; Memo re: Visit to Rockefeller Center Inc., Feb. 1, 1966, AO, F229-271-2, B381623.

142 Tremayne: Ground Lease Implications, May 5, 1966, and Appraisal and Recommendations re: Eaton Centre, Jun. 12, 1967, both in AO, F229-271-2, B381622-8.

143 Notes re: Friends of OCH, Feb. 22, 1966; McEachern to Weatherspoon, Apr. 11, 1966; Butler to Miss C., Mar. 6, 1967, all in AO, F229-162-0-371-1, B253778.

144 Turner Appraisal, Feb. 22, 1966, AO, F229-271-2, B381622.

145 Appraisal and Position Summary, May 19, 1967, AO, F229-162-0-373, B253778.

Chapter 3: A People Place

1 "People Take Over Yonge St.," *Toronto Star*, May 31, 1971; "A Sea of Strollers on the Mall," *Telegram*, May 31, 1971. Elements of this chapter were published in Ross, "The Politics of Public Space," 89–102.

2 The notion of "everyday politics" has its roots in scholarship on peasant societies in Southeast Asia, but as Benedict Kerkvliet suggests, it has a wider applicability to understanding day-to-day, unorganized, and often subtle political behaviours. See Kerkvliet, "Everyday Politics," 227–43.

3 For a discussion of this ambivalence in Canada, see Penfold, "'Are We to Go Literally?,'" 8–23. On automobility, see Featherstone, "Automobilities," 1–24.

4 On the era's car-dependent landscapes, see Christopher Wells, *Car Country*, 251–88.

5 On this retail strategy to downtown renewal, see Cohen, "Buying into Downtown Revival," 82–95.

6 Those plans are "The Eaton Centre" (Fall 1964), AO, F229-501-135, B382379. For a critical assessment of Gruen, see Hardwick, *Mall Maker.*

7 See, for example, Cheyne, "No Better Way?," 103–28. In the European context, see Feriel, "L'invention du centre-ville européen," 99–122.

8 Teaford, *The Rough Road,* 7.

9 "Downtown Gets Uplift," *Life,* October 26, 1959; "The Nation's First Downtown Shoppers' Mall," *Kalamazoo Gazette,* October 1959, quoted in Cheyne, "No Better Way?," 110.

10 Rubenstein, *Pedestrian Malls,* 180–85; Roberto Brambilla and Gianni Longo, *For Pedestrians Only: Planning, Design, and Management of Traffic-Free Zones* (New York: Whitney Library, 1977), 174–75. For further discussion of the various phases of mall development, see Robertson, *Pedestrian Malls and Skywalks,* 26–29.

11 City of Toronto Planning Board, *The Pedestrian in Downtown Toronto* (Toronto: CTPB, 1959); White, *Planning Toronto,* 186.

12 CTPB, *Plan for Downtown Toronto,* 31, 37.

13 Merchants to CTPB, Mar. 15, 1963, CTA, F2032, series 723-63.

14 On previous lobbying, see, for example, "Businessmen Continue Yonge Parking Fight," *Globe and Mail,* April 19, 1955.

15 Merchants to CTPB, Mar. 15, 1963, CTA, F2032, series 723-63.

16 Resumé of Meeting with Yonge Street Merchants, May 17, 1963, and Lawson to CTPB, Oct. 24, 1963, both in CTA, F2032, series 723-63.

17 Henderson, *Making the Scene.*

18 "'Jail-in' for 50 after Yorkville's Worst Brawl," *Toronto Star,* August 21, 1967.

19 O'Connor, *The First Green Wave,* esp. 40–45.

20 "Alderman Plans Leave-Car-at-Home Week," *Globe and Mail,* April 6, 1970.

21 Rome, "The Genius of Earth Day," 194–205.

22 On that debate, see Robinson, "Modernism at a Crossroad," 295–322.

23 "Archer to People Interested in a Pedestrian Mall," July 20, 1970, CTA, F1314-1029-1.

24 See Simon Hall, "Protest Movements in the 1970s."

25 A 1974 municipal study – itself the product of a citizen committee – listed more than fifty "organized interest groups" that were active in central Toronto. CTPB, *Core Area Task Force,* 224–25.

26 Ley, *The New Middle Class.*

27 A classic internal account of reform mobilization is Sewell, *Up against City Hall.* On municipal reform and its allies in Toronto, see also Caulfield, "'Reform' as a Chaotic Concept," 107–11.

28 "Are We Planning for *People* in Downtown Toronto?" (Mar. 1970), CTA, F20-54-1 (emphasis in original).

29 Mailout Labels, Aug. 1970; Notice of Public Meeting, Feb. 3, 1971, both in CTA, F200-2160-6.

30 "Archer Loses Wife to Mall Hoopla," *Telegram,* June 2, 1972; "The Mall: Seven-Day Miracle That Changed Toronto," *Toronto Star,* June 5, 1971; "Toronto Faces Future

as a People-Oriented, Loveable, Small Town," *Toronto Star,* June 3, 1971; "Architects Award to Citizens," *Globe and Mail,* May 18, 1972.

31 Statistics on vehicles from City People, *The Yonge Street Mall: A Feasibility Study* (Toronto: City People, 1974), 9; pedestrian counts from Development Department Mall Report Draft, Oct. 29, 1971, CTA, F1314-1029-1.

32 "A Miracle Is Happening on Auto-Free Yonge Street," *Toronto Star,* August 12, 1972.

33 On this ideal, see Isenberg, *Downtown America,* 4–6.

34 "Archer Loses Wife to Mall Hoopla," *Telegram,* June 2, 1972; "The Mall: Seven-Day Miracle That Changed Toronto," *Toronto Star,* June 5, 1971.

35 "Toronto Faces Future as a People-Oriented, Loveable, Small Town," *Toronto Star,* June 3, 1971.

36 "Toronto the Dreary: Mall Caps 10 Years of Change," *Telegram,* June 2, 1971.

37 "Permanent Malls," *Telegram,* June 7, 1971; "Groups Plan to Ask City to Retain Mall," *Globe and Mail,* June 5, 1971.

38 Statistics Canada, *Census of Canada,* 1951–71.

39 Iacovetta, "Immigrant Gifts," 34–73.

40 "The Yonge St. Mall: A People Place," *Telegram,* June 5, 1971.

41 On Metro Caravan, see David Wencer, "Historicist: The Caravan Is on Its Way," Torontoist.com, June 24, 2017, https://torontoist.com/2017/06/historicist-caravan -way/; Yonge Street Mall: Progress Report #2, Mar. 1972, CTA, F53-128-90.

42 "Dragon Mall Draws 135,000 Pedestrians," *Toronto Star,* September 7, 1971.

43 MTPD, *Strip Retail Areas,* 46–56.

44 "Toronto's Downtown Mall Is Here Again," *Toronto Star,* June 28, 1972.

45 Main Street Canada Pamphlet, 1973, CTA, F1314-1029-1.

46 See "How to Succeed as a City," *Detroit Free Press,* July 15, 1973; or, for echoes in journalism, "A City That Works," *Harper's,* December 1, 1974, 14–19.

47 Convention and Tourist Bureau of Metropolitan Toronto Press Release, Aug. 4, 1972, CTA, F200-1512-532; City People, *The Yonge Street Mall,* 43.

48 City People, *The Yonge Street Mall,* 43; Eglinton YPC Association Poll, Oct. 20, 1973, CTA, F200-1512-564.

49 "The Yonge Street Pedestrian Mall: Good Environment Equals Good Business," *BMR Comment* 125 (June 1971), 7–18; Downtown Council: Mall Survey Report (1971), both in CTA, F1314-1029-8; "Big, Small Businesses Divided on the Value of the Yonge Mall," *Globe and Mail,* June 2, 1971.

50 Archer to LLBO, Jun. 6, 1973, CTA, F1314-1029-39; "40,000 Love the Mall," *Toronto Star,* June 1, 1971.

51 "Donnie the Bootblack Lets You Set the Price," *Toronto Star,* May 21, 1969; "Shoe-shine Boy, China Merchant Salute the Mall," *Toronto Star,* August 18, 1971.

52 "Troubadours Who Play for Spare Change," *Toronto Star,* July 19, 1975.

53 Problems of Downtown Yonge Street, Dec. 1972, CTA, F220-11-842; "Capitalists of the Counterculture," *Toronto Star,* October 16, 1977.

54 Chief Inspector to Archer, Sep. 7, 1973, CTA, F1314-1029-34.

55 "Stanfield Sees the People on Yonge St Mall," *Globe and Mail,* June 4, 1971; "In Wake of Yonge St Mall, People Want More," *Globe and Mail,* June 7, 1971.

56 Commissioner to Mall Committee, Aug. 17, 1970, CTA, F220-11-842.

57 "Chaotic Traffic Jams Expected to Follow 1973 Yonge St. Mall," *Toronto Star,* June 2, 1973; "A Miracle Is Happening on Auto-Free Yonge St.," *Toronto Star,* August 14, 1972.

58 Press Release: Bike Power, May 26, 1971, AO, F1058, B253244, Bicycle Promotion.

59 "Cycle Army Converges on the Mall," *Telegram,* May 31, 1971.

60 See, for example, the *City Cyclist,* Toronto's first urban cycling newsletter, which began its run in 1978.

61 "Spadina Opponents Hold a Party in Pedestrian Mall, Of Course," *Toronto Star,* June 4, 1971; "Victory Party," *Globe and Mail,* June 4, 1971.

62 York-Toronto Tuberculosis and Respiratory Disease Association (YTTRDA), *Carbon Monoxide in Downtown Toronto* (Toronto: YTTRDA, May 1974); "Choke! Splutter! Gasp! Yonge St Is Hard on Your Lungs," *Toronto Star,* April 17, 1973.

63 City People, *The Yonge Street Mall,* 156.

64 Mahood, "Hitchin' a Ride in the 1970s," 205–27.

65 "The Yonge St. Mall Fights Off Its Sin Strip Image," *Toronto Star,* August 20, 1973.

66 Report of Chief of Police: Yonge Street Mall, Oct. 16, 1973, CTA, F200-1512-564.

67 Canadian Welfare Council, *Transient Youth: Report of an Inquiry in the Summer of 1969* (Ottawa: Canadian Welfare Council, 1970); "Youth on the Move," *Toronto Star,* July 10, 1971.

68 Jamie Bradburn, "Historicist: 'Sip 'n Sex'–Paul Godfrey's Origin Story," Torontoist. com, July 4, 2015, www.torontoist.com/2015/07/historicist-sip-n-sex-in-north-york; Henderson, "Toronto's Hippie Disease," 205–34.

69 "Once-Groovy Yorkville Has Now 'Gone Commercial,'" *Toronto Star,* May 22, 1971; "The Strip Has a Pastime to Suit Every Preference," *Globe and Mail,* July 13, 1971.

70 "Yonge Street," *Guerilla,* April 1971; "Showplaces for the Nation: Yonge Street Mall," *Guerilla,* August 1971.

71 See, for example, "Mall Degenerate Hangout, He Says," *Toronto Star,* July 24, 1973.

72 "I Got Beaten Up on Yonge St. While Hundreds Just Watched," *Toronto Star,* June 26, 1972.

73 Report of Chief of Police: Yonge Street Mall, Oct. 16, 1973, CTA, F200-1512-564; "Police Call Mall an 84-Day Orgy of Lawlessness," *Toronto Star,* November 9, 1973.

74 See letters in AO, RG33-4-49.10, B223692, Operations: Pedestrian Malls.

75 Martel, "'They Smell Bad,'" 218–20.

76 Police to Mayor: Crime Statistics, Yonge St., Oct. 31, 1978, CTA, F200-1818-95.

77 Co-ordinator's Report on 1973 Mall, May 18, 1973, CTA, F220-11-843.

78 On this practice, see T.P. to Archer, Sep. 11, 1972, CTA, F1314-1029-2.

79 Ranasinghe, "Reconceptualizing Vagrancy," 55–94.

80 Co-ordinator's Report on 1973 Mall, May 18, 1973, CTA, F220-11-843.

81 "Stop Knocking Yonge St. Mall, Architect Says," *Toronto Star,* August 25, 1973.

82 "TO's Downtown Mall Ending Third Year," *Province,* September 24, 1973; Questionnaire, 1973 Yonge Street Mall, Oct. 1973, CTA, F200-1512-564.

83 Grand Jury Report, Aug. 2, 1974; Board of Commissioners to Archer, Aug. 13, 1974, both in CTA, 1314-1029-33.

84 "This Mall Has Become a Nightmare," *Globe and Mail,* August 6, 1974; "This Is Requiem for the Yonge St. Mall," *Toronto Star,* August 15, 1974.

85 Survey Results, Dec. 29, 1972, CTA, F1314-1029-29; Surveys, 1972, CTA, F1314-1029-8; Survey Results, Aug. 15, 1973, CTA, F1314-1029-26.

86 Downtown Council Meeting Minutes – Pedestrian Mall, July 23, 1973, CTA, F1314-1029-26; "Merchants against 3-Month Yonge St. Mall, Restauranteur Claims," *Toronto Star,* February 20, 1973.

87 "Downtown Merchants' Head Expects a Smaller Mall in 1974," *Toronto Star,* August 20, 1973.

88 Eaton Centre Ltd.: History of Property Acquisitions, Feb. 15, 1966, AO, F229-501-135, B382473.

89 "Ancient Yonge Renews ... ," *Toronto Star,* November 29, 1973.

90 "Simpson's Digs In against Mall Idea," *Toronto Star,* April 1, 1978.

91 Kernaghan to Public Works, Sep. 30, 1970; Kernaghan to Archer, Dec. 15, 1970, both in CTA, F200-2160-5.

92 Government of Ontario, *The Expropriations Act, 1968–69* (Toronto: Queen's Printer, 1970).

93 City Solicitor to Committee on Public Works, Sep. 22, 1970, CTA, F220-11-843; Edison to Commissioner of Devt, Aug. 1, 1972, CTA, F1314-1029-7.

94 Claire Hoy, *Bill Davis: A Biography* (Toronto: Methuen, 1985), 88–89. On Davis as a centrist environmentalist, see Killan and Warecki, "The Algonquin Wildlands League," 1–27.

95 Cabinet Meeting Minutes 9-8/74, Feb. 13, 1974, AO, RG64-18, B222281, Cabinet Committee on Justice – Pedestrian Malls; White to Godfrey, Apr. 10, 1974, CTA, F220-11-842.

96 On the social construction of the motor-age street, see Davies, "Reckless Walking," 123–38; and Norton, *Fighting Traffic;* on pedestrians' place in it, see Blomley, *Rights of Passage,* esp. 3–4.

97 Correspondence with these and other cities was extensive. See, for example, the letters in William Archer's files, CTA, F1314-1029-35 and F1314-1029-15.

98 Robertson, "The Status of the Pedestrian Mall," 250–73.

99 City People, *The Yonge Street Mall,* 43.

100 "Mall Will Close to Help Drivers," *Star,* August 13, 1974; "Council Rejects Bid to Prevent All Future Malls," *Toronto Star,* August 16, 1974.

101 These proposals are outlined in City People, *The Yonge Street Mall.*

102 Cheyne, "No Better Way?," 127–28; Cole E. Judge, *The Experiment of American Pedestrian Malls* (Fresno, CA: Fresno Downtown Development Centre, 2013), 4.

Chapter 4: Fighting Sin Strip

1 J.M. to Mayor, Jan. 10, 1973, CTA, F200-1512-565. In this chapter, the names of citizens who wrote private letters to the mayor and other civic officials have been anonymized.

2 Crombie Reply Draft, Jun. 25, 1973, CTA, F200-1512-565.

3 On this emerging context of sexual regulation in Canada, see Lacombe, *Blue Politics;* and Brock, *Making Work.*

4 Two studies particularly focused on the spatial practices of prostitution are Gilfoyle, *City of Eros;* and Dunae, "Geographies of Sexual Commerce," 115–42.

5 On the postwar sex district, see especially Sides, "Excavating the Postwar Sex District," 355–79; Senelick, "Private Parts in Public Places," 329–53; Francis, *Red Light Neon;* and Lacasse, *La prostitution feminine à Montréal.*

6 Sides, "Excavating the Postwar Sex District," 356.

7 On prostitution's central role in the organization of the North American sex district at the turn of the twentieth century, see Levesque, "Éteindre le Red Light," 191–201.

8 Lance W. Roberts, Rodney A. Clifton, Barry Ferguson, Karen Kampen, and Simon Langlois, eds., *Recent Social Trends in Canada, 1960–2000* (Montreal and Kingston: McGill-Queen's University Press, 2005), 520.

9 See Nowlin, *Judging Obscenity,* esp. 47–132.

10 Bronstein, *Battling Pornography,* 63; "Hundreds Clamor to See Nude Film Free," *Toronto Star,* March 4, 1970.

11 Ralph Blumenthal, "Porno Chic: 'Hard-Core' Grows Fashionable – and Very Profitable," *New York Times Magazine,* January 21, 1973.

12 On theatres, see Moore, "Movie Palaces"; on changing modes of alcohol sales, see Heron, *Booze,* esp. 80–131, 300–48.

13 Data drawn from *Might's Greater Toronto City Directory* (Toronto: Might's, 1969 and 1970); "It's the Yonge Street Strip for the Saturday Night Action," *Toronto Star,* September 20, 1969.

14 See Hooper, "'Enough Is Enough,'" esp. 94.

15 A.E. LePage, *Toronto, 1975: Real Estate Market Survey* (Toronto: LePage, 1976), 12; Richard Baine and A. Lynn McMurray, *Toronto: An Urban Study* (Toronto: Clarke, Irwin, 1973), 45. Eaton's real estate development files demonstrate that other corporate investors were already competing for Yonge Street properties in the mid-1960s. See Spohn re: Toronto CBD Properties, Jun. 7, 1965, AO, F229-271-2, B381623.

16 Grattan Gray, "Who Owns Yonge Street?," *Toronto Life,* September 1974, 32.

17 Lyon, *Yonge Street Revitalization Project,* Appendix II. For one landlord's account of renting three Yonge Street properties to sex-related businesses, see S.M. to Crombie, December 6, 1977, CTA, F200-1512-1270.

18 Daphne Spain has given us tools for understanding spatial segregation by gender down to the micro level. Spain, *Gendered Spaces.*

19 Based on police Morality Bureau reports. Inspector Wilson to Emslie, Aug. 20, 1974, CTA, F1337-240; Stirling to Duffin, Jul. 7, 1975, CTA, F220-11-567.

20 See, for example, Charles Taylor, "Look What's Happened to Toronto the Good," *Toronto Life,* December 1972; "He Grosses $500,000 Selling City Sex," *Toronto Star,* July 2, 1975.

21 "Reform Caucus Seems to Have Wards 6, 7 Locked Up," *Toronto Star,* November 27, 1976.

22 Van der Meulen, "When Sex Is Work," 150–53.

23 Clipperton, "Work, Sex, or Theatre?," 32–34.

24 Schematic Drawing of Mr. Arnold's, 1977, CTA, F220-118-28, provides a police sketch of the interior of a parlour.

25 Holly Dale and Janis Cole's fascinating short *Cream Soda* depicts the daily workings of a Sin Strip parlour and these negotiations first-hand (Janis Cole and Holly Dale,

Cream Soda, no commercial release, 1975). For an interview with a body rub attendant, see Brock, *Making Work,* 14.

26 "Thrills for the Have-Nots at the Yonge Street Sex Cinemas," *Globe and Mail,* January 20, 1973; "Body Rub Girls Expose Issue of Law, Morals," *Toronto Star,* December 11, 1973.

27 Jack Batten, "The New Nudity Exposed," in W.E. Mann, ed., *The Underside of Toronto* (Toronto: McClelland and Stewart, 1970), 309.

28 See, for example, Donald Shebib's cult classic *Goin' Down the Road* (Toronto: Chevron, 1970); and Dale and Cole, *Cream Soda.*

29 R.B. to Crombie, Jan. 8, 1973, CTA, F200-1512-567.

30 "It's the Yonge Street Strip for the Saturday Night Action," *Toronto Star,* September 20, 1969; "The Strip Has a Pastime to Suit Every Preference," *Globe and Mail,* July 13, 1971.

31 See, for example, "Body Rub Girls Expose Issue of Law, Morals," *Toronto Star,* December 11, 1973.

32 The best account of this campaign and David Crombie's first year as mayor is in Caulfield, *The Tiny Perfect Mayor,* 19–37.

33 "Dennison Showed Lack of Leadership, Challengers Charge," *Toronto Star,* November 7, 1972; "O'Donohue: Let's Clean Up the Yonge St 'Strip,'" *Toronto Star,* November 23, 1972.

34 "Mayor Crombie: We've Got to Get People out of Cars," *Toronto Star,* December 23, 1972; Author interview with David Crombie, February 11, 2014.

35 Problems of Downtown Yonge Street, Dec. 1972, CTA, F220-11-842.

36 "Toronto Needs a Third Newspaper," *Telegram,* October 30, 1971.

37 "Yonge Strip Crackdown," *Toronto Sun,* December 29, 1972. Circulation figures from Audit Bureau of Circulations, *ABC Factbook, 1971/1972* and *1975/1976* (Toronto: ABC, 1973 and 1976).

38 Author interview with Crombie, February 11, 2014.

39 "Write to Me, Crombie Asks," *Toronto Sun,* December 29, 1972; "Clean Up Yonge," *Toronto Sun,* January 16, 1973.

40 I mapped a set of 1,025 addresses and created a database with other personal information – gender, occupation, marital status, reason for writing, type of letter – when available.

41 P.L. to Crombie, July 26, 1973, CTA, F200-1512-565.

42 Centennial United Church to Crombie, Jan. 17, 1973, CTA, F200-1512-567.

43 On this process of political maturation, see Fernandes, "Beyond the 'Politics of Toil,'" 59–72.

44 R.B. to Crombie, Dec. 29, 1972; R.D. to Crombie, Jan. 17, 1973; M.B. to Crombie, Dec. 29, 1972, all in CTA, F200-1512-567.

45 R.D. to Crombie, Jan. 17, 1973, CTA, F200-1512-567.

46 W.W. to Crombie, Jan. 4, 1973; M.G. to Crombie, Jan. 15, 1973 (Midway atmosphere); S.M. to Crombie, Jan. 3, 1973; D.B. to Crombie, Dec. 30, 1972, all in CTA, F200-1512-567.

47 "Yonge St. Must Be for All the People, Says Toronto Man," *Toronto Star,* January 27, 1973.

48 S.P. to Crombie, Jan. 16, 1973, CTA, F200-1512-568.

49 Lacombe, *Blue Politics*, 6.

50 S.P. to Crombie, Jan. 16, 1973, CTA, F200-1512-568; P. to Crombie, Jan. 5, 1973, CTA, F200-1512-567.

51 LCWT to Crombie, Mar. 10, 1973, CTA, F200-1512-566; Letter re: LCWT Petition, Nov. 18, 1975, CTA, F200-1512-792. On the group's influence in its heyday, see Mackintosh, "Scrutiny in the Modern City," 29–48.

52 Hunt, *Governing Morals*, 11.

53 D.B. to Crombie, Dec. 30, 1972, CTA, F200-1512-567.

54 On that discourse, see Beauregard, *Voices of Decline*.

55 "Yonge as Bad as Times Square," *Toronto Star*, January 23, 1973; M.K. to Crombie, Jan. 17, 1973, CTA, F200-1512-568; W.L. to Crombie, Jun. 21, 1973, CTA, F200-1512-565.

56 "Now Is Time to Act, Say Churches," *Toronto Sun*, January 5, 1973.

57 Sermon from H.C. Slade, "Toronto's Sin-Lane to Ruin," *Gospel Witness*, January 25, 1973; Avenue Rd. Church to Toronto Churches, Jan. 5, 1973, CTA, F200-1512-567.

58 Japanese United Church to Crombie, Jan. 9, 1973, CTA, F200-1512-567; Parkdale Baptist Church to Crombie, Feb. 14, 1973; G.K. [St. Michael's parent] to Crombie, Feb. 9, 1973, both in CTA, F200-1512-566; Form Letter 1 to Crombie, Jan. 1973, CTA, F200-1512-567.

59 On the "conservative sixties" in the United States, see Farber and Roche, *The Conservative Sixties*; on civility, see Cmiel, "The Politics of Civility," 263–90; for a key work on conservative populism, see Lassiter, *The Silent Majority*. The literature is less developed in Canada, but both Tillotson, *Give and Take*, and Hayday, *So They Want Us to Learn French*, engage with conservative activism and populism in the 1960s and 1970s.

60 A.K. to Crombie, Feb. 9, 1973, CTA, F200-1512-566.

61 "Born Again! The Evangelicals," *Newsweek*, October 25, 1976. On the shift away from mainline Protestantism in Canada, see Douville, "The Uncomfortable Pew," 479–80.

62 "Vigil against 'Ways of the World,'" *Toronto Star*, April 21, 1973 (photo); "Pornography Must Go," *Toronto Star*, July 5, 1975 (photo).

63 G.G. to Crombie, Jan. 5, 1973, CTA, F200-1512-567.

64 "No Crombie Crackdown on Yonge Street," *Toronto Star*, January 13, 1973; "Idea of Censorship Abhorrent, Writes Author Pierre Berton," *Toronto Star*, December 29, 1972.

65 "The Great Ones," *Globe and Mail*, January 15, 1973; "Clean Up Yonge," *Toronto Sun*, January 16, 1973.

66 S.P. to Crombie, Jan. 16, 1973, CTA, F200-1512-568.

67 See, for example, the opinion forum "Sordid or Folksy, City's Yonge St. Divides Opinion," *Toronto Star*, June 4, 1975.

68 Information on police strength is from Metropolitan Toronto Police Department, *Annual Statistical Report*.

69 Morton, *Mayor Howland*, 37; Marquis, "The Police as a Social Service," 338.

70 Chief to Metropolitan Board of Commissioners of Police, Sep. 8, 1977, CTA, F220-118-26; see also "Buzzers Give Warning," *Toronto Star*, July 26, 1973.

71 Inspector Stirling to Sparrow, Apr. 27, 1977, CTA, F220-118-26.

72 "Police Say Hands Tied on Yonge St. Clean-Up," *Globe and Mail*, March 4, 1973; "Powerless to Deal with Prostitutes – Chief," *Toronto Star*, December 9, 1977.

73 Author interview with Janis Cole, January 28, 2014.

74 Daniel Francis discusses this in reference to Vancouver in *Red Light Neon*, 51–54.

75 Hirt, *Zoned in the USA*, 2–3. On the history of zoning in Toronto, see Moore, "Zoning and Planning," 316–41.

76 For an overview of discussions related to these two cities, see Toronto City Council Special Committee on Places of Amusement, *Report and Recommendations*, (Toronto: City of Toronto, 1977), 105–10. On dispersal and containment, see Sides, "Excavating the Postwar Sex District," 369–70.

77 Buildings and Development Report No. 30, Oct. 1974, CTA, F220-118-28; "Planners Urge Body Rub Zoning," *Toronto Star*, September 23, 1974.

78 "Transfer Sleazy Commerce to Island," *Toronto Star*, June 6, 1975.

79 For an in-depth discussion of this, see Barker to Crombie, Oct. 31, 1977, CTA, F200-1618-111.

80 Data drawn from Morality Bureau to Duffin, Jul. 7, 1975, CTA, F200-1512-792.

81 "Lastman Declares War on Body-Rub Parlours," *Toronto Star*, August 31, 1973; Minutes of Metropolitan Toronto Council, December 12, 1973, CTA.

82 White to Joy, May 22, 1974, CTA, F220-118-28.

83 Joy to White, Jul. 31, 1974, CTA, F220-118-28; "Davis to Let Metro License Body Rubs by the End of June," *Toronto Star*, June 10, 1975; "Politics and Pornography: The Yonge Street Clean-Up," *Globe and Mail*, July 5, 1975.

84 "Crombie Sees Yonge Strip Clean in Year," *Toronto Star*, June 11, 1975.

85 Minutes of Metropolitan Toronto Council, August 26, 1975.

86 Backhouse, "Nineteenth-Century Canadian Prostitution Law," 390–91.

87 "Control – but with Extras," *Globe and Mail*, August 18, 1975.

88 List of Body Rub Owner Applications, Aug. 10, 1976, CTA, F220-118-28; "Fight Vowed by Body Rubs on Crackdown," *Toronto Star*, June 11, 1975.

89 Linetsky Deputation Text, Aug. 19, 1975, CTA, F220-11-567; Rust D'Eye to Joy, Aug. 19, 1977, CTA, F220-118-28.

90 Rust D'Eye to Joy, Aug. 19, 1977, CTA, F220-118-28; Minutes of the Metropolitan Toronto Council, March 8, 1977.

91 Toronto City Council Special Committee on Places of Amusement, *Report and Recommendations*.

92 Ibid., I–III, 3.

93 See ibid., 56.

94 See Caulfield, *The Tiny Perfect Mayor*, 9–12; and White, *Planning Toronto*, 293.

95 CORRA to Crombie, Jun. 15, 1977; NJCA to Crombie, July 14, 1977, both in CTA, F200-1512-793.

96 McLaughlin to Crombie re: Meeting with AG, July 5, 1977, CTA, F200-1818-96; Sheppard to Implementation Committee re: Injunctions, July 28, 1977, CTA,

F200-1512-793; "Crombie's Answer to City's Sex Shops: Lock 'Em Up," *Toronto Star*, July 22, 1977; "Davis Dallying on Sex Clean-Up: City," *Toronto Star*, July 26, 1977.

97   Inspector Stirling to Sparrow re: Places of Amusement, Apr. 27, 1977; Acting Inspector Shaw to Rust D'Eye, Sep. 8, 1977; Chief to Metropolitan Board of Commissioners of Police, Sep. 8, 1977, all in CTA, F220-118-26.

98   "Crombie Stand Smacks of Dictatorship: Reader," *Toronto Star*, July 27, 1977; "Appalled, Disgusted by Yonge St. Sex, Citizen Charges," *Toronto Star*, June 15, 1977.

99   On the impacts of the Jaques murder on citizen activism in Vancouver, see Francis, *Red Light Neon*, 96–97.

100   Rosenwein, "Worrying about Emotions in History," 842–43; for an excellent brief overview of emotions in urban history, see Kenny, "Emotions and City Life," 5–7.

101   Memo re: Calls about Yonge, Aug. 8, 1977, CTA, F200-1512-794 (emphasis in original).

102   S.L. to Crombie, Aug. 3, 1977; D.W. to Crombie, Aug. 4, 1977, both in CTA, F200-1512-794.

103   H.C. to Crombie, Aug. 3, 1977, CTA, F200-1512-794.

104   N.K. Petition, Aug. 8, 1977, CTA, F200-1512-795; W.W. Petition, Aug. 3, 1977, CTA, F200-1512-794 (hair salon).

105   On this, see Iacovetta, "The Sexual Politics," 361–89.

106   Fernandes, "Beyond the 'Politics of Toil,'" 59–72; De Sa, *Kicking the Sky*. On this, see also Bill Moniz, *The Shoeshine Boy* (Toronto: Vista-Global Productions, 2006), documentary film, 95 min.

107   "Angry Crowd Seeks Revenge for Emanuel," *Toronto Star*, August 9, 1977.

108   For two examples, see P.L. to Crombie, Aug. 11, 1977, CTA, F200-1512-795; and Mayor's Office Note, Aug. 3, 1977, CTA, F200-1512-794.

109   Valverde, *The Age of Light*, 90–91.

110   "Sex-Shop Slaying May Kill the Strip," *Toronto Star*, August 4, 1977; "Sin Strip Victim," *Toronto Sun*, August 3, 1977. Yvonne Chi-Ying Ng explores in detail how this slippage operated in the local media following the Jaques murder in "Ideology, Media, and Moral Panics."

111   "Homosexual Backlash Feared," *Toronto Star*, August 3, 1977; Coalition for Gay Rights in Ontario Press Release, Aug. 9, 1977, CTA, F200-1512-795.

112   Gerald Hannon, "Men Loving Boys Loving Men," *Body Politic* 39 (December 1977–January 1978): 29–33; Hooper, "'Enough Is Enough.'"

113   Author interview with David Crombie, February 11, 2014.

114   "He's Brains behind the Yonge St. Fight," *Toronto Star*, August 13, 1977.

115   See, for example, "Councils Could Have Hit Sex Shops: Ontario," *Toronto Star*, August 9, 1977; Joy to Godfrey, Aug. 24, 1977, CTA, F220-118-26.

116   Chief to Metropolitan Board of Commissioners of Police, Sep. 8, 1977, CTA, F220-118-26.

117   Ibid.

118   Inspection statistics drawn from Charges Laid as a Result of Police-MLC Cooperation, Aug 25, 1977; Chief to Crombie, Aug 10, 1977; and Medical Officer of Health to Crombie, Aug 19, 1977, all in CTA, F220-118-26.

119 Yonge St. Implementation Committee Interim Report, Oct. 28, 1977, CTA, F220-118-27.

120 "The Heat's on Czar of Strip Cleanup," *Globe and Mail,* April 26, 1978.

121 Manning Interim Report to Godfrey, Nov. 10, 1977, CTA, F220-118-27.

122 B.S. to Chief of Police, Aug. 4, 1977, CTA, F200-1512-795; "Body Rub Shops Give In to Raids and Close Down," *Toronto Star,* August 15, 1977.

123 Yonge St. Implementation Committee Interim Report, Oct. 28, 1977, CTA, F220-118-26.

124 Brock, *Making Work,* 25–43; "Police Open War on Sex 'Track,'" *Toronto Star,* May 4, 1978.

125 Margaret Dwight-Spore, "Speaking Up for Our Sisters: Decriminalization of Prostitution," *Fireweed* 1, 1 (1978): 23–26, describes the context of the group's founding. On the broader context, see Mathieu, "The Emergence and Uncertain Outcomes," 29–50.

126 "Yonge St. Clean but Sex Shows Sizzle in the Suburbs," *Toronto Star,* October 11, 1980; Ontario, Provincial Parliament, *Hansard,* 31st Parl., 4th Sess. (November 13, 1980) at 5:30 pm, https://www.ola.org/fr/affaires-legislatives/documents-chambre/legislature-31/session-4/1980-11-13/journal-debats.

127 "Protests, Fire End Plan for Body Rubs," *Toronto Star,* April 8, 1979; Sides, "Excavating the Postwar Sex District," 373–75.

128 Lyon, *Yonge Street Revitalization Project,* Appendix II, 1–4.

129 David Lewis Stein, "We'd Better Act Now – Yonge Is Dying," *Toronto Star,* November 6, 1977; "The Strip Is Alive with Smiles," *Toronto Star,* December 23, 1977; on redevelopment, see "Redevelopment Key to Yonge St. Future," *Toronto Star,* August 12, 1978. Quote from "Let's Give Yonge St. a New Kind of Style," *Toronto Star,* April 23, 1978.

Chapter 5: Malling Main Street

1 "Eaton Centre," *Toronto Star,* August 7, 1979.

2 "Eaton Centre Firmly Defended," *Globe and Mail,* March 17, 1979.

3 "Death of a Main Drag," *Globe and Mail,* March 10, 1979.

4 The rise of the development corporation deserves more study by historians. The standard business survey, Bliss, *Northern Enterprise,* devotes just three and a half pages to the topic; the best studies covering the 1960s and 1970s are contemporary, critical, and non-academic. The following discussion relies especially on Spurr, *Land and Urban Development;* Rudin, *The Changing Structure;* and Lorimer, *The Developers;* see also Collier, *Contemporary Cathedrals;* and Donald Gutstein, *Vancouver Ltd.* (Toronto: Lorimer, 1975).

5 Harris, *Creeping Conformity,* 129–54.

6 An early 1970s survey of Canada's hundred largest developers discovered that just twelve had been active prior to the 1950s and that more than half were founded in the 1960s. Graham Barker, Jennifer Penney, and Wally Seccombe, *High Rise and Superprofits* (Kitchener: Dumont Press, 1973), 17.

7 Stoffman, *The Cadillac Fairview Story,* 1.

8   The best analysis of the merger and the company's creation is Gluskin, *Royal Commission,* esp. 5–19.

9   See ibid., 14–17; and Spurr, *Land and Urban Development,* 194–201.

10 Spurr, *Land and Urban Development,* 194.

11 Numbers from Stoffman, *The Cadillac Fairview Story,* 14; and Gluskin, *Royal Commission,* 11.

12 Gluskin, *Royal Commission,* 34–35.

13 For a theoretical framing of the restructuring of urban space through capital investment and reinvestment, see Harvey, *The Urbanization of Capital.*

14 Diamond quoted in Stoffman, *The Cadillac Fairview Story,* 10–11; on the National Housing Act, see Harris, *Creeping Conformity,* esp. 133–36.

15 On capital switching, see Charney, "Three Dimensions of Capital Switching," 740–58.

16 A.E. LePage, *Annual Real Estate Market Survey, 1970, 1973, 1974* (Toronto: LePage, various years).

17 Gad, "Downtown Montreal and Toronto," 156–58 (largest in Canada). Other statistics drawn from CTPB, *Core Area Task Force.*

18 The value of buildings erected annually in Toronto more than tripled from $167 million in 1964 to $554 million in 1975, largely buoyed by the construction of office towers and apartment blocks. City of Toronto, *Municipal Handbook* (Toronto: City of Toronto, various years). For a sense of the excitement that accompanied the boom in certain City agencies, see City of Toronto Development Department, *Development in Toronto: Bulletin 1* (Toronto, City of Toronto, 1971).

19 Unless otherwise noted, information and quotations in this paragraph are drawn from Eaton's Future in Downtown Toronto, Apr. 1969, AO, F229-271-2, B381623-4.

20 Ibid.

21 MTPB, *Shopping Centres,* 32–35.

22 "Announcement – Pacific Centre," *Vancouver Sun,* July 23, 1968. On the project more generally, see Rhodri Windsor Liscombe, "A Study in Modern(ist) Urbanism: Planning Vancouver, 1945–1965," *Urban History* 38, 1 (2011): 147–48.

23 See Eaton's Future in Downtown Toronto, Apr. 1969, AO, F229-271-2, B381623-4; and 15-Year History of Eaton's Toronto CBD, 1969, AO, F229-162-0-381, B253779, on the conditions of negotiations.

24 Architect Harry Petroff, quoted in "Parting a Lobster and His Money," *Globe and Mail,* December 27, 1975 ("machines"); builder Edward DeBartalo, quoted in "Why Shopping Centers Rode out the Storm," *Forbes,* June 1, 1976 ("the best investment"). On profitability in the United States, see Hanchett, "U.S. Tax Policy and the Shopping Center," 1082–1110; for Canada, see Lorimer, *The Developers,* 186–215.

25 Fairview was an early member in the council. See Stoffman, *The Cadillac Fairview Story,* 25.

26 For an overview of mall planning, see Gillette, "The Evolution," 449–60.

27 Eaton's Future in Downtown Toronto, Apr. 1969, AO, F229-271-2, B381623-4, describes how refusal to move the store led to Eaton's rebuffing earlier development offers. Fairview's perspective on this point is discussed in Stoffman, *The Cadillac Fairview Story,* 61–62.

28 Frieden and Sagalyn, *Downtown, Inc.,* 61–86.

29 Filion and Hammond, "When Planning Fails," 1–27.

30 The partnership between Fairview and Eaton's was signed in May 1970; TD Bank joined as construction began, in spring 1974. Fairview to Dennison, May 7, 1970, CTA, F200-1512-464.

31 On this agenda in the United States, see Frieden and Sagalyn, *Downtown, Inc.,* 259–60.

32 "U of T to Sell Land to Centre Developer," *Globe and Mail,* October 19, 1973.

33 "Eaton's Wants to Demolish Church for Big Project," *Toronto Star,* May 1, 1970.

34 On the church's history and especially its social mission, see C. Ian P. Tate, *Church of the Holy Trinity, Trinity Square, Toronto* (Toronto: Church of the Holy Trinity, 1965); and Kevin Plummer, "Historicist: The Heart of the City," Torontoist.com, October 20, 2012, www.torontoist.com/2012/10/historicist-the-heart-of-the-city/.

35 Author interview with David Crombie, February 11, 2014; Churchill, "American Expatriates," 31–44.

36 "The Gay Archivist at Work," *Gay Archivist* 9 (1991), http://www.clga.ca/Material/Records/docs/chatlga9.htm, accessed March 2016.

37 An overview of Fairview's tactics from the church perspective is in Gibson to Wood re: Trinity Church, Apr. 13, 1971, CTA, F200-1512-464; "Eaton Plan Poses Tough Expropriation Questions," *Toronto Star,* February 9, 1971.

38 Public Relations Position: Toronto CBD, Apr. 30, 1970, AO, F229-162-0-373, B253778.

39 "Jelly Sandwiches Yowling Babies at Holy Trinity," *Toronto Star,* October 16, 1972.

40 "Church Small but Powerful Pawn in Development Game," *Telegram,* February 9, 1971.

41 "Holy Trinity Church Wants to Build a Downtown 'People Place,'" *Toronto Star,* March 13, 1971.

42 Aims and Criteria of the Church of the Holy Trinity, Apr. 21, 1971, AO, F1058, B253237-DE, Eaton Centre.

43 "Holy Trinity Church Wants to Build a Downtown 'People Place,'" *Toronto Star,* March 13, 1971.

44 Heaman, *A Short History,* 145.

45 For the city planning perspective on that decision, see Objectives for the Area Bounded by Dundas, Yonge, Queen and Bay Streets, May 11, 1971, CTA, F200-1512-464; on expropriation, see "Mayor Says MPPs Killed City's Chances to Aid Eaton Centre," *Toronto Star,* May 27, 1971.

46 On early opposition to apartments, see Dennis, "Interpreting the Apartment House," 305–22.

47 CTPB, *Core Area Task Force,* 292.

48 CORRA Constitution 1968, Revised 1973, CTA, F1337-200; for a developer attempting to organize tenants, see Cadillac Property Management – Dear Residents, Sep. 22, 1971, AO, F1058, B253237-$C, Cadillac.

49 J.L. Granatstein, *Marlborough Marathon: One Street against a Developer* (Toronto: Hakkert, Lewis, and Samuel, 1971), 118.

50 O'Connor, *The First Green Wave,* 114–16; the Downtown Action fonds are in the CTA, fonds 1026.

51 "Developers Series: A Beginning," *Guerilla,* December 1971. Spurr, *Land and Urban Development,* is the most comprehensive example of this approach.

52 See Ryan O'Connor's 2008 interview with Marilyn Cox, quoted in O'Connor, *The First Green Wave,* 115.

53 The "corporate city" idea is best elaborated in Lorimer, *The Developers,* 219–57.

54 See the fascinating City of Toronto Planning Board, *Public Attitudes to Downtown Development: A Newspaper Survey, October 1974* (Toronto: CTPB, 1974).

55 See, for example, James Lorimer, "It's a Champagne Time for Developers," *Globe and Mail,* March 20, 1972. Stein, *Toronto for Sale,* was largely based on two years of editorial columns in the *Toronto Star.*

56 See, for example, "Sewell Out 'to Scuttle' Eaton Centre Plan, Rotenberg Charges," *Toronto Star,* May 6, 1971.

57 Objections to the Fairview-Eaton's Proposal (Summer 1971), CTA, F1306-308-1-24; Eaton's Leaflet (Summer 1971), CTA, F1026-51; "Make Eaton Centre a Real City Affair," *Toronto Citizen,* July 8, 1971.

58 White, *Planning Toronto,* 194; on Manthorpe, see "Dreams of Toronto City Planner Turned Into a Nightmare of Red Tape," *Globe and Mail,* August 23, 2007.

59 "City Ends Business Group's Special Status," *Globe and Mail,* February 18, 1971; List of Briefs Received, Jul. 17 and 20, Toronto Reference Library, Eaton Centre Briefs 1972, 711.552 E135.

60 "Crombie First to Enter Race for Mayoralty"; "Defiant Tenants Vow to Continue Bleecker St. Fight," both in *Toronto Star,* July 7, 1972.

61 On the two opposed camps, see, for example, "How Mayoralty Candidates Voted since '69 – It's on the Record," *Toronto Star,* November 24, 1972; "David Crombie Cares (Fall 1972)," AO, F1058, B253237-CPP.

62 The best example is "Special Election Issue," *UDI Views,* December 1972; see also "People Power: A Vital Force for Good That Must Not Be Misunderstood or Abused," *UDI Views,* August 1972.

63 "Eaton Centre Plan Accepted by Trinity," *Globe and Mail,* October 12, 1972; "Fairview Cools It to Survive Heat on Eaton Centre," *Daily Commercial News,* July 26, 1972, captures the tone of the meetings well.

64 Agreement between Church of the Holy Trinity, Fairview Corporation and Eaton's, Nov. 14, 1972, AO, F299-501-135, B382473.

65 Downtown Council Submission, Jul. 17, 1972; Notes for Planning Board Presentation, Jul. 17, 1972, both in Toronto Reference Library, Eaton Centre Briefs 1972, 711.552 E135.

66 City of Toronto, *Appendix "A" to the Minutes of Proceedings for the Year 1972* (Toronto: City of Toronto, 1973), 4242–415.

67 "Eaton Centre Agreement Called Too Lax," *Globe and Mail,* November 23, 1972; City of Toronto, *Appendix "A,"* 4238 ("awkward").

68 "Mayor Lists Problems: Davis, Holy Trinity, and Protest Groups," *Toronto Star,* October 12, 1972.

69 "Special Election Issue," *UDI Views,* December 1972.

70 Notes: Speech to Building Owners and Managers Association, Oct. 16, 1973, CTA, F1326-302-74.

71 Richard White explores this change in detail in *Planning Toronto*, 302–19.

72 "Eaton's Downtown Suburbia Rears Its Head Again," *Toronto Citizen*, October 11, 1973; Presentation of Fairview-Eaton Proposal, Jul. 17, 1972, Toronto Reference Library, Eaton Centre Briefs 1972, 711.552 E135.

73 The main critiques are outlined in Better Downtown Planning Eaton Centre Memorandum, Jan. 28, 1974, CTA, F1026-51.

74 See Frieden and Sagalyn, *Downtown, Inc.*, 172–97.

75 Zeidler, *Building Cities Life*, 167–87.

76 Ibid., 168–69.

77 Mumford, *The City in History*, 439; on Houston's Galleria, see "Supercity: Supermall," *Architectural Forum* 136 (April 1972): 30–35.

78 Agreement between Church of the Holy Trinity, Fairview Corporation and Eaton's, Nov. 14, 1972, AO, F299-501-135, B382473.

79 See "Eaton Centre Slideshow, Glass Arch Dazzle Council"; and "City's Heart Is at Stake in Eaton Plan," both in *Globe and Mail*, November 6, 1973.

80 Public Relations Position: Toronto CBD, Apr. 30, 1970, AO, F229-162-0-373, B253778.

81 "At Last It's Go," *Eaton News*, May 1974.

82 "Ancient Yonge Renews ... ," *Toronto Star*, November 29, 1973. The *Toronto Sun* took the most nostalgic tack in "The Strip Won't Be Quite the Same," *Toronto Sun*, January 27, 1974.

83 "New Eaton's Opens with Trumpets, Pipes," *Toronto Star*, February 10, 1977.

84 Quotes in this paragraph are from A Company Dream Takes Shape, 1977, AO, F229-162-0-385, B253779.

85 "1½ Ton Eaton Statue Trundles up Street," *Toronto Star*, December 30, 1976; Special Programs Commemorate Closing, Jan. 1977, AO, F229-162-0-385, B253779.

86 Examples drawn from "I Mourn Loss of an Old Friend," *Toronto Star*, February 4, 1977; and "New Store Evokes Happy Memories in Old Eatonians," *Toronto Star*, February 10, 1977.

87 "Last Day at Eaton's: Buying Fever, Sadness," *Globe and Mail*, February 6, 1977.

88 Steve Penfold discusses the challenges of the 1970s for Eaton's and other Canadian department stores in *A Mile of Make-Believe*, 159–67.

89 TEC Merchandising Philosophy, Dec. 1965, AO, F229-501-135, B382479; "Eaton's Banking on High Productivity from New Centre," *Globe and Mail*, January 14, 1977.

90 "Eaton's Scraps Its Catalogue," *Toronto Star*, January 14, 1976; "Season's Greetings: You've Got the Boot!" *Toronto Sun*, December 12, 1976; "Eaton Centre: Six Months Later," *Toronto Sun*, August 21, 1977; "Santa's Parade Dies – After 77 Years," *Toronto Star*, August 9, 1982.

91 John Craig Eaton, "The Gamble That Paid Off," October 24, 1977, Canadian Club Toronto, http://www.canadianclub.org/Events/EventDetails.aspx?id=2135.

92 Stoffman, *The Cadillac Fairview Story*, 71–72.

93 On the merger, see Gluskin, *Royal Commission*, 14–20; on the developer and the centre's profitability, see "Developer's Assets $2 Billion," *Toronto Star*, August 10, 1979; "Eaton Centre II: Something to Smile About," *Business Journal*, September 1979, 13–18; and "Cadillac Fairview to Move Downtown," *Toronto Star*, September 26, 1979.

94 Data drawn from *Might's Greater Toronto City Directory* (Toronto: Might's, 1980). For profiles of a few property owners on Yonge, see Grattan Gray, "Who Owns Yonge Street?," *Toronto Life,* September 1974.

95 On mall shopping and experience, see Goss, "The 'Magic of the Mall,'" 21–25; and Crawford, "The World in a Shopping Mall," 8. Quotes from "Eaton Centre," *Toronto Star,* August 7, 1979.

96 "Life in the City: Giant Shopping, Eating Centre Proves It's Still Possible," *Toronto Star,* September 27, 1980.

97 For the tenant list from 1979, see the *Mews Eaton Centre Gazette,* Fall 1979, CTA, F70-1144-2-44; on rental costs, see "Eaton Centre: Six Months Later," *Toronto Sun,* August 21, 1977; on leasing practices, see "Will New Centre Concentrate Toronto Shopping?," *Financial Post,* December 25, 1976; and more generally Gareth Shaw, "Shopping Centre Developments in Toronto," in *Shopping Centre Development: Policies and Prospects,* ed. John A. Dawson and J. Dennis Lord (London: Croom Helm, 1985), 112–19.

98 "Will New Centre Concentrate Toronto Shopping?" *Financial Post,* December 25, 1976; "Eaton Centre Complex Will House 18 Theatres," *Globe and Mail,* October 19, 1978.

99 Downtown Business Council to Crombie, Mar. 3, 1977; TEC Merchants' Association to City Solicitor, Jun. 27, 1977, both in CTA, F200-1818-29.

100 The first mention of the project "killing Yonge" dates from 1971. "Eaton Plan Could Kill Yonge, 2 Aldermen Warn," *Globe and Mail,* May 6, 1971.

101 Statistics from "Eaton Centre: Six Months Later," *Toronto Sun,* August 21, 1977; and "Life in the City: Giant Shopping, Eating Centre," *Toronto Star,* September 27, 1980; statistics from Pedestrian Attitude Survey: Lower Yonge Street, Summer 1978, CTA, F200-1985-33; and "A Magnet in the City's Core," *Globe and Mail,* March 31, 1979.

102 "Eaton Centre Firmly Defended," *Globe and Mail,* March 17, 1979, suggests that traffic in and out of Dundas subway station more than doubled from thirty-two thousand daily users in 1975 to seventy-five thousand in 1979.

103 "Destruction of Yonge St Blamed on Centre," *Toronto Star,* March 1, 1979; "Centre Not to Blame," *Globe and Mail,* March 31, 1979.

104 The Downtown Council recognized this shift in its efforts to rebrand the area as a "cultural and entertainment centre." See Downtown Council Brief, June 1977, CTA, F200-1818-29.

105 "New Main Street: Eaton Centre," *Toronto Star,* August 7, 1979.

106 Terry Bush, "Life in the City (Starts at the Centre)," 1977 (jingle); for television spots, see "The Eaton Centre – Life in the City," 1983; and "Eaton Centre – My City, My Centre," 1985. For a selection of Eaton Centre TV ads, see retrontario.com, https://www.youtube.com/watch?v=6O6Qn2EUz5s&ab_channel=Retrontario.

107 Cohen, "From Town Center to Shopping Center," 1059.

108 "Eaton Centre Concept Blends Suburban, Downtown Shopping," *Toronto Star,* August 27, 1976.

109 Belisle, *Retail Nation,* 92–95; on the key place of the female consumer, see also Fahrni, "Explorer la consommation," 468–69.

110 Pedestrian Attitude Survey: Lower Yonge Street, Summer 1978, CTA, F200-1985-33.

111 "Meet Me for Lunch by the Fountain," *Toronto Star,* August 6, 1980.

112 "Eaton Centre Firmly Defended," *Globe and Mail,* March 17, 1979.

113 "Security – How to Defend Your Investment," *Shopping Center World,* November 1977.

114 "Protecting Shoppers Means Protecting Profits," *Shopping Center World,* October 1984; "Life in the City: Giant Shopping, Eating Centre," *Toronto Star,* September 27, 1980.

115 "Tougher Security Keeps Undesirables from Eaton Centre," *Toronto Star,* April 15, 1977; see "Wall-to-Wall Kids Scare Shoppers," *Toronto Sun,* March 30, 1980, for the targeting of Black teenagers.

116 Figures for the 1980 removals are from "Wall-to-Wall Kids Scare Shoppers," *Toronto Sun,* March 30, 1980. For the mid-1980s, see Gillespie to Layton, Jun. 14, 1985, CTA, F1361-1545-13. Numbers of trespass charges are from "Eaton Pickets Get Access to Mall," *Globe and Mail,* April 18, 1985.

117 Ontario Court of Appeal-843/86, Transcript, *R. v Layton,* 24, quoted in Tucker, "The Malling of Property Law?," 314.

118 "Police Call Mall an 84-Day Orgy of Lawlessness," *Toronto Star,* November 9, 1973. See Chapter 3 for more details.

119 See maps in City of Toronto, *Appendix "A,"* 4311–320.

120 These cases are covered in Tucker, "The Malling of Property Law?," 313–33.

Remaking Downtown Yonge Street

1 "The Radical Re-imagining of Yonge Street," *Toronto Star,* September 25, 2015.

2 "Toronto Reaches for 'Pause Button' on Yonge Street Redevelopment," *Metro News,* October 19, 2016.

3 Zeidler, *Buildings Cities Life,* 184–86.

4 In 2010, 53 percent of Canada's top retailers were foreign-owned and -operated, with the vast majority being American. Industry Canada, *Canada's Changing Retail Market, 2010* (Ottawa: Industry Canada, 2013).

5 Robert Allsop, "Are We Killing Yonge Street?" *Now Magazine,* July 6, 2016.

6 The story is related in Milroy, *Thinking Planning and Urbanism.*

7 "We Don't Deserve This Horrorchitecture," *Toronto Star,* January 14, 2008.

8 "Iconic Yonge-Dundas Square a Major City Asset," *Toronto Star,* February 4, 2008.

9 City of Toronto, *yongeTOmorrow Report* (Toronto: City of Toronto, 2020), 6–7.

10 City of Toronto, *Toronto Municipal Code 636: Public Squares,* revised June 2015.

11 Ruppert, *The Moral Economy of Cities;* Smith, "'Whose Streets?,'" 156–67.

12 A critical account of the crime and its aftermath is Arvast, *What Killed Jane Creba.*

13 "Police Cast Keen Eye on Videotapes," *Toronto Star,* December 28, 2005.

14 Forty of the fifty-two who were shot and killed in 2005 were African Canadian men. Chan and Chunn, *Racialization, Crime, and Criminal Justice,* 59–60.

15 See, for example, David Brady Productions' three-part documentary series *Yonge Street Rock and Roll Stories* (Toronto: David Brady Productions, 2011).

16 "That Time When Yonge and Dundas Was Cool," blogTO, August 19, 2020, http://www.blogto.com/city/2016/01/that_time_when_yonge_and_dundas_was_cool/.

17 Liz Worth, *Treat Me Like Dirt: An Oral History of Punk in Toronto and Beyond, 1977–1981* (Toronto: ECW Press, 2009), 195.

18 "12,000 Pinpricks of Light Online to Save Sam's Iconic Sign," *Toronto Star,* June 1, 2007; "Sam the Record Man Sign Back at Yonge-Dundas Square," *Toronto Star,* December 1, 2017.

19 Edward Keenan, "Don't Bring a Mall into the Municipal Temple," *Toronto Star,* September 30, 2015.

20 Robert Allsop, "Are We Killing Yonge Street?," *Now Magazine,* July 6, 2016.

21 City of Toronto/DIALOG, *Historic Yonge Street: Heritage Conservation District Plan* (Toronto: DIALOG, 2016).

22 Downtown Yonge Business Improvement Association, *YongeLove* (Toronto: DYBIA, 2015); on yongeTOmorrow, see "Council Approves Redesign of Busy Downtown Yonge St. for Pedestrians," *Toronto Star,* February 3, 2021, http://www.thestar.com/news/city_hall/2021/02/03/council-approves-redesign-of-busy-downtown-yonge-st-for-pedestrians.html.

Selected Bibliography

Archival Sources

Archives of Ontario (AO)
F 299 T. Eaton Company Fonds
F 1058 Pollution Probe Fonds
Legislature of Ontario Debates
RG 33 Ministry of the Solicitor General
RG 64 Ministry of Justice

City of Toronto Archives (CTA)
F 16 Toronto Transit Commission Fonds
F 20 Howard Walker Fonds
F 53 Community Folk Art Council of Metropolitan Toronto Fonds
F 70 Larry Becker Fonds
F 200 Former City of Toronto Fonds
F 220 Municipality of Metropolitan Toronto Fonds
F 1026 Downtown Action Fonds
F 1048 Friends of Old City Hall Fonds
F 1306 John Sewell Fonds
F 1314 William Archer Fonds
F 1326 Colin Vaughan Fonds
F 1337 David Crombie Fonds
F 1361 Jack Layton Fonds
F 2032 City of Toronto Planning Board Fonds

Toronto Reference Library
Baldwin Collection/*Toronto Star* Digital Archives
Might's city directories
Minutes of the City of Toronto Council
Minutes of the Metropolitan Toronto Council

Newspaper clippings files
Reference Stacks Toronto Collection
Urban Affairs Collection

Other Sources

Armstrong, Christopher. *Civic Symbol: Creating Toronto's New City Hall, 1952–1966.* Toronto: University of Toronto Press, 2015.

Arthur, Eric. *Toronto: No Mean City.* Toronto: University of Toronto Press, 1964.

Arvast, Anita. *What Killed Jane Creba: Rap, Race, and the Invention of a Gang War.* Toronto: Dundurn, 2016.

Backhouse, Constance. "Nineteenth-Century Canadian Prostitution Law: Reflection of a Discriminatory Society." *Social History/Histoire sociale* 18, 36 (1985): 387–423.

Beauregard, Robert A. *Voices of Decline: The Postwar Fate of US Cities.* Cambridge, MA: Blackwell, 1994.

Belisle, Donica. *Retail Nation: Department Stores and the Making of Modern Canada.* Vancouver: UBC Press, 2011.

Bliss, Michael. *Northern Enterprise: Five Centuries of Canadian Business.* Toronto: McClelland and Stewart, 1990.

Blomley, Nicholas. *Rights of Passage: Sidewalks and the Regulation of Public Flow.* London: Routledge, 2010.

Bocking, Stephen. "Constructing Urban Expertise: Professional and Political Authority in Toronto, 1940–1970." *Journal of Urban History* 33, 1 (2006): 51–76.

Brock, Deborah. *Making Work, Making Trouble: Prostitution as a Social Problem.* Toronto: University of Toronto Press, 1998.

Bronstein, Carolyn. *Battling Pornography: The American Feminist Anti-Pornography Movement, 1976–1986.* New York: Cambridge University Press, 2011.

Brushett, Kevin. "'People and Government Travelling Together': Community Organization, Urban Planning and the Politics of Post-War Reconstruction in Toronto, 1943–1953." *Urban History Review/Revue d'histoire urbaine* 27, 2 (March 1999): 44–58.

Bunting, Trudi, and Hugh Millward. "A Tale of Two CBDs I: The Decline and Revival(?) of Downtown Retailing in Halifax and Kitchener." *Canadian Journal of Urban Research* 7, 2 (December 1998): 139–66.

Careless, J.M.S. *Toronto to 1918: An Illustrated History.* Toronto: Lorimer, 1984.

Caulfield, Jon. "'Reform' as a Chaotic Concept: The Case of Toronto." *Urban History Review/Revue d'histoire urbaine* 17, 2 (October 1988): 107–11.

–. *The Tiny Perfect Mayor.* Toronto: Lorimer, 1974.

Chan, Wendy, and Dorothy Chunn. *Racialization, Crime, and Criminal Justice in Canada.* Toronto: University of Toronto Press, 2014.

Charney, Igal. "Three Dimensions of Capital Switching within the Real Estate Sector: A Canadian Case Study." *International Journal of Urban and Regional Research* 25, 4 (December 2001): 740–58.

Cheyne, Michael. "No Better Way? The Kalamazoo Mall and the Legacy of Pedestrian Malls." *Michigan Historical Review* 36, 1 (2010): 103–28.

Churchill, David. "American Expatriates and the Building of Alternative Social

Space in Toronto, 1965–1977." *Urban History Review/Revue d'histoire urbaine* 39, 1 (Fall 2010): 31–44.

Clipperton, Deborah. "Work, Sex, or Theatre? A Brief History of Toronto Strippers and Sex Work Identity." In *Selling Sex: Experience, Advocacy, and Research on Sex Work in Canada,* ed. Emily van der Meulen, Elya Durisin, and Victoria Love, 29–44. Vancouver: UBC Press, 2013.

Cmiel, Kenneth. "The Politics of Civility." In *The Sixties: From Memory to History,* ed. David Farber, 263–90. Chapel Hill: University of North Carolina Press, 1994.

Cohen, Lizabeth. "Buying into Downtown Revival: The Centrality of Retail to Postwar Urban Renewal in American Cities." *Annals of the American Academy of Political and Social Science* 611 (May 2007): 82–95.

–. "From Town Center to Shopping Center: The Reconfiguration of Community Marketplaces in Postwar America." *American Historical Review* 101, 4 (1996): 1050–81.

–. *Saving America's Cities: Ed Logue and the Struggle to Renew Urban America in the Suburban Age.* New York: Farrar, Straus and Giroux, 2019.

Collier, Robert. *Contemporary Cathedrals: Large-Scale Developments in Canadian Cities.* Montreal: Harvest House, 1975.

Crawford, Margaret. "The World in a Shopping Mall." In *Variations on a Theme Park: The New American City and the End of Public Space,* ed. Michael Sorkin, 3–30. New York: Hill and Wang, 1992.

CTPB (City of Toronto Planning Board). *Core Area Task Force: Technical Appendix.* Toronto: CTPB, 1974.

Davies, Stephen. "Reckless Walking Must be Discouraged: The Automobile and the Shaping of Urban Canada to 1930." *Urban History Review/Revue d'histoire urbaine* 18, 2 (October 1989): 123–38.

De Sa, Anthony. *Kicking the Sky.* Toronto: Doubleday Canada, 2013.

Dennis, Richard. "Interpreting the Apartment House: Modernity and Metropolitanism in Toronto, 1900–1930." *Journal of Historical Geography* 20, 3 (1994): 305–22.

Douville, Bruce. "The Uncomfortable Pew: Christianity, the New Left, and the Hip Counterculture in Toronto, 1965–1975." PhD thesis, York University, 2011.

Drouin, Martin. *Le combat du patrimoine à Montréal (1973–2003).* Quebec City: Presses de l'Université du Québec, 2005.

Dunae, Patrick. "Geographies of Sexual Commerce and the Production of Prostitutional Space: Victoria, British Columbia, 1860–1914." *Journal of the Canadian Historical Association* 19, 1 (2008): 115–42.

Fahrni, Magda. "Explorer la consommation dans une perspective historique." *Revue d'histoire de l'Amérique française* 58, 4 (Spring 2005): 465–73.

Farber, David, and Jeff Roche, eds. *The Conservative Sixties.* New York: P. Lang, 2003.

Featherstone, Mike. "Automobilities: An Introduction." *Theory, Culture and Society* 21, 4 (2004): 1–24.

Feriel, Cédric. "L'invention du centre-ville européen. La politique des secteurs piétonniers en Europe occidentale, 1960–1980." *Histoire urbaine* 42 (2015): 99–122.

Fernandes, Gilberto. "Beyond the 'Politics of Toil': Collective Mobilization and Individual Activism in Toronto's Portuguese Community, 1950s–1990s." *Urban History Review/Revue d'histoire urbaine* 39, 1 (Fall 2010): 59–72.

Filion, Pierre, Igal Charney, and Rachel Weber. "Downtowns That Work: Lessons from Toronto and Chicago." *Canadian Journal of Urban Research* 24, 2 (Winter 2015): 25–27.

Filion, Pierre, and Karen Hammond. "When Planning Fails: Downtown Malls in Mid-Size Cities." *Canadian Journal of Urban Research* 17, 2 (2008): 1–27.

Fogelson, Robert M. *Downtown: Its Rise and Fall, 1880–1950*. New Haven: Yale University Press, 2001.

Francis, Daniel. *Red Light Neon: A History of Vancouver's Sex Trade*. Vancouver: Subway Books, 2006.

Freiden, Bernard, and Lynne Sagalyn. *Downtown Inc.: How America Rebuilds Cities*. Cambridge, MA: MIT Press, 1989.

Fulford, Robert. *Accidental City: The Transformation of Toronto*. Toronto: Macfarlane Walter and Ross, 1995.

Gad, Gunter. "Downtown Montreal and Toronto: Distinct Places with Much in Common." *Canadian Journal of Regional Science* 22, 1–2 (Spring-Summer 1999): 143–70.

–. "Metropolitan Dominance." In *Historical Atlas of Canada*. Vol. 3, *Addressing the Twentieth Century*, ed. Geoffrey Matthews and Donald Kerr, 163–64. Toronto: University of Toronto Press, 1990.

Gad, Gunter, Elizabeth Buchanan, and Deryck Holdsworth. "Commerce in the Core: Toronto, 1881." In *Historical Atlas of Canada*. Vol. 2, *The Land Transformed*, ed. R. Louis Gentilcore, 153–54. Toronto: University of Toronto Press, 1993.

Gad, Gunter, and Deryck Holdsworth. "Corporate Capitalism and the Emergence of the High-Rise Office Building." *Urban Geography* 8, 3 (May-June 1987): 212–31.

–. "Large Office Buildings and Their Changing Occupancy: King Street, Toronto, 1880–1950." *SSAC Bulletin* 4, 85 (1985): 19–26.

Gilfoyle, Timothy J. *City of Eros: New York City, Prostitution, and the Commercialization of Sex, 1790–1920*. New York: W.W. Norton, 1992.

Gillette, Howard. "The Evolution of the Planned Shopping Center in Suburb and City." *Journal of the American Planning Association* 51, 4 (Autumn 1985): 449–60.

Gluskin, Ira. *Royal Commission on Corporate Concentration Study No. 3: Cadillac Fairview Corporation Ltd.* Ottawa: Minister of Supply and Services, 1976.

Gold, John. *The Practice of Modernism: Modern Architects and Urban Transformation, 1954–1972*. London: Routledge, 2007.

Goss, Jon. "The 'Magic of the Mall': An Analysis of Form, Function, and Meaning in the Contemporary Retail Built Environment." *Annals of the Association of American Geographers* 83, 1 (March 1993): 21–25.

Grant, Jill L., and Marcus Paterson. "Scientific Cloak/Romantic Heart: Gordon Stephenson and the Redevelopment Study of Halifax, 1957." *Town Planning Review* 83, 3 (2012): 319–36.

Greer, Allan. *Property and Dispossession: Natives, Empires and Land in Early Modern North America*. Cambridge: Cambridge University Press, 2018.

Gruen, Victor. *The Heart of Our Cities: The Urban Crisis: Diagnosis and Cure.* New York: Simon and Schuster, 1964.

Gunn, Simon. "The Spatial Turn: Changing Histories of Place and Space." In *Identities in Space: Contested Terrains in the Western City since 1850,* ed. Simon Gunn and Robert Morris, 1–14. Aldershot, UK: Ashgate, 2001.

Hall, Simon. "Protest Movements in the 1970s: The Long 1960s." *Journal of Contemporary History* 43, 4 (2008): 655–72.

Hanchett, Thomas. "U.S. Tax Policy and the Shopping-Center Boom of the 1950s and 1960s." *American Historical Review* 101, 4 (October 1996): 1082–1110.

Hardwick, M. Jeffrey. *Mall Maker: Victor Gruen, Architect of an American Dream.* Philadelphia: University of Pennsylvania Press, 2004.

Harris, Andrew, and Susan Moore. "Planning Histories and Practices of Circulating Urban Knowledge." *International Journal of Urban and Regional Research* 37, 5 (September 2013): 1499–1509.

Harris, Richard. *Creeping Conformity: How Canada Became Suburban, 1900–1960.* Toronto: University of Toronto Press, 2004.

Harris, Richard, and Peter Larkham, eds. *Changing Suburbs: Foundation, Form, and Function.* New York: Routledge, 1999.

Harris, Richard, and Martin Luymes. "The Growth of Toronto: A Cartographic Essay, 1861–1941." *Urban History Review/Revue d'histoire urbaine* 18, 3 (February 1990): 244–55.

Harvey, David. *The Urbanization of Capital: Studies in the History and Theory of Capitalist Urbanization.* Oxford: Blackwell, 1985.

Hayday, Matthew. *So They Want Us to Learn French: Promoting and Opposing Bilingualism in English-Speaking Canada.* Vancouver: UBC Press, 2015.

Heaman, Elsbeth. *A Short History of the State in Canada.* Toronto: University of Toronto Press, 2015.

Henderson, Stuart. *Making the Scene: Yorkville and Hip Toronto in the 1960s.* Toronto: University of Toronto Press, 2011.

–. "Toronto's Hippie Disease: End Days in the Yorkville Scene, August 1968." *Journal of the Canadian Historical Association* 17, 1 (2006): 205–34.

Heron, Craig. *Booze: A Distilled History.* Toronto: Between the Lines, 2003.

Hirt, Sonia A. *Zoned in the USA: The Origins and Implications of American Land-Use Regulation.* Ithaca, NY: Cornell University Press, 2014.

Hooper, Tom. "'Enough Is Enough': The Right to Privacy Committee and Bathhouse Raids in Toronto, 1978–83." PhD thesis, York University, 2016.

Hunt, Alan. *Governing Morals: A Social History of Moral Regulation.* Cambridge: Cambridge University Press, 1999.

Iacovetta, Franca. "Immigrant Gifts, Canadian Treasures, and Spectacles of Pluralism: The International Institute of Toronto in North American Context, 1950s–1970s." *Journal of American Ethnic History* 31, 1 (Fall 2011): 34–73.

–. "The Sexual Politics of Moral Citizenship and Containing 'Dangerous' Foreign Men in Cold War Canada, 1950s–1960s." *Histoire sociale/Social History* 33, 66 (November 2000): 361–89.

Isenberg, Alison. *Downtown America: A History of the Place and the People Who Made It.* Chicago: University of Chicago Press, 2004.

Jacobs, Jane. *The Death and Life of Great American Cities.* New York: Random House, 1961.

Kaplan, Harold. *Reform, Planning, and City Politics: Montreal, Winnipeg, Toronto.* Toronto: University of Toronto Press, 1982.

Kenny, Nicolas. "Emotions and City Life." *Urban History Review/Revue d'histoire urbaine* 42, 2 (Spring 2014): 5–7.

Kerkvliet, Benedict. "Everyday Politics in Peasant Societies (and Ours)." *Journal of Peasant Studies* 36, 1 (2009): 227–43.

Killan, Gerald, and George Warecki. "The Algonquin Wildlands League and the Emergence of Environmental Politics in Ontario, 1965–1974." *Environmental History Review* 16, 4 (Winter 1992): 1–27.

Klemek, Christopher. *The Transatlantic Collapse of Urban Renewal: Postwar Urbanism from New York to Berlin.* Chicago: University of Chicago Press, 2011.

Kopytek, Bruce Allen. *Eaton's: The Trans-Canada Store.* Charleston, SC: History Press, 2014.

Kruse, Kevin M., and Thomas J. Sugrue, eds. *The New Suburban History.* Chicago: University of Chicago Press, 2006.

Lacasse, Danielle. *La prostitution feminine à Montréal, 1945–70.* Montreal: Boréal, 1994.

Lacombe, Dany. *Blue Politics: Pornography and the Law in the Age of Feminism.* Toronto: University of Toronto Press, 1994.

Langer, Peter. "Sociology – Four Images of Urban Diversity: Bazaar, Jungle, Organism, and Machine." In *Cities of the Mind: Images and Themes of the City in the Social Sciences,* ed. Lloyd Rodwin and Robert M. Hollister, 97–118. New York: Springer, 1984.

Lassiter, Matthew. *The Silent Majority: Suburban Politics in the Sunbelt South.* Princeton: Princeton University Press, 2006.

Lavender-Harris, Amy. *Imagining Toronto.* Toronto: Mansfield Press, 2010.

Lefebvre, Henri. *The Production of Space.* Oxford: Basil Blackwell, 1991.

Lemon, James. "Plans for Early 20th-Century Toronto: Lost in Management." *Urban History Review/Revue d'histoire urbaine* 18, 1 (June 1989): 11–31.

–. *Toronto since 1918: An Illustrated History.* Toronto: Lorimer, 1985.

Levesque, Andrée. "Éteindre le Red Light: Les réformateurs et la prostitution à Montréal entre 1865 et 1925." *Urban History Review/Revue d'histoire urbaine* 17, 3 (February 1989): 191–201.

Lewis, Robert, and Paul Hess. "Refashioning Urban Space in Postwar Toronto: The Wood-Wellesley Redevelopment Area, 1952–1957." *Planning Perspectives* 31 (2016): 563–84.

Ley, David. *The New Middle Class and the Remaking of the Central City.* New York: Oxford University Press, 1996.

Lorimer, James. "Citizens and the Corporate Development of the Contemporary Canadian City." *Urban History Review/Revue d'histoire urbaine* 12, 1 (June 1983): 3–9.

–. *The Developers.* Toronto: Lorimer, 1978.

Lorinc, John, Michael McClelland, Ellen Scheinberg, and Tatum Taylor, eds. *The Ward: The Life and Loss of Toronto's First Immigrant Neighbourhood.* Toronto: Coach House, 2015.

Lyon, Barry. *Yonge Street Revitalization Project.* Toronto: Yonge Street Revitalization Project, July 1978.

Mackintosh, Phillip Gordon. *Newspaper City: Toronto's Street Surfaces and the Liberal Press, 1860–1935.* Toronto: University of Toronto Press, 2017.

–. "Scrutiny in the Modern City: The Domestic Public and the Toronto Local Council of Women at the Turn of the Twentieth Century." *Gender, Place and Culture* 12, 1 (2005): 29–48.

Mahood, Linda. "Hitchin' a Ride in the 1970s: Canadian Youth Culture and the Romance with Mobility." *Histoire sociale/Social history* 47, 93 (May 2014): 205–27.

Marquis, Greg. "The Police as a Social Service in Early Twentieth-Century Toronto." *Social History/Histoire sociale* 25, 50 (November 1992): 335–58.

Martel, Marcel. "'They Smell Bad, Have Diseases, and Are Lazy': RCMP Officers Reporting on Hippies in the Late Sixties." *Canadian Historical Review* 90, 2 (June 2009): 215–45.

Mathieu, Lilian. "The Emergence and Uncertain Outcomes of Prostitutes' Social Movements." *European Journal of Women's Studies* 10, 1 (February 2003): 29–50.

Micallef, Shawn. *Stroll: Psychogeographic Walking Tours of Toronto.* Toronto: Coach House Books, 2010.

Milroy, Beth Moore. *Thinking Planning and Urbanism.* Vancouver: UBC Press, 2010.

Monkkonen, Eric. *America Becomes Urban: The Development of U.S. Cities and Towns, 1790–1980.* Berkeley: University of California Press, 1988.

Moore, Paul. "Movie Palaces on Canadian Downtown Main Streets: Montreal, Toronto, and Vancouver." *Urban History Review/Revue d'histoire urbaine* 32, 2 (Spring 2004): 3–20.

Moore, Peter. "Zoning and Planning: The Toronto Experience, 1904–1970." In *The Usable Urban Past: Planning and Politics in the Modern Canadian City,* ed. Alan Artibise and Gilbert Stelter, 316–41. Toronto: Macmillan, 1979.

Morton, Desmond. *Mayor Howland: The Citizen's Candidate.* Toronto: Hakkert, 1971.

Mumford, Lewis. *The City in History: Its Origins, Its Transformations, Its Prospects.* New York: Harcourt, 1961.

Nerbas, Don. "William Zeckendorf, Place Ville-Marie, and the Making of Modern Montreal." *Urban History Review/Revue d'histoire urbaine* 43, 2 (Spring 2015): 5–25.

Neumann, Tracy. *Remaking the Rust Belt: The Postindustrial Transformation of North America.* Philadelphia: University of Pennsylvania Press, 2016.

Ng, Yvonne Chi-Ying. "Ideology, Media, and Moral Panics: An Analysis of the Jaques Murder." Master's thesis, University of Toronto, 1981.

Norton, Peter. *Fighting Traffic: The Dawn of the Motor Age in the American City.* Cambridge, MA: MIT Press, 2002.

Nowlin, Christopher. *Judging Obscenity: A Critical History of Expert Evidence.* Montreal and Kingston: McGill-Queen's University Press, 2003.

O'Connor, Ryan. *The First Green Wave: Pollution Probe and the Origins of Environmental Activism in Ontario.* Vancouver: UBC Press, 2015.

Osbaldeston, Mark. *Unbuilt Toronto: The History of the City That Might Have Been.* Toronto: Dundurn, 2008.

Penfold, Steve. "'Are We to Go Literally to the Hot Dogs?' Parking Lots, Drive-Ins, and the Critique of Progress in Toronto's Suburbs, 1965–1975." *Urban History Review/Revue d'histoire urbaine* 33, 1 (Fall 2004): 8–23.

–. "The Eaton's Santa Claus Parade and the Making of a Metropolitan Spectacle, 1905–1982." *Social History/Histoire sociale* 44, 87 (May 2011): 1–28.

–. *A Mile of Make-Believe: A History of the Eaton's Santa Claus Parade.* Toronto: University of Toronto Press, 2016.

Pevere, Geoff. "Flickering City: Toronto on Film until 2002." In Geoff Pevere, Piers Handling, Matthew Hays, Wyndham Wise, Brenda Longfellow, Steve Gravestock, and Justin D. Edwards, *Toronto on Film,* 19–66. Toronto: Toronto International Film Festival, 2009.

Peyton, Jonathan. *Unbuilt Environments: Tracing Postwar Development in Northwest British Columbia.* Vancouver: UBC Press, 2017.

Poitras, Claire. "Downtowns, Past and Present." *Urban History Review/Revue d'histoire urbaine* 37, 2 (Spring 2009): 3–5.

Ranasinghe, Prashan. "Reconceptualizing Vagrancy and Reconstructing the Vagrant: A Socio-Legal Analysis of Criminal Law Reform in Canada, 1953–1972." *Osgoode Hall Law Journal* 48 (2010): 55–94.

Relph, Edward. *Toronto: Transformations in a City and Its Region.* Philadelphia: University of Pennsylvania Press, 2014.

Robertson, Kent. *Pedestrian Malls and Skywalks: Traffic Separation Strategies in American Downtowns.* Aldershot, UK: Avebury, 1994.

–. "The Status of the Pedestrian Mall in American Downtowns." *Urban Affairs Quarterly* 26, 2 (December 1990): 250–73.

Robinson, Danielle. "Modernism at a Crossroad: The Spadina Expressway Controversy in Toronto, ca. 1960–1971." *Canadian Historical Review* 92, 2 (2011): 295–322.

Rockwell, Margaret. "The Facelift and the Wrecking Ball: Urban Renewal and Hamilton's King Street West, 1957–1971." *Urban History Review/Revue d'histoire urbaine* 37, 2 (Spring 2009): 53–61.

Rome, Adam. "The Genius of Earth Day." *Environmental History* 15, 2 (March 2010): 194–205.

Rose, Albert. *Governing Metropolitan Toronto: A Social and Political Analysis, 1953–1971.* Berkeley: University of California Press, 1972.

Rosenwein, Barbara H. "Worrying about Emotions in History." *American Historical Review* 107, 3 (2002): 821–45.

Ross, Daniel. "The Politics of Public Space: Toronto's Yonge Street Pedestrian Mall, 1971–1974." *Urban History Review/Revue d'histoire urbaine* 47, 1–2 (Fall-Spring 2018–19): 89–102.

Rubenstein, Harvey. *Pedestrian Malls, Streetscapes, and Urban Spaces.* New York: John Wiley and Sons, 1978.

Rubin, Elihu. *Insuring the City: The Prudential Center and the Postwar Urban Landscape*. New Haven, CT: Yale University Press, 2012.

Rudin, Jeremy. *The Changing Structure of the Land Development Industry in the Toronto Area*. Toronto: Centre for Urban and Community Studies, 1978.

Ruppert, Evelyn. *The Moral Economy of Cities: Shaping Good Citizens*. Toronto: University of Toronto Press, 2006.

Santink, Joy. *Timothy Eaton and the Rise of His Department Store*. Toronto: University of Toronto Press, 1990.

Saulnier, Pierre-Yves, and Shane Ewan, eds. *Another Global City: Historical Explorations into the Transnational Municipal Moment, 1850–2000*. New York: Palgrave Macmillan, 2008.

Scadding, Henry. *Toronto of Old*. Toronto: Adam, Stevenson, 1873.

Sendbuehler, M.P. "Battling 'The Bane of Our Cities': Class, Territory, and the Prohibition Debate in Toronto, 1877." *Urban History Review/Revue d'histoire urbaine* 22, 1 (October 1993): 30–48.

Senelick, Laurence. "Private Parts in Public Places." In *Inventing Times Square: Commerce and Culture at the Crossroads of the World*, ed. William R. Taylor, 329–55. New York: Russell Sage, 1991.

Sewell, Jessica. *Women and the Everyday City: Public Space in San Francisco, 1890–1915*. Minneapolis: University of Minnesota Press, 2011.

Sewell, John. *Up against City Hall*. Toronto: James Lewis and Samuel, 1972.

Shapely, Peter. "Civic Pride and Redevelopment in the Post-War British City." *Urban History* 39, 2 (May 2012): 310–28.

Sides, Josh. "Excavating the Postwar Sex District in San Francisco." *Journal of Urban History* 32, 3 (2006): 355–79.

Smith, Christopher. "'Whose Streets?': Urban Social Movements and the Politicization of Public Space." *Public: Art, Culture, Ideas* 29 (2004): 156–67.

Spain, Daphne. *Gendered Spaces*. Chapel Hill: University of North Carolina Press, 1992.

Spurr, Peter. *Land and Urban Development: A Preliminary Study*. Toronto: Lorimer, 1976.

Stein, David Lewis. *Toronto for Sale: The Destruction of a City*. Toronto: New Press, 1972.

Stoffman, Daniel. *The Cadillac Fairview Story*. Toronto: Cadillac Fairview, 2004.

Strange, Carolyn. *Toronto's Girl Problem: The Perils and Pleasures of the City, 1880–1930*. Toronto: University of Toronto Press, 1995.

Teaford, John C. *The Metropolitan Revolution: The Rise of Post-Urban America*. New York: Columbia University Press, 2006.

–. *The Rough Road to Renaissance: Urban Revitalization in North America, 1940–1985*. Baltimore, MD: Johns Hopkins University Press, 1990.

Terranova, Charissa N. "Ultramodern Underground Dallas: Vincent Ponte's Pedestrian-Way as Systematic Solution to the Declining Downtown." *Urban History Review/Revue d'histoire urbaine* 37, 2 (Spring 2009): 18–29.

Tillotson, Shirley. *Give and Take: The Citizen-Taxpayer and the Rise of Canadian Democracy*. Vancouver: UBC Press, 2017.

Tilly, Charles. "What Good Is Urban History?," *Journal of Urban History* 22 (1996): 702–19.

Tucker, Eric. "The Malling of Property Law?: The Toronto Eaton Centre Cases, 1984–1987, and the Right to Exclude." In *Property on Trial: Canadian Cases in Context,* ed. Eric Tucker, James Muir, and Bruce Ziff, 303–52. Toronto: Irwin Law, 2012.

Valpy, Michael. "Timothy Eaton's Stern Fortifications." In *The Ward: The Life and Loss of Toronto's First Immigrant Neighbourhood,* ed. John Lorinc, Michael McClelland, Ellen Scheinberg, and Tatum Taylor, 135–39. Toronto: Coach House Press, 2015.

Valverde, Mariana. *The Age of Light, Soap, and Water: Moral Reform in English Canada, 1885–1925,* 2nd ed. Toronto: University of Toronto Press, 2008.

van der Meulen, Emily. "When Sex Is Work: Organizing for Labour Rights and Protections." *Labour/Le Travail* 69 (Spring 2012): 150–53.

Walker, Richard, and Robert D. Lewis. "Beyond the Crabgrass Frontier: Industry and the Spread of North American Cities, 1850–1950." *Journal of Historical Geography* 27, 1 (2001): 3–19.

Weaver, John C. "'Tomorrow's Metropolis' Revisited: A Critical Assessment of Urban Reform in Canada, 1880–1920." In *The Canadian City: Essays in Urban and Social History,* ed. Gilbert Stelter and Alan Artibise, 456–77. Ottawa: Carleton University Press, 1984.

Wells, Christopher. *Car Country: An Environmental History.* Seattle: University of Washington Press, 2012.

Wetherell, Sam. *Foundations: How the Built Environment Made Twentieth-Century Britain.* Princeton: Princeton University Press, 2020.

White, Richard. *Financing the Golden Age: Municipal Finance in Toronto, 1950 to 1975.* IMFG Papers on Municipal Finance and Governance 29. Toronto: Munk School of Global Affairs, 2016.

–. *Planning Toronto: The Planners, the Plans, Their Legacies, 1940–80.* Vancouver: UBC Press, 2016.

–. "Urban Renewal Revisited: Toronto, 1950 to 1970." *Canadian Historical Review* 97, 1 (Spring 2016): 1–33.

Winter, James. *London's Teeming Streets, 1830–1914.* New York: Routledge, 1993.

Young, Jason. "Searching for a Better Way: Subway Life and Metropolitan Growth in Toronto, 1942–1978." PhD thesis, York University, 2012.

Zeckendorf, William, with Edward McCreary. *The Autobiography of William Zeckendorf.* New York: Holt, Rinehart and Winston, 1970.

Zeidler, Eberhard. *Building Cities Life: An Autobiography in Architecture.* Vol. 1. Toronto: Dundurn, 2013.

Zipp, Samuel. "The Roots and Routes of Urban Renewal." *Journal of Urban History* 39, 3 (May 2013): 366–91.

Index

(f) after a page number indicates an illustration or map.

Acland, James, 58, 59, 60, 66–67
activism. *See* citizen activism
Adamson, Harold, 90–91
A.E. LePage realtor, 103, 137
African Canadians, 23, 176–77, 205*n*14
Allen, William, 57
Ambrose, Tommy, 2, 3
American Marketing Association, 31
Andrews, Don, 108
Annex Ratepayers' Association, 147
Archer, William, 11, 80, 86, 92, 142
Arthur, Eric, 58–59
Athens Restaurant, 39

Banz, George, 65
Barton, George, 56
BEAVER (Better End All Vicious Erotic Repression), 131
Belisle, Donica, 45
Berton, Pierre, 52–53, 63, 116
bicycling, 86–87, 192*n*60
Blumenfeld, Hans, 58
Body Politic newspaper, 127
body rub parlours: arson, 132; exterior (advertising), 107(f); interior, 194*n*24; municipal licensing and inspection bylaw, 119–21, 128–29; police raids, 117–18, 128–30, 167; police raids

criticism, 130; sex businesses closures, 130; sex workers, 105–6, 194*n*25. *See also* sex entertainment district ("Sin Strip")
Bourne, Larry, 53–54
Brock, Deborah, 131
Bronfman family, 137, 138
Burton, Edgar, 94
Burton, G. Allan, 45, 157(f)

Cadillac Development, 135–37, 154
Cadillac Fairview real estate developer: about, 135–37; finances, 154; property portfolio, 173; rent hierarchy, 155–56; shopping centre advertorial, 133; shopping centre plan, 134–35
Callaghan, Barry, 116
Canada: corporate development, 135–37; residential development finance program, 136–37; retail ownership, 173, 205*n*4; urban renewal funding, 42
Canada Housing and Mortgage Company, 136
Canadian Architect, 58, 69
Canadian Equity and Development, 54, 135–37, 154
Canadian Facts, 10, 67

Canadian Pacific Railway Building (1913), 25

Centennial United Church, 110

Central Area Plan (1976), 171

Charlie's Angels, 124, 127, 130

Chinatown, 82

Christian and Missionary Alliance church, 113, 125

Church of the Holy Trinity: about, 49, 140–41; aerial view, 142(f); demolition plans, 141; gay rights advocate, 141; preservation plan, 50, 63–64, 141–44; real estate development negotiations, 143–44; Trinity Square public space, 143, 148, 150–51, 162, 172

Cinema 2000 movie theatre, 104(f)

citizen activism: associations and interest groups, 58–60, 65–67, 78, 123, 147, 190n25; church preservation, 141–44; conservative populism, 113–14, 196n59; corporate vs democratic city, 145; design award, 80; expressway bans, 87; Friends of Old City Hall, 58–60, 65–67; influence (Yonge Street transformation), 167–68; pedestrian malls, 11, 77–78, 80; record store nostalgia, 177–78; sex district (churches against), 110, 113–15; sex district (demonstrations against), 115(f); sex district (letter-writers against), 99–100, 109–16, 123, 195n40; sex district (letter-writers support), 116; sex district (petitions against), 109, 113, 120; shoeshine boy murder, 124–26(f), 127; vs urban redevelopment, 144–48; youth, 144–45

City Beautiful ideal, 26

City Hall (New): aerial view, 56(f); civic square (Nathan Phillips Square), 44, 62, 63, 139; costs, 48, 58; design competition, 46, 60; planning, 44, 47, 49

City Hall (Old): civic ceremonies, 24; clock tower, 64; demolition proposal, 55–56(f), 63, 67; demolition reaction, 57–60, 66(f)–67, 70; letter of intent (purchase), 58; nostalgia for, 178; preservation proposals, 50, 59–60; real estate sale negotiations, 57–58

City Hall newsletter, 145

City Magazine journal, 146

City of Tomorrow. *See* Eaton Centre (first project (1956–67))

City of Toronto: associations and interest groups, 58–60, 65–67, 78, 123, 147, 190n25; building survey, 49; *Central Area Plan* (1976), 171; civic symbol, 44; governance restructuring (Metro Toronto), 29–30(f); incorporation (1834), 16; influence (Yonge Street transformation), 165–67; municipal archives, 9, 10–11; municipal elections, 68, 105, 107–9, 148; *Official Plan* (1949), 43–44; Places of Amusement report recommendations, 122–23; planning controls, 149; Planning Department, 44, 146–47, 149, 166; planning policies, 48–50, 171–72; planning publication *(Plan for Downtown Toronto),* 45, 49, 53, 71, 75; political alliances, 122; public housing projects, 42, 58, 125; ratepayer associations, 147; tax assessment and revenues, 27, 43–44, 57; urban bicycling lobbying, 87, 192n60; urban redevelopment debate (Eaton Centre), 146–48. *See also* Crombie, Mayor David; Dennison, Mayor William; Givens, Mayor Phillip; Lastman, Mayor Mel; Metro Toronto (Municipality of Metro Toronto – 1953); Phillips, Mayor Nathan; Redevelopment Advisory Council (RAC); Toronto Transit Commission (TTC)

Clark, Peter, 94, 158

Clark Shoes, 158, 173

Coalition for Gay Rights, 127

Cole, Janis, 11, 118
College Park complex, 171
Colonial Tavern, 37
Commerce Court (1931), 25
Community Folk Arts Council, 82
Confederation of Residents' and Ratepayers' Associations (CORRA), 123,
  144, 146, 147
corporate development: concentration,
  135–36; financialization, 136–37; influence (Yonge Street development),
  168–69; integration, 136; public-
  private partnerships, 42, 52, 71, 166,
  175–76; urban development, 135–37,
  199n4, 199n6. *See also individual
  names of real estate developers*
Cox, Marilyn, 144
Creba, Jane (murder victim), 176–77
Crombie, Mayor David: alliances, 122;
  letter-writers to (against sex district),
  99–100, 109–16, 123, 195n40; letter-
  writers to (shoeshine boy murder),
  124–25; mayoral candidacy, 147;
  planning controls, 149; on sex district, 108, 109, 120, 122, 123; on
  Yonge Street anniversary, 1

Davidson, True, 58, 122
Davies, Jim, 90
Davis, Premier William, 87, 95, 120,
  123
De Sa, Anthony, 125–26
demonstrations: bicycling parade, 86–
  87; Old City Hall demolition, 66(f);
  pedestrian malls, 77; sex district,
  115(f); shoeshine boy murder,
  125–26(f)
Dennison, Mayor William, 58, 61(f),
  68–69, 148
department stores. *See* Eaton's Department Store; retail trade; Simpson's
  Department Store
Development Department (1962), 45,
  71, 146
Diamond, Ephraim, 136

Dineen, William, 27
Disorderly Houses Act, 129, 130
downtown (concept of), 19–20, 182n12
Downtown Action project, 144–45, 146
Downtown Businessmen's Association,
  31
Downtown Council (former Downtown Businessmen's Association):
  archive, 12; downtown renewal, 2,
  156, 157–58, 204n104; pedestrian
  mall, 80, 82–83(f), 93–94; sex district, 108; street anniversary, 2
Downtown Yonge Business Improvement Association, 178
Dragon Mall, 82
Drawing Room restaurant, 106
Dundas Square, 174, 175–76, 178

Earth Day, 77
Eaton, John Craig, 154, 157(f)
Eaton, John David, 68
Eaton, Timothy, 20, 152, 172
Eaton Centre (first project (1956–67)),
  40–71; about, 62; analysis, 70–71;
  archives, 11; branding, 55; buildings
  naming, 63; cancellation, 13, 67–70;
  criticisms and opposition toward,
  57–60, 65–66(f), 67, 70; demonstrations against, 66(f); financial problems, 69; master plan reaction,
  64–67; master plan scale model, 60–
  61(f); media coverage, 61, 64, 69;
  municipal negotiations, 57–58; Old
  City Hall plans, 58, 63; opinion polls,
  64, 67; vision, 40–41, 62–63, 65. *See
  also* Project Viking (redevelopment
  project)
Eaton Centre (second project (1970–
  79)), 133–64; about, 14, 133–35;
  analysis, 162–64, 169; archives, 11;
  church real estate negotiations, 140–
  44; criticisms and opposition toward,
  133, 140–44, 146–48; design concessions, 139–40, 148, 200n27; design
  criticisms, 149–50; designs, 139–40,

148, 149–51, 155; development
agreement, 148; exterior (first phase),
134(f); galleria design, 150–51, 155;
as "killing Yonge," 156, 204*n*100;
media coverage, 151–52; merchants'
association, 156; movie theatre, 156;
newspaper advertorial, 133; opening
ceremony (first phase), 152–53(f);
opening ceremony (second phase),
157(f); pedestrian survey, 159; positive reaction to, 133, 152–53; private
space as public space, 158–62; public
art, 155; redesign, 150–51; rent hierarchy, 155–56; retail store chains,
156; security surveillance, 160(f)–62;
street access, 162, 172; trespassing,
161; visitor exclusions, 161–62;
visitor safety (women), 159; visitors,
153(f), 154, 156–57, 159, 161–62;
Yonge Street relationship, 155–62,
163–64, 172, 204*n*100
Eaton Centre Limited (formerly
Sunjam Limited), 55, 56–57, 69
Eaton News newsletter, 64, 151
Eaton's department store (T. Eaton
Company): archives, 11; bankruptcy,
172; beginnings, 20–21; buildings
demolition, 66, 94; chair, 68, 154,
157(f); College Street store, 36, 45–
46, 47, 171; competition, 20–21, 139,
157(f); corporate citizenship identity,
45–46, 55, 71, 152; corporate restructuring, 153–54; employees, 153–54,
162; factory complex, 47; founder,
20, 152, 172; influence, 36; land bank
(property portfolio), 8, 46–47(f),
55–56, 66, 94, 103, 138, 194*n*15;
locations, 36; mail-order catalogue,
154; market share, 48; marketing
strategies, 21, 48, 83; newsletter,
64, 151; newspaper ownership, 64;
pedestrian mall marketing, 83; public
exhibit ("City for Tomorrow"), 46;
Queen Street store, 3, 20, 47, 48, 139–

40, 152–53; real estate subsidiary
(Sunjam/Eaton Centre Ltd.), 55, 56–
57, 69; redevelopment lobbying, 46–
47; redevelopment project (Project
Viking), 48–50; retail vs real estate
role, 69–70; sales, 154; Santa Claus
Parade, 24–25; shopping centre
approval, 151; shopping centre development partnership, 138–40, 151,
201*n*30; statue relocation, 152, 172;
store closings, 152–53, 172; suburban expansion, 48; subway station,
75; traditions, 152–53; union drive,
162; valet parking, 29; women consumers, 21
Edison Hotel, 37
Expropriations Act (Ontario), 95

Fairview Mall, 149
Fairview real estate developer: beginnings, 137; church demolition plans,
141; church negotiations, 143–44,
147–48; council member, 200*n*25;
design planning, 149–50; development agreement, 148; development
partnership (Eaton's), 138–40, 151,
201*n*30; merger, 135, 136, 154; planning concessions, 148
Fernandes, Gilberto, 125
Fogelson, Robert, 19
Fort York, 59
Friar's Tavern, 173
Friends of Old City Hall, 11, 58–60,
65–67

Galeries d'Anjou shopping centre, 139
Galleria Vittorio Emanuele II shopping
centre, 150
Gardiner, Frederick "Big Daddy," 42
Gardiner Expressway, 34, 170
gay community, 127, 128, 141
Givens, Mayor Phillip, 57, 65–66, 68
Globe and Mail newspaper: circulation,
10, 181*n*23; database, 9, 10, 181*n*21;

downtown as heart, 6; Eaton Centre cancellation, 68; Eaton Centre criticism, 133; Eaton Centre opinion survey, 64; redevelopment terminology, 184*n*9; sex district bylaw, 121; sex district criticism, 106–7; subway construction, 31

Globe newspaper, 19, 21, 23, 25

Godfrey, Stephen, 133, 159

Gold, John, 50

Group Action to Stop Pollution (GASP), 77, 86

Gruen, Victor, 50, 56, 74

Guerilla alternative newspaper, 89, 145

Haggart, Ron, 65–66, 145

Hamilton (Ontario) building demolition, 66

Harris, Richard, 135

Heron, George, 153

Hess, Paul, 46–47

Hislop, George, 127

Holy Trinity Church. *See* Church of the Holy Trinity

Honey Dew Restaurant, 151

Hudson's Bay Company, 173

Hunt, Alan, 113

Iacovetta, Franca, 81

International Council of Shopping Centers, 139, 200*n*25

International Family Association, 115(f)

Jacobs, Jane, 133, 150, 159

Jaques, Emanuel (shoeshine boy murder), 13, 124–26(f), 127, 176

Jarvis Street ("the Track"), 131

Johnson, Jack, 131

Kalamazoo (Michigan) pedestrian mall, 74, 75, 78

Kinnear, Greg, 61–62

Kumove, Leon, 112

Lastman, Mayor Mel, 119

Lawson, Matthew, 48–50, 53, 64–65

Le Coq d'Or tavern, 37, 84

Leave the Car at Home Week, 77, 86

Lewis, Robert, 46–47

Ley, David, 78

Linetsky, Arnold "Mr. Arnold," 105, 121

Local Council of Women (Toronto), 113, 120, 125

Loew, Marcus, 22

London (Ontario) shopping centre, 52, 152

Lorimer, James, 145, 146

Lyle, John, 26, 27

Manning, Morris, 129

Manthorpe, Walter, 57, 65, 146

Massey, Vincent, 58

Massey Music Hall, 22

McArthur, Jack, 81

Meridian real estate developer, 146, 147

Metro Toronto (Municipality of Metro Toronto – 1953): body rub licensing bylaw, 119–22, 129, 132; chair, 42, 57; commercial strip plazas, 31; freeway network, 34, 170; growth, 30(f); incorporation, 29–30(f); planning, 166; shopping centres, 33; tax revenue and assessment, 43. *See also* City of Toronto

Metropolitan United Church, 145

Micallef, Shawn, 34

Mirvish, "Honest" Ed, 37

Mister Arnold's body rub parlour, 105, 107(f), 121, 194*n*24

Montreal: Galeries d'Anjou shopping centre, 139; vs Toronto as economic capital, 25, 182*n*30; urban redevelopment (Place Ville Marie), 51, 52, 54

Moore, Paul, 22

Mumford, Lewis, 150

Municipal Act (Ontario), 120

municipal government (Toronto). *See* City of Toronto

Municipality of Metro Toronto. *See* Metro Toronto (Municipality of Metro Toronto – 1953)

Murray, James, 63

Nathan Phillips Square, 44, 62, 63, 139

National Housing Act (1938), 136

Nerbas, Don, 51

New City Hall. *See* City Hall (New)

newspapers: archives, 9–10, 181n21, 184n9; circulation, 10, 181n23; readership surveys, 10, 64, 181n22; sex district reaction, 106–9; urban development, 42–43, 145–46; urban renewal terminology, 184n9. *See also specific names of Toronto newspapers*

Nordstrom retail store, 173

O'Donohue, Tony, 108

Official Plan (1949), 43–44

Old City Hall. *See* City Hall (Old)

180 Years Yonge Week, 1–2, 3, 8

Ontario Association of Architects, 80

Ontario government: legislation, 95, 120; pedestrian mall, 95; sex district, 120, 123; transportation, 87

Ottawa Sparks Street pedestrian mall, 74, 75, 78

Owen, David, 56–57, 62, 65, 69

Pacific Centre (Vancouver), 138, 152

Parkdale Baptist Church, 113

Parkin, John C., 81

pedestrian malls: automobile bans, 77, 86–88; beginnings, 7, 73–74, 75; economic benefits, 74; failures, 74; lobbying for, 75–76, 78; planning approaches, 73–74. *See also* Yonge Street pedestrian mall

Peoples' Information Service, 88–89

Phillips, Mayor Nathan, 44–45, 146

Pier 27 project, 170

Place Ville Marie (Montreal), 51, 52, 54

Places of Amusement report, 122–23

Planning Department, 44, 146–47, 149, 166

police: arrests report, 90–91; bathhouse raids, 127; body rub parlour raids, 117–18, 128–30, 167; body rub parlour raids criticism, 130; morality squad, 117, 123, 128, 167; pedestrian mall criticisms, 90–92; pedestrian mall crowd control, 91–92; sex district policing task force, 123; street policing methods, 161–62

Pollock's Shoes, 151

Pollution Probe, 11, 77, 80, 86–87, 144, 145

Ponte, Vincent, 63

Portuguese Canadians, 125–26(f)

Project Viking (redevelopment project): about, 48–50; aerial view, 56(f); media coverage, 52–53; name change (Eaton Centre), 54–55; risks, 50–51; sketches, 53. *See also* Eaton Centre (first project (1956–67))

public space: atmosphere, 23–25, 80–82, 97; bicycling, 86–87; church square (Trinity Square), 143, 148, 150–51, 162, 172; civic square (Nathan Phillips Square), 62, 63, 139; as democratic, 23, 168; everyday politics of, 73, 189n2; pedestrian mall as dysfunctional, 93(f); plazas (Dundas Square), 174, 175–76, 178; private space as public space, 158–62; public art, 155; public-private partnerships, 175–76; sex district as, 101; Yonge street as, 22–25

public transit. *See* Toronto Transit Commission (TTC)

public-private partnerships, 42, 52, 71, 166, 175–76

Radical Humanist newspaper, 85

real estate: speculation, 55, 103, 155, 168–69; surveys, 137. *See also* corporate development; urban development; *and individual names of real estate developers*

record stores, 173, 177–78

Redevelopment Advisory Council (RAC): about, 44–45; beginnings, 45, 71; chair, 45; downtown decline, 76; Eaton Centre plans, 64; real estate investment, 54; status, 147. *See also* City of Toronto

Regent Park public housing project, 42, 58, 125

research methodology (sources), 9–12, 181*nn*21–23

Retail Merchants Association, 27

retail trade: associations, 27, 31; attitudes toward youth, 90; consumer survey, 36; department stores, 20–21; discount stores, 84; evolution of, 20–21; global vs local, 173–75, 205*n*4; pedestrian mall criticisms, 85, 93–94; pedestrian mall lobbying, 75–76, 78; pedestrian mall marketing, 82–83(f); record stores, 173, 177–78; store chains, 156; vs street vendors, 85; suburban, 31, 33, 84; subway construction disruption, 31–32(f); subway effect, 75; tax assessments, 27. *See also specific names of retail businesses*

Revell, Viljo, 44

Rio Cinema, 39

Robinson, Gerald, 143

Rochdale College, 85

Rockefeller Center commercial complex, 55, 69

Rosenwein, Barbara, 124

Royal Commission on Corporate Concentration, 136

Ruppert, Evelyn, 176

Ryerson University, 172, 173, 177–78

Salvation Army building, 140

Sam the Record Man, 173, 177–78

Santa Claus Parade, 24–25

Scadding, Henry, 17, 34

Sears department store, 172

Sewell, John (as city councillor), 145

sex entertainment district ("Sin Strip"), 99–132; about, 13, 100–2; alliances against, 122; and American organized crime, 122; clientele, 106; decentralization (to suburbs), 131–32; demonstrations against, 115(f); emergence, 100–6; gay and lesbian bars, 103; gender dynamics, 104(f)–5, 112–13, 194*n*18; letter-writers support for, 116, 130; media portrayals and criticisms, 106–9; movie theatres, 104(f), 105, 117; municipal election issue, 107–9; municipal licensing regulation, 116–21, 128–30; murder, 124–26(f), 127; nostalgia for, 177; obscenity law, 102; opposition (citizen activism), 99–100, 109–14, 115(f)–16, 120, 123, 195*n*40; Places of Amusement report recommendations, 122–23; police raids, 117–18; police task force, 123; political alliances against, 122, 128; prosecution process, 129; prostitution, 123, 128, 131; sex businesses closures, 130; sex shop entrepreneurs, 104(f)–5, 130, 194*n*24; sex workers, 105–6, 194*n*25; sex workers advocacy group, 131; shoeshine boy murder, 124–26(f), 127. *See also* body rub parlours

sexual revolution: adult magazines and movies, 101–2, 104(f); commercial sex, 101–2; emergence, 100–2

shoeshine boys, 13, 38, 124–26(f), 127, 176

shopping centres: designs, 139–40, 149–51; downtown vs suburbs, 5, 52, 73–74, 84, 139–40; "dumbbell" design,

139; statistics, 33. *See also specific names of shopping centres*

Simcoe, Lieutenant-Governor John Graves, 1–2

Simpson, Robert, 20

Simpson's department store: beginnings, 20–21; buildings, 3, 24(f), 54; chair and president, 20, 45, 94, 157(f); competition, 139, 157(f); influence on downtown, 36; location, 36; marketing strategies, 21; parking, 29, 94; pedestrian mall opposition, 94–95; subway station, 75; successor to, 173; women consumers, 21

Skidmore, Owings, and Merrill, 56

Smith, Larry, 31, 48

Spadina Expressway, 77, 78, 86, 95

Sparrow, Alan, 122, 157

St. Jamestown apartment complex, 147

St. John's Ward, 23, 44, 47

St. Michael's Choir School, 114

Starvin' Marvin's strip club, 105

Stein, David Lewis, 132, 145, 146

Stephenson, Gordon, 48

subway: commercial development, 137; construction, 31–32(f), 34; property values, 48, 185n33; retail stores reaction, 75; stations, 75, 204n102; users, 204n102

Sunjam Limited (later Eaton Centre Limited), 55, 56–57, 69

Taylor, E.P., 54, 137

Telegram newspaper, 9, 10, 64, 69, 181n21

Toronto: American visitors, 83–84; armouries, 59; automobile ownership statistics, 29; automobile traffic, 24(f), 28–29, 32–33, 86–87(f), 88; business district, 19–20, 25; commercial development, 17, 28, 31, 35, 137, 200n18; commuters, 39, 170–71; decentralization, 5–8, 28–34, 180n7; downtown (concept of), 19–20, 182n12; downtown map, x(f);

economic expansion, 25–28; gang violence, 176–77, 205n14; gay community, 127, 128, 141; heritage conservation district, 178; history, 2–3, 15–18; immigration, 23, 29, 81, 125; modernist development, 13, 48–50, 54, 71; vs Montreal as economic capital, 25, 182n30; as multi-ethnic, 81–82; murders, 13, 124–26(f), 127, 176–77, 205n14; parking, 29, 32–33, 47, 94; pollution, 32, 86–88; as polycentric, 34; population statistics, 2, 16, 20, 21, 28, 29, 171; poverty, 23; private redevelopment, 53–54; racism, 176–77; railways, 16, 170–71; redevelopment areas, 44, 46, 166; as service vs private city, 27–28; street prostitution ("the Track"), 131; suburban development, 29–34, 135, 137; urban bicycling, 87, 192n60; urban expansion critiques, 25–28; urban transformation, 5–9; urban types, 23; vertical expansion (skyscrapers), 25, 35; women's council, 113, 120, 125

Toronto (municipal government). *See* City of Toronto

Toronto Board of Trade, 64, 76

Toronto Citizen community newspaper, 145, 146

Toronto Eaton Centre Merchants' Association, 156

Toronto Islands, 34, 119

Toronto Japanese United Church, 113

Toronto Life magazine, 69

Toronto Star newspaper: circulation, 10, 181n23; database, 9, 181n21; Eaton Centre (first) proposal reaction, 64, 65–66, 67; letters to (against sex district), 112; pedestrian mall reaction, 81, 90, 92; on redevelopment, 132, 145, 147; redevelopment terminology, 184n9; sex district, 106; shoeshine boy murder, 84, 124; shopping centre advertorial, 133

Toronto Sun newspaper: about, 10; alliances (against sex district), 122; circulation, 181n23; database, 9, 181n21; letters to (against sex district), 109; sex district criticisms, 108–9; shoeshine boy murder, 124

Toronto Transit Commission (TTC): beginnings, 28; streetcars, 20, 28; strike, 96; subway and commercial development, 137; subway and property values, 48, 185n33; subway and retail stores reaction, 75; subway construction, 31–32(f), 34; subway stations, 75, 204n102; subway users, 204n102

Toronto-Dominion Bank: shopping centre development partnership, 138, 140, 201n30; TD Centre, 54, 55, 137, 138

Trinity Square, 143, 148, 150–51, 162, 172

Tucker, Eric, 162

United States: commercial and retail centres, 55, 69, 150; municipal zoning ordinances (sex districts), 118–19; organized crime, 122; pedestrian malls, 74, 75, 78; urban renewal funding, 42

University Avenue Armouries (1891), 59

University of Toronto real estate, 140

urban development: citizen activism against, 144–48; commercial, 17, 28, 31, 35, 137, 200n18; consultants, 6; corporate developers, 52–55, 135–37, 199n4, 199n6; criticisms toward, 25–28, 57–60, 144–48; downtown (concept of), 19–20, 182n12; limitations, 42–43; media reaction, 42–43, 145–46; modernist, 13, 48–50, 54, 71; planning, 43–44, 73–74, 78, 146–47, 149, 166; "planning for people," 78; postwar decentralization, 5–8, 12–13, 180n7; power and politics,

4–5, 43–45; proposals, 41–42; public housing projects, 42; public-private partnerships, 42, 52, 71, 166, 175–76; suburban, 5–6, 28, 29, 31, 33–34, 135, 137; terminology, 184n9

Urban Development Institute, 147, 148

urban transit. *See* Toronto Transit Commission (TTC)

Valverde, Mariana, 126–27

van der Rohe, Mies, 54

Vancouver (Pacific Centre), 138, 152

Viking redevelopment project. *See* Project Viking (redevelopment project)

Vintage Toronto Facebook group, 177

Walsh, David, 157–58

Wanless, John, 21

Webb and Knapp Canada, 51–53, 54

Wellington Square (London, Ontario) shopping centre, 52, 152

Whose City? newsletter, 145

Winter, James, 6

women: consumers, 21, 159; gender dynamics, 21, 104(f)–5, 112–13, 194n18; local council, 113, 120, 125; sex workers, 105–6, 194n25

Wood, Neil, 159

Yonge, Sir George, 15

Yonge Street: aerial view, 142(f); anniversary (180 Years Yonge Week), 1–2, 3, 8; attitudes toward, 3–4, 159; automobile traffic, 24(f), 28–29, 38(f), 86–87(f), 88; buildings demolition, 21, 94, 151, 169; centrality of place, 7–8, 19, 22, 31, 102; ceremonies and celebrations, 24–25; Christmas lights, 38(f); cinemas, 22; citizen activism influence, 167–68; cocktail lounges, 37; commercial corridor, 3, 17–18(f), 35–37, 94, 132, 137, 174–75, 194n15, 194n17; contemporary transformations, 170–79; corporate influence on, 168–69; critiques of, 25–28; decline, 3–4, 7, 76, 94, 103, 113, 132; as democratic public space, 22–25, 168; downtown map, x(f); Eaton Centre as "killing Yonge," 156, 204n100; Eaton Centre relationship, 155–62, 163–64, 172, 204n100; electric lights, 18, 21–22, 38(f); entertainment district, 21–22, 37–38(f); future planning, 178–79; as "great northern highway," 2–3; heritage buildings designation, 59, 173–74, 178; identity as heart of city, 4, 6–7, 17; as key artery, 3, 15; land values, 20, 27, 36, 103; municipal government influence, 165–67; murders, 124–26(f), 127, 176–77; naming of, 15; nostalgia for, 177–78; office and financial services district, 20, 25, 35, 171; pedestrians, 37, 159, 175; planning survey (1978), 132; plaque (longest street), 170; police enforcement, 161–62; public plaza, 151, 157, 174, 175–76, 204n102; real estate speculation, 55, 103, 155, 168–69; record stores, 37, 173, 177–78; redesign planning ("yongeTOmorrow"), 178; reputation, 176–77; residential development, 171; retail trade, 17–18(f), 36–37, 94, 132, 151; safety, 176–77; song about, 2; street railway, 17, 18(f); subway construction, 31–32(f), 34; theatre, 22; traffic congestion, 24(f), 28–29; transformation challenges and influences, 165–70; transformation process, 4–5, 8, 12–14, 15, 170–79; unplanned growth, 26, 27; walking the street (*flâneurs*), 34–39, 170–71; width, 17, 26, 28; Yonge and College intersection, 35, 36, 46, 87(f), 171; Yonge and Dundas intersection, 89, 125, 151, 157, 174, 175, 177, 204n102; Yonge and King intersection, 20, 25, 35; Yonge and Queen intersection, 20, 22, 24(f), 36, 88, 139, 157; Yonge and Wellesley intersection, 103. *See also* sex entertainment district ("Sin Strip")

Yonge Street Adult Entertainment Association, 121

Yonge Street pedestrian mall, 72–98; about, 13, 72–73; analysis, 97–98; anti-mall lobbying, 92–93(f), 94–96; atmosphere, 80–82, 97; attitudes toward, 89–90, 95–96; automobile free, 86–88; beginnings, 11, 75–78; branding as "Main Street Canada," 83; buskers, 84–85; as citizen project, 80; as counterculture ideas space, 85–86; crowds and crowd control, 79(f), 80, 91–92; demonstrations for, 77; discount retail, 84; as dysfunctional public space, 93(f); entertainment firsts, 84–85, 102; as environmental symbol, 86–88; ethnic festivals, 82; failure, 96–98; gathering points, 88–89(f); intersections, 88, 89; marketing strategies, 78, 82–83(f); mass bicycling parade, 86–87; media reaction, 81, 86; as nightlife destination, 84–85; outdoor drinking, 84; pedestrian counts, 80; pedestrian surveys, 83–84, 96; pedestrian types, 80; pedestrians, 79(f), 80, 83–84, 88–89(f), 90, 96; as "people's freeway"/"people place," 72, 73, 78, 80, 95, 98, 152; police enforcement, 90–92; press release, 78; promotional postcard, 83(f); provincial government guarantor, 95; retail trade lobbying for, 75–76, 78; as retail trade marketplace, 82–85; shoeshine boys, 84; street vendors, 84–85; suburban pedestrians, 84; and "transient youth," 88–89; violence, 90–92; youth, 88–89(f), 90; youth information bureau, 88

York County grand jury (on pedestrian mall), 92–93

Yorkdale shopping centre, 33, 48, 52, 139
Yorkville "Village," 76–77, 89–90
youth: activism, 144–45; attitudes toward, 89–90; counterculture, 76–77; police profiling, 91; Yonge

Street mall pedestrians, 88–89(f), 90

Zanzibar Tavern, 115, 173
Zeckendorf, William, 51–52
Zeidler, Eberhard, 150–51, 172